A World
Without
Jews

A World Without Jews

The Nazi Imagination

from Persecution

to Genocide

ALON CONFINO

Yale UNIVERSITY PRESS
New Haven and London

Published with assistance from the Louis Stern Memorial Fund.

Yale University Press books may be purchased in quantity
for educational, business, or promotional use. For information,
please e-mail sales.press@yale.edu (US office) or
sales@yaleup.co.uk (UK office).

Epigraph: Nathan Ausubel, ed., *A Treasury of Jewish Folklore*
(New York, 1948), 17.

Printed in the United States of America.

The Library of Congress has cataloged the hardcover edition
as follows:
Confino, Alon, author.
A world without Jews: the Nazi imagination from persecution
to genocide / Alon Confino.
pages cm Includes bibliographical references and index.
ISBN 978–0–300–18854–7 (hardback)
1. Jews—Germany—History—1933–1945. 2. Jews—
Persecutions—Germany. 3. Holocaust, Jewish (1939–1945)—
Germany. 4. Germany—Politics and government—1933–1945.
5. Germany—History—1933–1945. 6. Germany—Ethnic
relations—History. I. Title.
DS134.255.C66 2014   940.53'18—dc23   2013041276

ISBN 978–0–300–21251–8 (pbk.)

A catalogue record for this book is available from the British
Library.

To Paolo and Davidi

and their worlds

A group of Nazis surrounded an elderly Berlin Jew and demanded of him, "Tell us, Jew, who caused the war?" The little Jew was no fool. "The Jews," he answered, then added, "and the bicycle riders." The Nazis were puzzled. "Why the bicycle riders?" "Why the Jews?" answered the little old man.

A Jewish joke told during the Second World War

Contents

Illustrations

Acknowledgments

I have come to think that writing a history book has an affinity with playing music. A music piece has, in one sense, a strict narrative in the form of the notes that comprise it and cannot be changed. But each time the score is played—that is, each time its story is told—it sounds a little bit different. Tightening and loosening of notes, slowing down or moving fast, disconnecting or linking the phrases—all these and others add up to a range of possible expressions and to different interpretations. History also has, in a sense, a strict narrative in the form of facts. Things have happened in the past, and we cannot change them (although, unlike in a musical composition, we may add new facts to the story as new archives are opened and new information is revealed). These facts are the building blocks of every historical narrative. But each time the historian crafts a story from the facts, it is a little bit different. He or she chooses different contexts, methods, or ways to relate cause and effect—and the result is a different interpretation.

Much as the musician tries to capture the tone and sentiment of a given piece, the historian listens to people in the past, attempting to capture their values and motivations, the rhythms of their life, often broken amid contradictions, unpredictability, and the constraining structures of history. And much as there are different kinds of music, from the military march to jazz, so there are different kinds of history, from economic to cultural. Each, when properly done, tells us something different but valuable about music and about people in the past, about the musician and the historian, and sometimes, when touched by the beauty and grace of art, about ourselves.

What a pleasure it is to thank the friends and colleagues who shared with me their wisdom, criticism, and time as I worked on this project. Amos Goldberg shared with me his deep insights and friendship, which have enriched me. Paul Betts and Monica Black read the entire final manuscript, and I am very grateful for their comments and conversations over the years. Dan Stone read the first draft and shared with me his knowledge of Holocaust history and historiography. Mark Roseman shared with me his sagacity over many a conversation. Ilana Pardes, who read an earlier draft, encouraged me to continue thinking about Freud. Halfway through the project I had the good fortune to get to know Tom Kohut, whose insights on history and psychology have been important. I am equally thankful to Asher Biemann, Alexandra Garbarini, Jeffrey Grossman, Allan Megill, and Dirk Moses for their insights.

I am deeply grateful to the John Simon Guggenheim Memorial Foundation for a generous fellowship that jazzed up this project. I wrote the first draft of this book as a Visiting Fellow at the Department of History and Civilization of the European University Institute in Florence in 2009–2010. I thank Gerhardt Haupt and Bartolomé Yun-Casalilla for making this possible and the members of the department for their gracious hospitality. A resident fellowship at the Institute for Advanced Studies in Culture at the University of Virginia in 2012–2013 allowed me to finish the book in a splendid environment. I am indebted to Jennifer Geddes, James Hunter, and Josh Yates. I am thankful to the University of Virginia for two summer research grants in 2011 and 2012 that helped me move the project along, and to the Dean of the College of Arts and Sciences and the Vice President of Research and Graduate Studies for a grant to defray photography costs.

I feel very fortunate for the gifted staff of Yale University Press who made the production of this book possible and for Laura Jones Dooley, who edited it with care.

I owe a tremendous amount to two people who believed in this project and provided constant attention and support. Will Lippincott, my agent, encouraged me throughout, and Jennifer Banks, my editor at Yale University Press, applied her splendid skills to the manuscript. It has been such a pleasure working with and befriending them.

The book is dedicated to my two most important worlds, to Paolo and Davidi.

A World
Without
Jews

Introduction
A Nazi Tale of Germans, Jews, and Time

S cenes of biblical fury combining audacity and transgression took place all across Germany.

The small town of Fürth could be a tourist destination. Located just a few miles from Nuremberg, in northern Bavaria, it's a scenic medieval settlement of tall, spiky houses and red tiled roofs, with a town hall modeled on the Palazzo Vecchio in Florence. In the old town, around the Church of Saint Michael, stand buildings with adorned facades dating from the seventeenth and eighteenth centuries. The historic center nestles between the rivers Rednitz and Pegnitz; to the west of town, on the far side of the Main-Danube Canal, is the municipal forest, and to the north lies a fertile area known as garlic country.

At around 2 o'clock in the morning on Thursday, November 10, 1938, groups of local young males dressed in brown uniforms roamed the streets of Fürth, knocking on the doors of their Jewish neighbors, classmates, and former friends. They entered the apartments, smashing furniture and objects, throwing possessions out the windows, and tearing books to shreds. Oskar Prager, then aged nine and a half, recalled that he saw the men take "my books, tear them up and throw them around the room. They were not Hebrew books but standard German reading books which children had at the time."[1]

All across town, Germans forced Jews from their homes and marched them to Schlageter Square, where the old train station had once proudly stood; earlier that year, the Nazis had knocked it down to create a parade ground. The square is known today as the Fürther Freiheit, Fürth's Freedom Square. "My mother was pushing the pram where the twins were crying or screaming," recalled young Oskar. "My constant questions to my father were answered with a sharp 'don't talk.'" If the night was cold and foggy, as would be expected in mid-November, something else was in the air. It "smelled of burning and I could see that the sky was reddish. Because of the fog I couldn't see clearly if something was burning because it was some distance away."²

In 1938 about two thousand Jews lived in Fürth, a town of approximately eighty thousand inhabitants. Jews had resided in the town as early as 1440. By the seventeenth century, there was a local Yeshiva, or Talmudic academy, of considerable repute, and in 1617 a synagogue was erected. In 1653, the first Jewish hospital in Germany was built in town. The Jewish cemetery on Weiher Street, created in 1607, is one of the oldest in Germany. At this time there were four main synagogues in town; some of them were already burning when the Jews made their silent march through the streets of their hometown accompanied by the threatening presence of their neighbors. The Nazis, members of the Storm Division (the brown-shirted SA, or Sturmabteilung, paramilitary group), collected Jews from all corners of town, even taking sick patients from the Jewish hospital and fifty children from the Jewish orphanage. On the way to the square, some Jews were rerouted to one of the synagogues, where they were forced to sing the Nazi anthem "Horst Wessel" and the rabbi was made to read from Hitler's *Mein Kampf.*

At midmorning, some of the Jews assembled in the square were driven to a nearby theater at the community center (ironically, until 1933 named for its Jewish donor), where in a dark hall, on a brightly lit stage, the men were whipped. Other Jewish men were taken to the police station and from there to Dachau, the concentration camp near Munich. As a new morning greeted the inhabitants of Fürth, many residents lined up along the streets to watch the paraded Jews. "With the sporting Brown Shirts setting the pace," recalled Edgar Rosenberg, who was thirteen at the time, "the walk from Schlageter Square to the community center—it leads past the Park Hotel [and] the downtown cinema . . . —takes no more than ten minutes; it leaves plenty of time and room for my nosy townsmen to crowd into the streets, spitting, yodeling, screaming, 'Well, high time!' and 'none too soon!' and bursting into a chorus of 'Jew Sows' and 'Croak Judas.' One of our town wits even stepped right up to the director of the Jewish Hospital, Medical Councilor Frank, to ask him whether he hadn't forgotten to bring his stethoscope."[3]

But earlier that Thursday, as dawn broke over the town's elegant houses, something else had happened in Schlageter Square. By now, all Jews had been assembled. Some, like Oskar and his family, had been standing there for some four hours. A good-sized crowd of citizens had also gathered. At the center of the square the Nazis had piled Jewish ritual objects from the synagogues along with items from the Jewish community house, which had been destroyed earlier. Clearly visible on the pole in the middle were the synagogues' Torah scrolls. There, after first rolling out the scrolls in the square and forcing the rabbis to walk on them, the Nazis hung the Torah. Then, before the assembled crowd, they set the pyre ablaze (simultaneously with one of the synagogues, it seems): the Hebrew Bible, one of the most sacred symbols of European-Christian civilization, was thus publicly burned.

Why did the Nazis burn the Hebrew Bible?

This is a good question because in European-Christian civilization the torching of the Bible is bound to be significant. However we choose to understand it, the act demands explanation. But the scholarship on Kristallnacht—the Night of Broken Glass on November 9, 1938, when the Nazis burned hundreds of synagogues—and the Holocaust as well as accounts of the Third Reich have all but ignored the burning. It is mentioned only sporadically as an illustration of Nazi brutality but is not made part of the story. This silence, too, deserves an explanation.

Recent accounts of the Third Reich, however sophisticated, do not pose this question because they view Nazi racial ideology as the fundamental source of the motivations, beliefs, and values that led to the Holocaust. According to this view, Nazi motivations sprung from the aim to build a racial biological society. There is no doubt about the importance of racial ideology in understanding Nazism, but the anti-Jewish identity the Nazis created was more complex. In burning the Bible the Nazis directed their wrath against a religious, not a racial, symbol. Other dominant directions in Holocaust research have also not been helpful, viewing the Germans' motivations as embedded in the administrative state process of extermination culminating in Auschwitz. This view has explored in meticulous detail the bureaucratic machinery of the German state that made the Holocaust possible, from the trains used to deport the Jews to the workings of the labor and death camps. Another important approach emphasizes the brutalization of the Second World War, which led the German soldiers to perpetrate mass murders. Scholarship on these topics certainly helps us capture and understand aspects of the Holocaust, but it cannot assist us in interpreting the burning of the Bible.

When we consider the Holocaust as emerging from racial ideology and a state-run administrative process during a brutal war, it becomes difficult to place Kristallnacht and the burning of the Bible within this framework. Historians have viewed November 9, 1938, as a dramatic rupture in Nazi policies, a downpour of mad violence that does not quite fit within either the racial ideology and legal discrimination of the prewar years or the state-run, bureaucratic extermination during the war. It does not fit because race and religion, which have often been viewed as separate categories, commingled in Kristallnacht; because by burning the Bible Germans conveyed a preoccupation with ancient roots and moral authority that cannot make sense within an exclusively racial explanation; and because the dramatic burning of a book holy also to Christianity seems hardly revealing about the extermination of Jews in the death camps. The point is not that racial and other accounts of the Third Reich portray Kristallnacht inadequately but that their history of the persecution and extermination of the Jews holds together much better once Kristallnacht is excluded. The burning of the Bible does not fit in these accounts.[4]

A world of meaning is lost when these views of racial ideology, the brutalization of war, and the state-run process of extermination dominate our understanding of the Holocaust because the question "Why did the Nazis and other Germans burn the Hebrew Bible?" demands a historical imagination that captures Germans' culture, sensibilities, and historical memories. When we change our perspective and view the burning of the Bible as part of the creation by Nazis and other Germans of a new German identity, when we acknowledge that this act involved a set of emotions that cannot be ignored or separated from the Holocaust, then new possibilities that challenge our perceptions emerge to help us understand the Holocaust. Burning the Bible was an intentional act: it happened all over Germany, in public for all to see, and both those who perpetrated the act and those who watched it perceived it as a transgression whether they supported or opposed the burning. The act was part of a larger story Germans told themselves during the Third Reich about who they were, where they came from, how they had arrived there, and where they were headed.

This story placed the Third Reich within German, European, and Christian history, providing a moral justification and a historical meaning, and outlined the creation of a European civilization with a new sense of morality and humanity. Precisely because Nazism saw itself as a radical, novel historical departure, it paid particular attention to the past, that protean and essential factor of life in all societies. The more radical the break with past conduct and morality—as the Nazis set out to build an empire based on the systematic persecution and extermination of groups of people—the greater the need for a new national story to make sense of what was happening. According to this story the Jews reflected a historical past—historical origins, to be exact—that needed to be extirpated in order for a new Germany to arise. To create a Nazi civilization, a new European order and form of Christianity, Jewish civilization had to be removed. Germany's historical origins needed to be purified down to the Jews' shared past with Christianity via the canonical text.

We should pause for a moment and consider that by telling a story about themselves, Nazis and other Germans behaved much as we do. We all tell stories about ourselves, individuals as well as national collectivities, in order to give our lives purpose and meaning. These stories are the bedrock of our identity, although we often tell our national stories not in order to get the facts right but in order to get them wrong, to explain our history and justify our motivations for doing things, the good deeds and especially the bad ones. (The same is also true for individual stories, of course.) One can think of the American story of a shining city on a hill that is a beacon of freedom and a land of opportunity, a narrative that often glosses over the Indian conquest, slavery, Jim Crow, and imperialism that are also part of American history. We often embellish our past, repress, change, or even lie about it; that is why our national stories are selective in choosing the facts, jumping from the past to the present, using anachronism and avoiding chronology. Telling stories makes us human, but not all our stories are humane. This is the kind of Nazi story we are after.

Burning the Bible stirred emotions and imaginations. A history of the Holocaust must include the history of emotions and imagination of Germans during the Third Reich, for the fundamental reason that the persecution and extermination was built on fantasy, in the sense that anti-Jewish beliefs had no basis in reality. In persecuting and exterminating the Jews, Germans waged a war against an imaginary enemy that had no belligerent intentions toward Germany and possessed no army, state, or government. The essential motivations for this war were not practical, for Germans and Jews did not have a conflict over territory, land, resources, borders, or political power that often characterizes cases of ethnic cleansing and genocide in the modern world. In the mind of the Nazis, this was a war about identity. Nazi anti-Semitism was all fantasy: nothing about it was driven by a desire to provide a truthful account of reality. Yet it was nonetheless believed by many Germans and therefore was for them real and truthful.

A key to understanding this world of anti-Semitic fantasies is no longer to account for what happened—the administrative process of extermination, the racial ideological indoctrination by the regime, and the brutalizing war—because we now have sufficiently good accounts of these historical realities. Rather, a key is to account for what the Nazis *thought* was happening, for how they imagined their world. What was this fantasy created by Nazis and other Germans during the Third Reich, and the story that went along with it, that made the persecution and extermination of the Jews justifiable, conceivable, and imaginable?

The Holocaust was a multifaceted event with multiple causes that cannot be reduced to a single explanation. The interpretation presented in this book should be placed alongside other accounts that emphasize political, military, or ideological history. Research on the Holocaust has become so vast that it is now a big-enough tent for different interpretations that shed light on the Holocaust from varied angles. Still, the story told in these pages does differ in some key points from current interpretations of the Holocaust, and I would like to articulate these differences.

An innovation in Holocaust scholarship in the last generation has been the emphasis on the regime's racial ideology and its biological, scientific worldview that categorized human beings according to putative racial genes with Aryans at the top and Jews at the bottom. There is no doubt about the importance of racial ideology in the Third Reich, but this view has now become so prevalent that it obscures a set of identities, beliefs, and memories that made Nazi Germany. It is inconceivable that a body of racial ideas, which was present but not dominant before 1933, was received and internalized by Germans so quickly thereafter while successfully marginalizing other important identities. This is not how identities work. In human affairs, even the most radical transformations are maintained by previous memories, beliefs, and habits of mind. Germans did not simply toss away their previously held religious, national, and local beliefs.

The view of Nazi beliefs as guided by modern racial science gave Nazi anti-Semitism a rational slant, even though it was all fantasy. In fact, Nazi racial science, similar to every science, had an element of mystery, a poetic side, that the Nazis themselves were aware of. When we look closely we see that their idea of race was nuanced and multifaceted and went beyond science and biology. J. Keller and Hanns Andersen, two university-educated German experts on the Jewish Question, wrote in their 1937 book *The Jew as a Criminal:* "Just like the spirochete bacteria that carries syphilis, so are the Jews the carriers of criminality in its political and apolitical form. . . . The Jew is the true opposite to a human being, the depraved member of a subracial mixing. . . . He is the embodiment of evil that rises against God and nature. Wherever his miasma strikes, it causes death. He who contends with the Jews, contends with the devil."[5] This hallucinatory, phantasmagoric text moved seamlessly between modern science, the idea of race, God, and the devil, combining scientific, moral, and religious metaphors into a fantasy about past, present, and future.

Once we make space for other ideas besides race in the making of Nazi identity, then religious, Christian sentiments come into sharp relief. The relations between Nazism and Christianity have been extensively debated. The emphasis on racial ideology often put race and religion as antinomies because, in principle, racial anti-Semitism contradicted religious doctrine, for Christianity had supported the conversion of Jews, whereas Nazism, based on the unchangeability of biological traits, denied this possibility. This opposition is true on the level of formal doctrine, of Church and regime dogma, but real life is more complicated (and therefore more interesting). Many Germans found ways to commingle successfully racial and religious sentiments. I argue for an intimate link between Nazism and Christianity beyond what current scholarship proposes: being a (certain) good Nazi and being a (certain) good Christian went hand in hand in the Third Reich, as racial and Christian anti-Jewish ideas complemented one another in many respects. The idea of race could not have been received by Germans, and could not have thrust them to commit such crimes in so short a time without the legitimacy it received from Christian, religious sentiments. If Germans supported Nazism it is also because it allowed them to remain a certain kind of Christians while becoming a new kind of Germans, as Nazis.

"Sentiments" and "sensibilities" are key words in the book to capture the Nazi imagination because they are subtle enough to capture nuances. In the discussion of the relation between race and religion, for example, they convey a habit of mind about Christianity that goes beyond whether someone went to church every Sunday or what the official position of the churches was during the Third Reich (although this is also part of our story). They reveal a Christian culture in German society that identified German nationhood with Christianity and which lent legitimacy that derived from anti-Semitic tradition to Nazi anti-Jewish prejudices.

A fundamental problem in interpreting the Holocaust has been how to explain the daunting gap between the anti-Jewish persecution of the prewar years and the almost unimaginable extermination during the war. If we look for Auschwitz in prewar Nazi culture we assume that Auschwitz was already clearly imaginable, which was not the case. If we emphasize racial ideology we assume a causal relation that explains too little because it is still not clear how the jump was made from hatred to extermination. Some approaches to Nazism simply avoid this problem by focusing on the administrative state process of the persecution and extermination as if this reveals the meaning of the event, as if a process can kill, and not human beings who love, hate, and murder.

Debates on the motivations of the killers have also tended to sidestep the problem of how the persecution of the 1930s turned to the genocide of the war. Some scholars view the Holocaust as a result of a deeply ingrained, historically unique, and centuries-old German anti-Jewish obsession; they thus assume that the genocide had been inscribed in German history centuries before Auschwitz.[6] Nor can the problem be illuminated by focusing on the social-psychological and group dynamic processes of the soldiers in the Second World War. According to this view, the circumstances of war transformed Germans into killers much more than their Nazi experience between 1933 and 1939 or a presumed atavistic anti-Semitism that goes back hundreds of years. Among the key factors were wartime brutalization, peer pressure, routinization of the killing, careerism, obedience to orders, and deference to authority. But focusing only on the extreme conditions of a brutal war severs the perpetrators from German culture that created these conditions. If the perpetrators were a product of extreme combat conditions and of the group dynamic of the soldiers in the crucible of war, then there is little to link them to the Nazi culture of the prewar years.[7]

My approach is different. I follow in this book the way Germans imagined a world without Jews. This is the leading metaphor that drives our story. Our starting point is the intentions of the Nazis and the policy of the German state starting on January 30, 1933: the construction of a Germany, and later a world, without Jews. This perspective captures the search in the Third Reich for a Germany without Jews while taking cognizance of the different policies (such as emigration or segregation), opinions, and sentiments of the project, its complexity, probability, and uncertainty. Some supported the idea, some opposed it, while some were left indifferent, but it was and remained a goal of the Third Reich from the beginning, a whole larger than the sum of Germans' views about the Jews. As we follow the story of a Germany without Jews in the 1930s we are not required to know the story's final destination (the extermination beginning in 1941); in fact, we ought to follow the story in much the same way that Germans did after 1933, when they did not know where their imagination would lead them. Our only firm point is January 30, 1933: a moral, historical, post-Enlightenment break was made then, not by planning an eventual extermination, but by thinking that a German world without Jews could be a reality, somehow.

Placing the imagination of a Germany without Jews at the center of the history of the Holocaust means shifting the focus from a story that ends in Auschwitz to the gradual making of a culture in which a Germany, and later a world, without Jews made sense to Germans. It is jarring to speak about "making sense" of the Holocaust, but it is the right phrase and the right investigation if we wish to uncover how Germans made sense of their world in the Third Reich, however morally objectionable this world was. "Made sense" also does not mean that everybody agreed to it. Rather, it means that Germans were able to imagine it, to internalize it, to make it part of their vision of the present and future, whether they agreed, opposed, or were indifferent to it. Because, in reality, it is not Auschwitz that stands at the center of the historian's study of Nazi anti-Semitism but the making of a German world without Jews. Imagining this world was not a consequence of the war; Auschwitz was. The idea of a Germany without Jews had been in the process of being realized already before the war from 1933: it would have been created with or without Auschwitz. How did it settle in Germans' imagination?

The imagination of a Germany without Jews links anti-Semitic actions and ideas in the prewar and war years because it describes Nazi anti-Semitism as a work in progress, built gradually over the years between 1933 and 1945. I thus challenge the mainstream view in popular and scholarly understanding of the Holocaust that the mass murder of the Jews during the war had not been anticipated, that victims and perpetrators alike scarcely believed what was happening, that it was unimaginable and unrepresentable. Primo Levi expressed this idea in one of the twentieth century's most profound statements: "Today, at this very moment as I sit writing at the table, I myself am not convinced that these things really happened."[8] The sentiment cannot be denied. At the same time, historians know that all that happened was, in some way, somehow, imagined, not literally, not exactly, but it was put into images and words that made it possible. No historical event springs from thin air, none is unique, because this implies having no links to context, past, and present. Of course, on November 9, 1938, no one could imagine the gas chamber of Auschwitz, not even Hitler himself. But on that day one could imagine a German world in which Jews and Judaism were terminated by fire and violence. Our aim is to seek patterns of meaning and purpose in a world of fantasies that made the extermination possible precisely because it was, somehow, imaginable and representable.

The Nazis imagined the Jew by using anti-Semitic ideas from their present-day German society. This statement may seem obvious, but it has consequences for our understanding of the Holocaust. A key approach to the Holocaust has been to focus on anti-Semitism as the primary motivation of the Nazis and to view Nazi racial ideology as the modern form of the old hatred. On one level, this argument is unassailable, for any account of the Holocaust that denies or minimizes anti-Semitism is bound to be unsatisfactory. But beyond this broad agreement, my argument here is in some respect fundamentally different from some trends in the anti-Semitism approach to the Holocaust. A central tenet of many studies of this approach, explicitly or implicitly, has been that an accumulation of the ancient hatred through the centuries paved the way and ultimately produced the Holocaust. I argue the opposite. It is not that the past (of anti-Semitism) *produced* the present (of the extermination), not that the ancient hatred led to the Holocaust, but that the Nazis interpreted anew the past of Jewish, German, and Christian relations to fit their vision of creating a new world. The Nazis, as we shall see, told a story of national origins at the center of which were the evil Jews. But in telling this story they picked and chose from the history of Jewish, German, and Christian relations elements that fit their narrative while creating anew their own present. It is the Nazis who made sense of, and gave new meaning to, past anti-Semitism, not so much the other way around. It is always people in the present who give meaning to the past, while the past itself can never give meaning to a future not yet born.

At the same time, the Holocaust cannot be understood without consideration of the history of European colonialism. Colonial genocides of the nineteenth and twentieth centuries were part of a process of accelerated violence related to nation-building at home and imperial territorial expansion abroad. The Nazi notions of race and of inferior groups who had no right to live belonged in the tradition of European colonialism, which, long before 1933, provided popular, "scientific," and political legitimacy to British, French, Dutch, Belgian, and others to rule over and kill millions around the world. What set the stage for the Nazi genocides were the broken taboos of earlier decades: the Holocaust was thinkable because, to give but one example, of the prior German extermination of the Herero and the Namaqua between 1904 and 1907 in South-West Africa (present-day Namibia) and the realization that wiping out peoples was a possibility.

Similarly, the enmity against and extermination of the Jews was part of a Nazi universe of racial enemies and exterminations. The Jewish genocide was bound up with a set of racial ideas that produced other Nazi mass killings and genocides of, among others, mentally ill patients, Ukrainians, and Russians. The Nazis were determined to build an empire, extending from the Atlantic in the West to the Pacific shores of Siberia in the East, devoted to expansion and the annihilation of entire populations. The Holocaust was only one in a series of genocides committed by the Nazis, and it can be understood only when placed within the comparative history of modern genocides.[9] It belongs squarely within the genre of genocides and was not an exceptional, stand-alone historical event. (That said, it has its own particularities because not all genocides are identical, though they all share certain common denominators that group them together as genocides.)

But in themselves the European traditions of modern colonialism and racial ideas cannot account for the Holocaust, and at some point I part way with the scholarship on comparative genocides and on the Nazi empire. Some scholars question in various ways the extent to which the Holocaust was central to understanding National Socialism. In making the Nazi empire, some argue, the Holocaust was a result rather than a goal of Nazism, growing out of the specific circumstances of the war.[10] Others integrate the Holocaust into a history of totalitarian genocides committed by Hitler and Stalin in eastern Europe, implying that the Holocaust was a result of the linked policies of the two dictators as they pushed each other to commit ever-worsening crimes.[11]

The limits of these arguments should also be made clear. If the Holocaust was a result of mass murders in eastern Europe between Hitler and Stalin, why did the Nazis choose to exterminate the Jews of Corfu, and by extension of western Europe, who had no direct relation to this conflict? If the Holocaust was essentially only part of mass murders such as the premeditated starvation of Ukrainian peasants by Stalin in the early 1930s, then why was it that the NKVD, Stalin's secret police, did not seek to kill all Ukrainians in the Soviet Union or indeed the world, whereas the Gestapo searched for every single Jew in occupied Europe to be murdered and, beyond that, asked the king of Bulgaria and the sultan of Morocco to hand over to the Nazis "their" Jews in order to send them to Auschwitz (both rulers refused)? The genocides in eastern Europe by Stalin and Hitler were bounded by territory, space, and time and had political, social motivations in the mind of the perpetrators. Why did the Nazis target the Jews as the only group that was hunted all over the Continent, as a sort of a spaceless and timeless enemy, whereas other victims of genocide in this period, such as, for example, mentally ill or asocial groups, were not considered existential threats that demanded deportation to Auschwitz from Athens or Rome? The problem with the arguments that the Holocaust was not central to understanding National Socialism is that they view a close description of the circumstances of the Second World War—that is, of what happened—as an explanation to what people believed and imagined—that is, of why things happened. According to these views, implicitly and at times explicitly, anti-Jewish sensibilities were not of major importance in the making of the Holocaust. I wonder about that. Empire building, multiple genocides, and other wartime circumstances cannot account for Germans' culture and motivations, much as the Nazi immigration policies to push the Jews out of Germany before November 1938 cannot account for burning the Bible.

My view is different. The Holocaust should be placed within a history of Nazi war and occupation, empire building, and comparative genocide. The Holocaust was not unique. But it was *perceived* during the war as unique by Germans, Jews, and other Europeans, and if we want to understand why the Holocaust happened, we ought to explain this. The comparative approach to genocide sharpens the similarities but also the differences between the Holocaust and other genocides. On the one hand, the idea of exterminating racial groups had been building in European culture and politics for a century before the Third Reich. But on the other hand, it is evident that for the Nazis the persecution and extermination of the Jews was more urgent and historically significant than other genocides they committed. Although they set out to kill all the Jews immediately during the war, they did not have a similar policy for other groups of victims. This only begs the question: Why did the Nazis view the extermination of the Jews as so urgent and fatal to their survival? Why did Germans, Jews, and Europeans perceive during the war the extermination of the Jews as unlike any other genocide perpetrated by the Nazis?

My answer, briefly stated without preempting the story that is to unfold, is that for the Nazis and other Germans, Jews represented time, symbolizing evil historical origins that had to be eradicated for Nazi civilization to arise. The Nazis chose as their main enemy the Jews, an ancient people, with a long history and fundamental role in Christian, European, and German society, and a source of a long tradition of positive and negative moral, religious, and historical symbols. The Jews stood at the origins of the Bible, of Christianity, and, for many in Germany and Europe, of modernity's liberalism, communism, and capitalism. Origins is a metaphor of being in time that implies legitimacy, roots, and authenticity. By persecuting and exterminating the Jews, the Nazis eliminated the shackles of a past tradition and its morality, thus making it possible to liberate their imagination, to open up new emotional, historical, and moral horizons that enabled them to imagine and to create their empire of death.

There was nothing peculiar in Europe about the Nazi view of the Jews as representing ancientness and historical origins; the idea goes back to Augustine of Hippo in the fourth century. But the Nazis set out to destroy the Jews as possessors of origins for two particular reasons: first, they deemed these origins evil and an immediate danger to Nazi Germany— according to them, Jewish powers extended over centuries and across the world, and only a radical uprooting would cure the world; and second, they aimed at building a civilization that owed no historical and moral debt to the Jews. These are the reasons the Nazis persecuted and exterminated the Jews using not only a language of racial inferiority but also one that ascribed awesome powers to the Jews. An enemy worth total annihilation must possess tremendous power, real or imagined. Some of this power was attributed to Jewish political and economic influence on capitalism and bolshevism in Washington, London, and Moscow. But, then, why burn the Bible if the influence of the Jews was manifested in the political and economic spheres? What was the power of the Bible that so disturbed the Nazis? There was in the Nazi persecution and extermination of the Jews an element of fear, almost terror, of the Jews. The notion of historical origins captures the Nazi mentality: the awesome power assigned to the Jews, the sentiment that the Jews held a key to German identity and empire.

By telling a story of national origins the Nazis fit within broad patterns of modern history. All nations in the modern world construct historical narratives that combine facts and inventions, and all crave the legitimacy that comes with a historical pedigree. The Nazis also sought the legitimacy that comes with roots. They constructed their story as they went along from 1933, building it in stages, linking their increasingly radical policies against the Jews to their expanding ambitions to remake Germany and Europe. Their imagination about the Jews was not coherent or closely knit but rather, like all fantasies, a blend of different and often opposing elements: it comprised racial, religious, and historical elements present in German culture, as well as the idea of *Heimat,* or homeland, which was the ultimate concept of German roots (we shall discuss it later on). From these cultural ingredients, the Nazis picked and chose what suited their aims. These aims changed as the Third Reich progressed because what the Nazis thought of the Jews in 1933 was different from what they thought in 1938 and again in 1942. Their story therefore was built piecemeal, and because the Reich was so short and tumultuous, they did not have the time to present their story in a systematic and comprehensive way. They planned on doing it after the victory.

But the Nazis did imagine a clear narrative arch of the relations between Germans and Jews from the dawn of history to the present. Right from the beginning they were certain about one thing, which did not change until the last day of the Reich: the Jews and their historical roots, real or invented, from the Bible down to the modern period, must be eliminated at all costs and whatever the consequences. The Nazis did not leave standing one cultural edifice that implied a cultural debt to the Jews: this amounted to making a new civilization by uprooting a key element of their own roots.

Here lies a deep significance of Nazism. The Nazis' dream of a clean historical slate has been one key reason that since 1945 the Holocaust has been so unsettling in our culture: by violently rejecting their own roots, the Nazis brought the question of what it means to be human to a new level of existential meaning. A historical importance of the Holocaust lies in one trait that characterized it: it was the first experiment in the total creation of a new humanity achieved by extermination, a humanity liberated from the shackles of its past. Of course, on one level the dream of setting oneself free from the past has always stalked the human imagination. And all modern revolutionary regimes have attempted to liberate themselves from some past: the French Revolutionaries set themselves apart from the Old Regime, the Bolsheviks from authoritarian, exploitative czarist Russia. The Third Reich fit squarely within this spectrum of revolutions that invented new pasts. What set it apart was the choice of enemy. The Jews provided a past that was chiefly measured not in political, economic, and social deeds but in moral, historical attributes. They formed part of German history but, well beyond that, of Christian and European history as well, embodying a certain idea of origins and the past. Eliminating them was not about inventing a new element in the national past, such as by depicting unfavorably the Old Regime and czarist Russia, but about rethinking anew the idea of human origins itself.

The Holocaust was about the Nazi dream of conquering historical time, past, present, and future. The Nazi empire in Europe was made possible by imagining first an empire of time. The Nazis had a revolutionary spatial policy to conquer the entire Continent, enslaving and exterminating millions. What, then, was the revolutionary concept of time that accompanied this revolutionary policy of space? What was the imagination of time and of history that gave meaning and legitimacy to their radical exterminatory policies?

This question cannot be answered by exploring solely the policies of the Nazi leadership and the rhetoric of its propaganda; it also demands an investigation of how the anti-Jewish imagination was made, experienced, and acted by Germans on the street level. To capture this, I focus on public actions that carried emotional and moral weight, were highly visible, and left rich documentation in diaries, letters, eyewitness testimonies, speeches, posters, images, films, travelogues, newspaper accounts, and records of government, military, Nazi Party, and religious organizations. I analyze specific acts of violence against Jews, local German parades representing Jews (such as Carnival), parades of humiliation, historical processions, the burning of books, including the Bible, and of synagogues, legal acts of discrimination, the process of marking Jews, and the actions embedded in ghettoization, mass murder, and extermination. I also use photographs from the period. They tell something about the past that we cannot access by literary means, and I present them as a lens to a world that was visible to contemporaries at the time, showing what Germans saw when they walked in the street, drove on the road, or made their way to work on the morning of November 10, 1938.

More important is the approach applied to understanding these sources. The history of the Holocaust is often written too close to the documents. This almost positivist attachment to facts has a good explanation: it has answered the difficulty of narrating the story of the Holocaust because a major historical task since 1945 has been simply to describe aspects of the historical reality of the persecution and extermination of the Jews between 1933 and 1945. The basic task of all history writing—to tell what the story was—was immensely difficult. After 1945 the Holocaust was generally not considered in public and scholarly circles as a foundational past in European history; the term itself became synonymous with the extermination of the Jews only around 1960. Primo Levi's *Se questo è un uomo* was rejected in 1946–1947 by Einaudi and five other Italian publishers for lack of interest before it was accepted by a small publishing house in Turin.[12] Few major historical works were devoted to the Holocaust until the 1970s. Then, ever since historians finally began, in the 1970s and then with growing persistence and meticulousness from the 1980s onward, to tell the story of the Holocaust, doubts have been expressed in scholarly and public discourse about the possibility of producing a historical representation of the Holocaust at all. On this issue, historians have reflected, more than they have shaped, popular perceptions about the special character of the Nazi past and the uniqueness of the Holocaust.

But this historical evaluation has worked as an emotional, moral, and professional bulwark against telling the story of the Holocaust. Accumulation of facts (often massive) cannot craft narratives of the Holocaust that carry their own truth. Scholars have turned to amassing facts in order to overcome the difficulty of writing about the Holocaust; facts from documents help domesticate this past and undo the strangeness of a racist and murderous world. They have thus banished the strangeness of the period from the story of the Holocaust. By "strangeness of the past" I mean those elements that can be captured through an analysis of culture, mentalities, and sensibilities. My point is not that the Holocaust is strange in a particular historical way; for the historian, all pasts are strange. Rather, my point is that the task of the historian ought to be to elucidate the strangeness of the past, not to attempt to overcome it.

That is what I seek to do in exploring Nazi imagination. To achieve this I attempt to capture emotions and sensibilities expressed in public actions. I look at what the Nazis did because beliefs cannot always be articulated, not even in private letters and diaries, while motivations are often hidden, subterranean, or contradictory. We often tell ourselves stories that we would like to believe about ourselves but that in fact obscure more than they reveal. We ought to look across documents and public actions to establish relations of meaning, to reveal what was thought and believed but was at times kept under wraps because of guilt, shame, repression, or a sense of transgression. Germans' behavior was both explicit and conscious—that is, what Germans said they were doing, the evidence historians can hope to access easily—and at times inexplicit or unconscious but perhaps more fundamental. By thinking about the Holocaust along these lines, we liberate ourselves from the tyranny of the documents and free our interpretative imagination, as we expect ourselves to do with respect to any other historical exploration.

The history of emotions is significant here. What was communicated emotionally in these public acts was just as important as what was said in words, indeed often much more important. There is a common view of the persecution and extermination of the Jews as a cold, administrative, industrial process epitomized by Auschwitz. This is of course true, but only in part. There is a tradition in Holocaust historiography of leaving the human element out. The approach called functionalism has interpreted the Holocaust as a result of impersonal administrative, structural state processes, as if history is made by structures, not human beings. Hannah Arendt's depiction of Adolf Eichmann as the banality of evil contributes to this ultimate view of the Holocaust as made by men lacking qualities and emotions. This image is wrong. The persecution of the Jews in the prewar years was characterized by massive, raw, personal violence, and during the extermination, some two and a half million victims were killed in face-to-face shootings. The persecution and extermination of the Jews were fueled by emotions, and all interpretations that avoid, deny, or ignore this must end up in a dead end as to a fundamental human element embedded in the event.

For it is not that the essence of the genocide was emotionless anti-Semitism, but instead that some of the perpetrators *presented* their actions in such a way. The denial of emotion was a mechanism to deal with feelings of moral unease, transgression, guilt, or shame. Murdering people cannot be an emotionless activity, for human beings, for the most part, are moral beings and like to think of themselves as such. Emotions may be hidden, denied, or subterranean, but they lurk somewhere; they were fundamental to Nazi anti-Semitism at all times, levels, and policies. The question for the historian is how to retrieve them.

In telling the story of Nazi imagination and how in the 1930s it anticipated the destruction in the 1940s, I have had to make choices of narrative and argumentation. The Third Reich is now the most-written-about topic in history: a standard bibliography of National Socialism listed twenty-five thousand titles in 1995 and a whopping thirty-seven thousand in 2000.[13] What has emerged is just how complex the Holocaust actually was. It was not simply a German event but a European and a North African one (Libyan and Tunisian Jews were sent to Auschwitz). It did not involve just Hitler and his cronies but German society, economy, and culture as a whole. And it did not involve only the Jews but was tied to a series of Nazi resettlement plans and murderous policies to redraw the map of Europe, which involved Poles, Russians, Roma and Sinti, and others. Some subjects, such as the timing of the decision of the Final Solution between the fall of 1941 and the winter of 1942, have become so big as to constitute by themselves a comprehensive body of work. A lasting contribution of Holocaust scholarship has been, then, to tell in detail aspects of the military, institutional, ideological, and political history of the Holocaust. One problem this remarkably specialized, massive historiography has presented, for the historian who wants to narrate the Holocaust and for the layperson who wants to understand what happened, is that, studied in such detail, it is at times difficult to see the forest for the trees.

My aim has been to cut through this vast, complex historiography in pursuit of Nazi imagination. There is a give and take in this approach: we lose at times the twisted roads, the intricate relations, and the Nazi changes of heart and of policy, while we gain an insight into the conscious and unconscious making of Nazi fantasies. Thus, for example, whereas I show how Nazi imagination of the Jews was reflected in the relations between Nazism and Christianity, in the policy of ghettoization during the war, and in popular participation in the regime's crimes, I have not discussed in detail all the aspects of these topics, such as the regional variations between Catholics and Protestants, the multiple changes to the policy of ghettoization, and the motivations of numerous distinct social groups at different periods to oppose or support the regime.

Detailing these topics would have taken me far afield from the story I wish to craft and the historical insight I seek to gain. These details are of course important to present certain historical aspects of the Third Reich. Different histories present diverse historical realities of the Third Reich, each contributing something to our overall understanding. In telling the story of Nazi imagination I strive to depict the past in its rich texture while also keeping in mind that one of the central tasks of the historian is not simply to narrate the past as infinitely rich and complex but also to render it comprehensible, to identify patterns by reducing a great deal of detail into a concerted story, and to find a narrative meaning within a universe of seemingly unrelated events.

In thinking about my overall approach, several scholars who combine intellectual erudition with literary elegance have inspired me. Saul Friedländer has written about the Holocaust with admirable thoughtfulness. He has emphasized redemptive anti-Semitism as paramount to the Nazi drive to exterminate the Jews. It "was born from the fear of racial degeneration and the religious beliefs in redemption. . . . [It was] a story of perdition caused by the Jew, and of redemption by a total victory over the Jew."[14] My work owes much to this insight about Nazi redemptive ideas, though I present a different interpretation as to why the Nazis thought that exterminating the Jews would bring apocalyptic deliverance. For Friedländer, the idea of race binds together the various Nazi beliefs in political, social, and cultural renewal that would follow the end of the Jews. I stress the element of historical time. Renewal would be the result of the eradication of any historical debt, real or invented, owed to the Jews. This idea of a new beginning via a clean historical slate bears the weight of the Nazi apocalyptic deliverance offered by the extermination of the Jews more accurately than the notion of race. I do not think that our views are necessarily contradictory as much as that they emphasize different facets of Nazi sensibilities. Another difference is that although Friedländer views the redemption as religious in nature, he has not linked the experience of Nazism and Christianity in any significant way, whereas I see specific elements of the two as mutually reinforcing.

Carlo Ginzburg has sought in his variegated historical work, focused on but not limited to Renaissance and early modern Europe, the limits and possibilities of the historical discipline. His writing on what constitutes historical evidence, on the relations between literature and historical narrative, and on the historian as a kind of detective in search of clues and traces left behind by historical actors have been for me insightful. I use standard historical sources (for example, anti-Jewish propaganda), but I am also interested in evidence that does not seem to fit overarching patterns and is revealing because of its uniqueness (the burning of the Bible). I have sought sources that connect Nazi actions with their emotions and imagination. These sources suggest relationships that are not always directly expressed but existed nonetheless.

One book has been from time to time on my mind as I engaged in this project, Sigmund Freud's *Moses and Monotheism*. I am not suggesting that we should understand the Holocaust via Freudian psychoanalytic method, not at all; my interest has been different. Freud's thesis in this book is that Moses, an Egyptian nobleman, creates the Hebrew nation by freeing it from bondage and imposing on it a monotheistic religion. But the demands of the new religion are too much. Moses is murdered, and the Jews adopt a powerful volcanic deity named Yahweh. The memory of Moses' murder is repressed, though an undercurrent tradition of his faith remains, gains force, and finally surfaces many centuries later. The awakened memories of Moses' faith commingle with the deity Yahweh to create Jewish monotheism, though the memory of the murder of Moses remains repressed among the Jews. How extravagant and fantastic! The book is a fable made into a sequence of historical arguments. It is conveyed (strenuously) in the language of evidence but is dominated by the language of fantasy. It is a work that requires from us time and again to suspend our historical disbelief and just go with the story. More than a study, it is a novel.[15]

Why, I have asked myself, do I return to this book? Freud wrote *Moses* in the mid-1930s, and it was published in full in 1939, after Freud had fled Vienna for London and shortly before he died. The immediate impulse to write the book sprang from the rise of the Nazis and Freud's shock at the massive anti-Jewish violence, which made urgent the questions of what it meant to be a Jew and of what the origins were of Jewish hatred and of Christianity's anti-Semitism. For Freud the extraordinary virulence and endurance of anti-Semitism could be explained only by an unconscious psychological truth embedded in it. His answer is that the relation between Christianity as the Son Religion and Judaism as the Father Religion is an application of the Oedipus complex. The New Testament and Christianity usurp the Old Testament and Judaism just as the Son usurps the Father. It also means that in spite of its claim to antiquity, Christianity remains historically and theologically an offspring of Judaism. Anti-Semitism ultimately exists because of envy, and the Jews are hated because they refuse to be saved by the Son and choose to remain Chosen. Freud felt that he uncovered a fundamental truth about anti-Semitism, and because this truth is based on the psychological unconscious, it implies that anti-Semitism is not secondary but essential to Christianity.

It is impossible and futile to attempt to prove this argument. Its power lies in the ideas it raises and the connections it makes. Underlining Freud's argument is the notion that an extreme contextualization of Nazi anti-Semitism (and we can add with hindsight "the Holocaust," though Freud was spared this knowledge) as originating only from the specific circumstances of the post–First World War period, the 1930s, and the Second World War is insufficient, for this argument assumes explicitly or implicitly that Nazi anti-Semitism had little to do with the rich past of anti-Semitism and Christian-Jewish relations. Freud's approach—to look at repressed memories at the dawn of time—is a nonstarter for the historian, as is the approach that directly links the Nazis to an event that happened centuries or millennia ago. But Freud's insight is fundamental—namely, the cultural importance of the presence of the past, of the idea of historical origins, and of the fabled stories nations tell themselves to make sense of their history.

I had this insight somewhere in my mind when I first encountered the sources about the burning of the Bible: I read them with shock that such a radical event took place, with surprise that it has not been made part of Holocaust history, and with uncertainty as to how to integrate the event into that history. But then things began to fall into place. Nazism's apocalyptic vision, I thought, was about crafting a new creation that by extension demanded new historical origins. For Germans in 1938 the Bible represented, among others, Jewish and Christian tradition and past; in burning the Bible, Germans expressed conceptions of historical time and origins. My approach has been to start from the Nazis in the Third Reich and look at (some of) their perceptions of the Jewish past and origins, and then to follow backwards the story the Nazis told about themselves and the Jews to wherever the Nazis took this story into the past. In this way I avoided the pitfalls of ahistorical repressed memories and of "discovering" Nazism hundreds of years before 1933. I have explored how the Nazis looked at the past, not how the past produced the Nazis.

Let me articulate this fundamental idea in different words. I do not believe, as mentioned, that centuries of anti-Semitism produced the Holocaust. But I do believe that the Holocaust cannot be explained without the deep tradition of anti-Judaism—and how the Nazis understood, recrafted, and used it. The Germans could conceive, justify, and imagine the persecution and extermination of the Jews because their ideas of Jews and Judaism in the Third Reich were part of a rich, familiar symbolic universe of past anti-Semitism and Christian-Jewish relations.[16]

But there is more. It soon became clear that Freud and the Nazis shared an important belief—namely, that the past is the key to the nature of national groups. This idea presumes kinship between present and past, and a historical continuity of national character and tradition over centuries. In fact, this way of describing nationhood fits very well within European ideas of the nation at the time. In 1882, before Freud invented psychoanalysis and Hitler was born, Ernest Renan, the French scholar of ancient languages and civilizations, gave a foundational lecture at the Sorbonne entitled "What Is a Nation?" His answer was that a nation "is a soul, a spiritual principle . . . [based on] the possession in common of a rich legacy of memories. . . . The nation, like the individual, is the culmination of a long past of endeavors, sacrifice, and devotion. Of all cults, that of ancestors is the most legitimate, for our ancestors have made us what we are."[17] Here are the basic elements of Europeans' view of national identity at the time, evident also in Freud's description of the Jewish nation in *Moses and Monotheism* and in the Nazis' view of the German nation: the search for origins; the nation as an organic entity endowed with soul or psyche or racial attributes; the parallel between the life of the individual and that of the collectivity; and the importance of memory and the transmission of legacy over many centuries.

My aim in pointing out this similarity between Freud and the Nazis is to highlight that in their era a certain way of thinking about national identity and origins was prevalent in Europe among very different nations and peoples. The Nazi tale of historical origins was not unique but an inherent part of the way Europeans conceived of national identity. The Nazis' peculiarity was to view the Jews as the linchpin in their story. And here, too, Freud and the Nazis share a resemblance. When Freud searched for the causes of Nazi anti-Semitism, he sought the answer, not in Nazi actions and thoughts, but in the Jewish past. And the Nazis, when they searched for the essence of their identity, ultimately found the Jews, whose history and origins seemed to define for them who they were and what they were seeking.

PART I

1933–1938
The Jew as the Origins of Modernity

A New Beginning by Burning Books

Of all man's instruments, the most astonishing is, without any doubt, the
book. The others are extensions of his body. The microscope . . . the plow and
the sword. . . . But the book is something else: the book is an extension of
memory and imagination because what is our past other than a set of dreams?
Which difference exists between remembering of dreams and remembering of
the past? This is what a book does.

Jorge Luis Borges, "El libro"

Now do you understand why I've been getting migraines?"
wrote Betty Scholem from Berlin on April 18, 1933, to her son
Gershom, the renowned kabbalah scholar at the Hebrew
University in Jerusalem. "A small event: the Zernsdorf bus
normally stops on our street *before* the bus stop, so we don't have to walk
so far. This time, someone called out to the driver as he lowered the steps
for us: 'So, for this pack of Jews you're making an extra stop!!' "[1]

When Adolf Hitler was appointed chancellor of Germany on January
30, 1933, Betty Scholem knew immediately that things were bad, but she
could not have imagined how quickly they would turn significantly worse.
The Scholems were a typical German-Jewish middle-class family, steeped
in German culture. In the decades following 1900, they had good reason to

feel that their place in Germany was secure. Arthur, Betty's husband, was a self-declared atheist, a "modern man," and a devoted patriot. At Christmastime the family home was decorated with a tree as a symbol of German national identity. The two oldest sons, Reinhold and Erich, followed in their father's footsteps and joined the family printing business, sharing Arthur's respectable, bourgeois values. But the two youngest sons, Werner and Gerhard, as Gershom was then called, opposed the First World War, so enraging Arthur that he threw Gerhard out of the house. Werner ultimately became a communist and gained election to the Reichstag in 1924 as a member of the party, while Gershom became a Zionist and emigrated to Palestine in 1923. The optimism that once characterized the Scholem family as German Jews shattered before Betty's eyes. Arthur died in 1925. The Nazis arrested Werner and his wife on February 23, 1933, and Gershom was far away in the Levant. The normal, safe, everyday neighborhood life she had taken for granted all those years collapsed around her, as it did for all German Jews.[2]

And so it went all over the Reich. In small Creglingen in Württemberg, a hamlet of a few thousand souls, including seventy-three Jews, members of the SA, allegedly searching for weapons in Jewish homes, attacked the local synagogue on Sunday, March 25, 1933. Interrupting the service, they took sixteen men and marched them in a parade of degradation to the town hall, where they severely beat and whipped them. Two did not survive; sixty-seven-year-old Hermann Stern and fifty-two-year-old Arnold Rosenfeld died in their native city, next to those they regarded as neighbors.[3] In Breslau, on the other side of the Reich, young Nazis assaulted Jewish judges and lawyers in the courthouse on March 11. They moved from room to room, screaming at Jews to get out, chasing judges and lawyers, some in official garb, into the street. The court closed for three days, and when it reopened, the president of the court ruled that only 17 of the 364 Jewish lawyers who practiced law in Breslau would be allowed to enter the building and appear in court. Ludwig Foerder, a veteran who was wounded in the First World War, and a man named Geldfeld, chairman of the Board of Governors of the Jewish community, were among those chased from the building. Outside, Geldfeld turned to Foerder: "Just tell me, to whom will it be possible to complain about this outrage?" "Distinguished Privy Councilor," came the answer, "I fear there is no longer any such place."[4]

Knowing with hindsight the end of the story of Jewish persecution in the Third Reich more than ten years later, we often view 1933 as the beginning of a gradual process of discrimination. In fact, it was an avalanche. The Third Reich began, not with a slow increase of violence against Jews, but with a massive, explosive attack on their civil, political, and legal rights in precisely the everyday places where one feels most secure—buses, workplace, home, one's own body. After January 30, 1933, on a daily basis Nazis desecrated synagogues, smashed windows of Jewish shops, and subjected Jews to acts of degradation in Königsberg, Chemnitz, Cologne, Krefeld, Munich, Berlin, and many other localities all over the Reich.[5] Jewish life became expendable, killing Jews a nonpunishable offense: a Jew was lynched in Kiel on April 1, 1933, while on April 11, guards from the SS (Schutzstaffel, Protection Squad, the elite unit of the Nazi Party) in Dachau removed four Jewish inmates from the newly established concentration camp and shot them out in the open. Adolf Hitler had been chancellor for a mere ten weeks.

In one respect, the violence against Jews following January 30 wasn't new. After the First World War anti-Jewish acts had been widespread in German society.[6] The violence markedly increased after the Reichstag elections of September 1930, which saw the electoral breakthrough of the Nazi Party. On the Jewish New Year on September 12, 1931, there were bloody skirmishes on Berlin's elegant Kurfürstendamm. Stormtroopers habitually assaulted synagogues and Jewish shops and attacked Jews in public. There was some continuity between the anti-Jewish violence of the Nazis in the Weimar Republic and in the immediate years after the seizure of power.[7]

At the same time, January 30, 1933, did represent a turning point. The Weimar Republic, which lasted from 1919 to 1933, was a democracy based on the rule of law and on a constitution that was one of the most progressive in the world. Jews were protected by the police and defended by the courts, even if individuals within these two institutions harbored anti-Semitic sentiments. The Third Reich, in contrast, permitted and encouraged violence against Jews. On February 22, 1933, Hermann Göring, the second in command in the Nazi Party who was nominated Prussian minister of the interior in Hitler's new government, used his authority to enroll fifty thousand SA men into the police as auxiliary force. These stormtroopers, key perpetrators of anti-Jewish violence, were now invested with official authority to carry out their brutality. After January 30 it was common for police officers to refuse to lend succor to Jewish victims, asserting that "police duties do not include the protection of Jews." On July 22 the government announced an amnesty for all crimes committed during the "National Socialist Revolution," and as a result all pending cases of murder, assault, and house break-ins were closed.[8]

For Nazis and other Germans, "the Jew" represented different and often contradictory things. Some SA men of humble origins resented the Jews as rich capitalists and greedy bankers and wanted to do away with the Jews as well as with much of capitalist industrial society, going back to a bucolic idea of premodern, small hometown existence, which one Nazi Party leader called "anti-capitalist nostalgia."[9] Others resented the Jews' role as owners of large companies such as the department store chain Tietz, which had fourteen thousand employees, or the Berlin-based Ullstein publishing empire. But many businesspeople and middle-class Germans shared none of these ideas; instead, they saw the Jews as carriers of insidious communist ideas to bring about a Bolshevik revolution in Germany. For still others, such as Achim Gercke, a specialist for race research in the Ministry of the Interior, the racial issue was paramount. To him, the anti-Jewish laws promulgated by the ministry were important to educate Germans that "the national community is a community of blood" that must reject Jews regardless of their political affiliation.[10] Many Germans resented the overrepresentation of Jews in key areas of public and professional life, such as the universities, medicine, and the law. Others simply saw the Jews as plotters par excellence, as conspirators united in a worldwide cabal to control the world, be their aim communist, capitalist, religious, or something else altogether.

Adolf Hitler epitomized the ability of anti-Semites to believe simultaneously in a mishmash of imaginary, diverse, and contradictory views about the Jews. For him, the Jewish conspiratorial activity spanned the entire globe and all of history. His anti-Semitism had Christian and metaphysical elements—he talked about the Jews as devils, as enemies of truth and virtue—as well as economic and political components—he ranted against the Jews as instigators of the French Revolution, equal rights, communism, and capitalism. Hitler saw the Jews as a race, a biological fact that cannot be altered by any change of name, belief, or religion, but he also viewed his anti-Semitism in religious terms: "Today I believe that I am acting in accordance with the will of the Almighty Creator," he mused in *Mein Kampf*, which he wrote in the mid-1920s. "By defending myself against the Jew, I am fighting for the work of the Lord."[11]

Everyone in Germany had his or her own idea of "the Jew." But there was a common denominator in the first months and years of the Nazi regime of all these disparate and conflicting views. The Nazi anti-Jewish story had an internal unity and shared a central motif: the idea that the Jews were the creators of an evil modernity that soiled present-day Germany. The adjective *jüdisch*, or Jewish, was attached to every phenomenon of the modern world objectionable to the Nazis, and then some. Jews were responsible for bolshevism, communism, Marxism, socialism, liberalism, capitalism, conservatism, pacifism, cosmopolitanism, materialism, atheism, and democracy; for Germany's defeat in the First World War, the 1918 November Revolution (which brought an end to the war and the German Empire), and the Weimar Republic; for Weimar's culture of entertainment in the cabaret and club scene, as well as for sexual freedom, psychoanalysis, feminism, homosexuality, and abortion; for modernist, atonal, and jazz music, for Bauhaus architecture, and for abstract painting represented in impressionism, postimpressionism, cubism, Dadaism, and expressionism.

The accusation against Jews as rootless cosmopolitans, a people whose loyalty is not to any specific nation but to an abstract ancient religion, had been common in Europe since the French Revolution. Nationalists in different countries, from France via Hungary to Russia, denounced Jews as alien to the intrinsic identity and culture of the homeland and as unable to shed their inherent rootlessness. The Nazis adopted this idea while fitting it to their own period. In 1933, the Nazis did not have in mind genocide and extermination—this came only later. What they did begin to imagine was a new, improved, pure Germany without the Jews and the modern vices caused by them. What was imperative was the total destruction of Weimar democracy, of the rule of law, and of German liberalism as well as communism.

The Nazis promoted their own modernity, a racial society of pure Aryans based on the idea of a strong leader and of a nation poised for

European hegemony, an alternative ideology to liberalism in the West and communism in the East. They proposed a united national community devoid of class and party political strife and of aristocratic and bigwig privileges, the benefits of technology, communication, and modern science in the service of the people, a national will embedded in Hitler, and support for a style of representational art. What concerned the Nazis and their supporters in 1933 was the present. They pinned their hopes on a transformation of current politics, culture, and identity, and they thus made the Jews into the enemy in the fight for a new German society: the campaign against them in the early years of the Third Reich was tied up with the campaign against democracy, liberalism, and communism— against all that the name Weimar Republic represented. The persecution of the Jews not only involved anti-Semitism but clinched the anti-Marxist and antiliberal vision of modernity shared by Nazis as well as by many Germans who did not identify themselves as Nazis.

If the Jews were the chief enemy of the Nazi revolution, the linchpin in the crushing of one modernity and the making of another, it is because only they represented in the minds of the Nazis and other Germans at one and the same time different, and often opposing, enemies. They could represent Marxism and liberalism, democracy and bolshevism, communism and cubism (not quite the artistic style for social realists). The idea of "the Jew" was powerful precisely because it added up into a whole that was bigger than the sum of its parts. Of course, not all Germans and Nazis linked Jews to all these attributes. But this is precisely the point: the Jew symbolized different enemies of a German regeneration to different people. The formidable image of the Jew as the origin of an evil modernity was precisely that it could mean many things to many people while still providing a common denominator of redeeming Germany from its present decline.

Betty Scholem, Hermann Stern, Arnold Rosenfeld, and Ludwig Foerder were victims of a wave of Nazi violence that not only targeted Jews but engulfed all of German society in 1933. The terror was widespread, against communists, socialists, trade union leaders, and left-leaning liberals, and more comprehensively against all those who expressed dissent in public, were regarded by the Nazis as ideological enemies, or were nonconformists of some kind. On March 25, at the same moment Jews in Creglingen were savagely beaten, stormtroopers, SS, and police units in forty-five other localities across the Reich occupied and demolished trade union offices. On the same date that Jewish lawyers were terrorized in Breslau, Felix Fechenbach, former secretary of the socialist leader Kurt Eisner and the current editor of the Social Democratic newspaper in Detmold, was taken into custody at the other end of the Reich together with other socialist leaders in the province of Lippe. He was shot dead on August 8 while allegedly being transferred to Dachau.[12]

When Hitler was appointed chancellor on January 30, 1933, his power was by no means absolute, and many in Germany believed that his political career would be brief. Yet within seven weeks a Nazi revolution swept Germany carried out by enthusiastic Germans, and Hitler became a dictator. In the weeks leading to January 30, Field Marshal Hindenburg, the old, ill, conservative president of the Weimar Republic, had not been prepared to sanction Hitler's appointment until he was satisfied that the chancellor's power would remain limited. Hitler headed a government in which all the posts but two were held by conservatives, with Franz von Papen, a key conservative wheeler-dealer, as deputy chancellor. The conservatives, who included aristocrats, army officers, big landowners, and industry captains, wanted to use the Nazis as legitimation and support for the destruction of Weimar democracy, but without handing actual political power to Hitler and his party. Many upper-class conservatives disdained the Nazi Party's populist, mass appeal and the humble social origins of its leaders, including Hitler. Von Papen, confident in Hitler's limited room for political maneuver, is purported to have said to a friend, "In two months we'll have pushed Hitler into a corner so hard that he'll be squeaking."[13] He was not the only one who thought so. "Nobody thinks [Hitler's cabinet] can last till the spring," wrote Christopher Isherwood, the British writer who lived in Berlin at the time and whose stories on the last days of Weimar inspired the musical *Cabaret*.[14]

But Hitler had several key advantages. Political realism forced the conservatives around President Hindenburg to work with him, and in truth they needed him more than he needed them. They wanted to replace the Weimar Republic with an authoritarian regime with limited political rights and aggressive policies against liberals, socialists, and communists.

They had key social and economic roles yet lacked the political power and mass following that Hitler enjoyed. He was the leader of Germany's largest political party. At the end of January 1933 the National Socialists boasted 719,446 members organized in ten thousand local branches in dozens of communities big and small all over the Reich.[15] These followers were determined to make their mark on history when on Monday, January 30, shortly after one o'clock in the afternoon, the radio announced Hitler's appointment. At eight o'clock that evening the Nazi masses displayed their tremendous power in a torchlit parade from Berlin's largest park, the Tiergarten, passing under the triumphal arch of Brandenburg Gate and on along the Wilhelmstrasse, where the Reich Chancellery and Hitler's hotel, the Kaiserhof, were located. Hitler reviewed the parade from a hotel window; President Hindenburg stood and observed the crowds at the next window. The French ambassador, André François-Poncet, watched the event from the embassy on Pariser Platz, by the Brandenburg Gate:

> The torches [the marchers] brandished formed a river of fire, a river with hastening, unquenchable waves, a river in spate sweeping with a sovereign rush over the very heart of the city. From these brown-shirted, booted men, as they marched in perfect discipline and alignment, their well-pitched voices bawling warlike songs, there rose an enthusiasm and dynamism that were extraordinary. The onlookers, drawn up on either side of the marching columns, burst into a vast clamor. The river of fire flowed past the French Embassy, whence . . . I watched its luminous wake.[16]

Others had different emotions. Earlier that day, at about five o'clock, as darkness began to set, Berlin's bustling boulevards filled with newspaper boys yelling the freshly printed headline of the evening papers: "Cabinet of National Unity Formed—Hitler Reich Chancellor." Sebastian Haffner, the celebrated German author and historical journalist, was then twenty-five: "For about a minute [my reaction was] icy horror. . . . It was so bizarre, so incredible, to read it now in black and white. . . . For a moment I physically sensed the man's odor of blood and filth, the nauseating approach of a man-eating animal—its foul, sharp claws in my face."[17]

Hitler knew that his position was solid: he had been appointed chancellor legally without destroying the constitution and with the support of the establishment and the army. He enjoyed broad public support. The challenge now was how to transform German politics quickly into a dictatorship. He lost no time in putting his stamp on events. Within twenty-four hours of his appointment as chancellor, new Reichstag elections had been called for March 5. The campaign for the final Reichstag elections in the Weimar Republic took place in an atmosphere of Nazi violence and terror. The SA men who joined the police as an auxiliary force went wild, beating up communists and socialists, dissolving their meetings, harassing them in taverns, and destroying party and newspaper offices. Public expression of opposition was thereby reduced to a minimum, while the Nazis enjoyed a decisive advantage by using the organs of local and state agencies.

A bizarre chance event then strengthened the Nazi hand further. On February 27, as the election campaign moved toward its climax, the Reichstag building was set on fire by a lone, young Dutch communist, Marinus van der Lubbe. By the next day Hitler had persuaded the well-disposed president and cabinet that a communist revolution was imminent. The Communist Party was suppressed and its leadership arrested. Hindenburg signed an emergency decree suspending civil liberties and permitting the government to take any measures necessary to protect public safety.

In this climate of intimidation and rumors, Germans went to the polls on March 5. Hitler's opponents felt fear and foreboding, while his supporters sensed exhilaration. Still, Hitler's party fell short of an absolute majority, as the Nazis increased their vote from 33 percent to 44 percent. The Catholic Center Party received its customary 11 percent, the Social Democrats 18 percent, also close to its usual number of votes, and even the Communists still won 12 percent. This was a political blow to Hitler because any change in the existing Weimar constitution required a two-thirds majority in the Reichstag. Hitler planned to propose an Enabling Act in the new Reichstag that would effectively do away with parliamentary procedure and legislation and instead transfer full power to the chancellor and his government for the next four years. In this way his dictatorship would be grounded in legality.

Hitler's delicate parliamentary situation in fact concealed the enormous political legitimacy and authority enjoyed by the Nazis. Broad swaths of Germans from all walks of life who did not vote for Hitler still supported his resolute suppression of socialism and Marxism, believed that the alternative to Hitler was a civil war or a communist coup, and identified with the robust nationalism of the Nazis. A sentiment of national rebirth after years of gloom and pessimism swept across Germany.

On March 23, in the Kroll Opera House, the Reichstag's new provisional home, Hitler made it clear who was in charge. The entire group of Nazi deputies entered the chamber in their brown-shirted paramilitary uniforms. Dressed similarly, Hitler presented the Enabling Act as the deputies cheered him on and jeered and ridiculed their enemies. Those communists who were not already imprisoned were refused admittance to the building. The Social Democrats announced that they would vote against the act, so passage lay with the Catholic Center Party, which shamelessly decided to support the act following Hitler's promises to sign a concordat with the papacy safeguarding the rights of Catholics and of the Roman Catholic Church in Germany. Supporters of the Enabling Act numbered 444; only the 94 Social Democrats present voted against it. Hitler thus became dictator created by democracy and appointed by parliament. The Enabling Act was the constitutional foundation stone of the Third Reich. In purely legal terms the Weimar constitution was never abolished. The Enabling Act was renewed in 1937 and again in 1939 and was made permanent in 1943. Within seven weeks Hitler had legally transformed Germany from a constitutional democracy to a dictatorship. He could not have done this without the enthusiastic support of Germans who marched and cheered under his window on January 30.

What followed in the coming months was a massive purge of German society and the elimination of those institutions and structures of the Weimar Republic that no longer served a useful purpose in a National Socialist state. In a process known as "synchronization" (*Gleichschaltung*), one by one every independent source of political, social, and cultural power in Germany was abolished. The trade unions' offices were ransacked and then closed in early May and a new Nazi organization called the German Labor Front put in their place. With the labor movement crushed and the

Social Democratic and Communist Parties destroyed in a whirlwind of violence, the key political opposition to Nazism was removed and the road to one-party state cleared. On July 14 a government decree formally proclaimed the Nazi Party the only legal political party in Germany. The new, modern, future-looking one-party Nazi dictatorship came into being on the same date as the Bastille fell in 1789: for the Nazis, their revolution replaced the French one as history's new promise.

The legal destruction of the Weimar Republic and the violence against the left in 1933 significantly increased the popularity of the regime. The arrests of political opponents were widely publicized in the press, as was the building of concentration camps, such as Dachau, the largest and best known. There was nothing secret about the camps, and they were there for all to see. Marion and Peter Yorck von Wartenburg married in 1930 and after the Nazis came to power witnessed and participated in the resistance against the regime. Later on Peter would be a member of the Kreisau Circle that carried out the assassination attempt against Hitler on July 20, 1944. In her diary Marion Yorck von Wartenburg recounted that in 1933 "we once went to Torgau (in Saxony, not far from Leipzig) and traveled past a camp that was fenced in with thick barbed wire, the lower part a big fence and above it barbed wire inside and out, and Peter said, 'That is a concentration camp.'"[18] Publicity about the camps served as a Nazi warning for loyalty and conformism. Many Germans were horrified by the violence, but many others greeted it with a sense of anti-leftist and antidemocratic relief and support.

The terror was not only political but touched every part of and everyone in German society, in cultural activities and at educational institutions, in every locality from Berlin to small, provincial villages. Social life was Nazified down to the most ordinary local associations. Thus, for example, sport, nature, and philatelic local associations with no political affiliation had to reorganize, throw out their Jewish members, and profess loyalty to the regime if they wished to continue their activities. Open dissent and resistance were dangerous, and public social life outside of Nazi organizations became very difficult.

Everything was done in the name of Nazism. Here lay Germany's new horizons, beyond Weimar, democracy, socialism, communism—and beyond their Jewish influence. It is within this picture of the Nazi revolution

and the massive purge of German society that the discrimination of
Jews made sense to the Nazis and other Germans. On one level, the Jews
were one enemy among others in the Nazi broad political and cultural
realignment in the heady months of 1933. But on another level, only the Jews
represented all the different modern enemies of the Nazi revolution. Their
persecution made sense within the political anti-democratic and anti-leftist
Nazi revolution, but it went beyond that because it was not dependent on
their political belief: being Jewish was reason enough to be an enemy of the
Nazi revolution.

The general meaning of the Nazi revolution emerged from the par-
ticularity of the Jewish persecution. The purges in the arts were typical.
Detesting many of the musical styles of the early twentieth century,
whether modern, atonal, or jazz, the Nazis moved to ban certain music
and musicians and to expunge avant-garde composers and their work
from the repertoire. Jewish musicians, singers, and administrators in
operas and orchestras, as well as music professors, immediately lost their
jobs. Concerts by Jewish musicians were canceled all over Germany. Bruno
Walter, the principal director of the Leipzig Gewandhaus Orchestra, was
denied access to the concert hall on March 16 and was told that were he to
conduct a special concert in the Berlin Philharmonic several days later the
building would burn down. Joseph Goebbels stipulated that the concert
would take place only under a non-Jewish conductor. Walter withdrew his
participation and left Germany.[19] But Jews symbolized a larger phenomenon, for not only Jews were hounded out, but all modernist and other
kinds of culturally and politically offensive music. Early on, measures
against jazz were taken by local and regional authorities, while the fox-
trot, Charleston, and other jazz-inspired dances were banned in all western German youth hostels as of August 1933.[20] For every Kurt Weill, who
was banned for his collaboration with Bertholt Brecht, there was a Hanns
Eisler, a non-Jew who was banned for his collaboration with Brecht and
for being a student of the atonal composer Arnold Schoenberg. That many
of the persecuted musicians were Jewish only made them into a clearer
target and symbol of the greater cause—the fight against the evils of modern influences that soiled the Nazi revolution.

Similar purges took place in other areas of German life and with
similar results: the principal aim was to remove communists, socialists,

and politically unreliable persons, along with all Jews regardless of political belief. The important decree of April 7, the Law for the Restoration of a Professional Civil Service, was aimed at forcibly ejecting different state employees: officials appointed after the 1918 November Revolution, Jews, and particularly anyone whose political opinions and activities did not ensure their political reliability. It targeted Jews but above all communists and socialists. Similar policies took place on local and community levels. The Nazification of the Federation of German Women's Associations, the national organization of the moderate German feminists, thus included the coerced dissolution of provincial chapters deemed suspicious by the Nazis, as happened in Baden on April 27, as well as demands for the exclusion of all Jewish members.[21]

The purge in the universities followed a similar pattern. The list of academics dismissed from university positions because they were Jewish or had Jewish wives is illustrious. Twenty present or future Nobel laureates had to leave Germany, among them Albert Einstein. Fritz Haber, who worked on the development of poison gas in the First World War, was not dismissed because of his war record, but he resigned on April 30 in protest of the sacking of Jewish colleagues. Jews were not the only ones who lost their positions; because academics in Germany were civil servants, the law of April 7 influenced all those regarded by the Nazis as politically unreliable. Even so, a third of university teachers who lost their posts were Jewish.[22]

Setting out to create a new German identity, the rulers of Germany took the fight against the "un-German spirit" very seriously. That is why the Nazis turned with such vehemence to the cultural domain, determined to cleanse the "Jewish spirit" from modern Germany. One event epitomized the meaning of this new German identity: the burning of books across the Reich on May 10, 1933. The Nazis showed panache in announcing their identity by burning books, before they burned people, and a penchant for the hissing, crackling sound of pages devoured by fire.

In Heidelberg, the book-burning ceremony began at the university with an evening lecture by the director of the Militant League for German Culture, Joseph Behringer, on "The Disparagement of German Art Between 1919 and 1933."[23] Heidelberg University, established in 1386, is

Germany's oldest. It had evolved in the nineteenth century into a cosmopolitan and liberal institution. Several professors were leaders of the liberal movement in the German 1848 Revolution, while after 1900 luminaries such as Max Weber in sociology, Ernst Troeltsch in theology, Gustav Radbruch in constitutional law, and Karl Jaspers in psychiatry and philosophy held posts there. Its professors were famous for being innovative. Located in Baden, with its tradition of liberalism, the university attracted foreign students, including many Jews. But in the later years of the Weimar Republic anti-democratic trends brought changes to the campus; the university could not exist as an island unto itself. The students and faculty became radicalized, and many supported the Nazi Party. In the summer of 1932 the statistician Emil Gumbel, a pacifist and a Jew, was hounded from the university by his intolerant nationalist colleagues and their supporting students (he ended up at Columbia University). By January 1933, Heidelberg University was all too eager to embrace the Nazi revolution.[24]

Present at the ceremony that evening were university professors and students, as well as members of the National Socialist German Students' Association, of the German Students' Body, and of the Nazi Party and other organizations. Behringer immediately drew the historical fault lines between the new Germany and its enemies. Following the French Revolution, he told the audience, a foreign element entered German art. And after 1918, "German soul and German spirit increasingly disappeared, influenced by dominating foreign isms, starting with Impressionism, Expressionism, then Futurism, Cubism, and Dadaism, . . . Now the good old German art returns—German again are our art, soul, and spirit."[25]

The real festivities began following the lecture, at around 9:30 p.m. A procession took off from Jubilee Square in front of town hall: by now darkness had fallen, and the students' torch parade lit the streets from Neckarstaden into Sofienstrasse, Hauptstrasse, and University Square. Marching in the procession with flags and insignia were professors, students, members of the Steel Helmets (a right-wing paramilitary organization of First World War veterans), the SS and SA, and several music bands. It must have been a sight when the procession of fire, music, and flags entered the crowded square. At one point, it was said, the police had to close the overcrowded area. At the center, earlier that afternoon, the students had erected an impressive pyre, supported by scaffolding poles, more than twelve feet high. The base, more than six feet wide, was made of bundled left-wing journals and newspapers. Hanging from the poles were communist and socialist newspapers, posters, books, pamphlets, and flags. At the top were caps of socialist organizations that led the fight against the right wing and the Nazis: the Black, Red, Gold Banner of the Reich, made of the colors of the Weimar Republic's flag, and the Iron Front, along with a Soviet sickle and star.

The books slated for burning had been confiscated in the preceding weeks. Already on March 12 stormtroopers had ransacked the local trade union library. On April 12, the town council announced that all "Bolshevik-pacifist, atheist and Marxist" books and newspapers should be removed from local libraries. A thorough cleansing of public libraries followed. On April 25, the Heidelberg Students' Body called all students to cleanse their personal libraries. Now, in front of the pyre, the leader of the students gave one last speech against the "Jewish-corrosive, Marxist-Bolshevik, frivolous writing . . . criminals against the German spirit," before, finally, the fire devoured the insidious books.[26]

Similar ceremonies took place in university towns across Germany, in Bonn, Darmstadt, Dresden, Freiburg, Giessen, Göttingen, Greifswald, Halle-Wittenberg, and others, some twenty-four in all.[27] The "initiative against the un-German spirit," as the burning of the books was known, was conceived by the National Socialist German Students' Association and the German Students' Body. On April 13, large white posters with bright red print appeared all over Germany with a manifesto, *The Twelve Theses*, announcing the initiative: "The German Students' Body organize from April 10 to May 10 1933 an enlightening campaign 'against the un-German spirit.' The Jewish spirit . . . together with liberalism as a whole must be uprooted."[28] On April 19, they announced the creation of a pillar of shame in all German universities—large columns centrally placed on campus that encouraged posted denunciations of professors who did not give full support to the Nazi revolution.

Throughout April and May students all over Germany cleaned out thousands of objectionable books from libraries. So did bookstores, which had to post the announcement of the upcoming book-burning on their windows. The forbidden books could not be bought or checked out during the Third Reich. The public library on the Kurfürstendamm had between

ten and a hundred copies of novels by Thomas Mann, Stefan Zweig, and
Erich Maria Remarque in 1932. In May 1933 the librarian was sacked, and the
objectionable books were replaced by numerous copies of Hitler's *Mein
Kampf* and Goebbels's *Struggle in Berlin* (*Kampf in Berlin*).[29] Many banned
books were taken off the shelves but remained in libraries. The reasons for
this were diverse: either to follow the new masters or to protect the books by
hiding them, or because the sole librarian had too many copies to purge
them all. Private homes continued to keep their copies, of course.[30] Blacklists
of books were drafted by different Nazi authorities, organizations of students, and universities, but there was no master list decided by the regime.[31]

In Frankfurt, the auto-da-fé at the Römerberg attracted fifteen thousand spectators.[32] In Berlin's Opera Square, twenty-five thousand masterpieces of Western culture were jubilantly consumed in a conflagration.
Ten thousand of them came from the Institute for Sexual Science, which
had been ransacked several days earlier. Photographs of Opera Square give
an idea of the atmosphere that evening.

German, Jewish, and non-German authors whose work was
devoured by the flames included Sholem Asch, Henri Barbusse, Franz

Boas, Bertholt Brecht, Max Brod, John Dos Passos, Ilya Ehrenburg, Albert Einstein, Lion Feuchtwanger, Sigmund Freud, André Gide, Heinrich Heine, Ernest Hemingway, Theodor Heuss, Helen Keller, Siegfried Kracauer, V. I. Lenin, Karl Liebknecht, Jack London, Rosa Luxemburg, Thomas Mann, Karl Marx, Robert Musil, Erich Maria Remarque, Arthur Schnitzler, Upton Sinclair, Ernst Toller, H. G. Wells, and Stefan Zweig.

Book-burnings are not unknown in German history. Repressive authorities had sought in the past to stifle ideas and intimidate authors. In the Third Reich book-burnings took place in the months before May 10 against socialist and communist literature and political writing.[33] But the burning of the books on May 10 represented a wider agenda about remaking German identity because it was initiated by students and academics, whose professions are based on the reading and writing of books, and because it took place as a public ritual in citadels of learning. "The flames blaze all over German universities tonight as symbol of [spiritual] purification," cried Gerhard Fricke in the ceremony in Göttingen.[34] Germanists especially were prominent among the academics who participated. Only one Germanist, Max Hermann, openly opposed the initiative, and he protested for national reasons; in 1942 he was deported to Theresienstadt, where he died in 1944.[35] Prominent German scholars including Franz Schultz in Frankfurt, Gerhard Fricke in Göttingen, and Hans Naumann in Bonn supported the book-burning, as did such organizations as the Militant League for German Culture of Alfred Rosenberg, the self-designated ideologue of the Nazi regime, the Center of German Libraries and Librarians, and the National Socialist Association of Teachers.[36]

Stormtroopers, literati, librarians, and teachers joined academics and students in what became a popular initiative from below. State authorities adhered only later. The Reich education minister, Bernhard Rust, was actually against the initiative, not for any moral reasons—he was a member of the Nazi Party since 1922 and an anti-Semite—but because his ministry did not play a leading role. Goebbels's Ministry for Popular Enlightenment and Propaganda, founded on March 13, likewise did not originate the initiative. Goebbels himself told a gathering of German booksellers on May 16, 1933, that he supported the students' initiative but that in future the students should synchronize their actions with the general policies of the regime. Still, he praised the act of burning the books as such, which his audience greeted with resounding applause.[37] Even though the public burning could not have happened without the regime's approval, participants were not coerced from above but acted enthusiastically from below.[38] In the burning of the books following the Nazi revolution, Germans redefined concepts of nationhood, Germanness, and history.

History was very much a part of the event, invoking traditional forms of celebrating German identity. The ceremonies leading to the burning—the celebratory speech, the procession, and the participation of various associations with flags and music—belonged to a pattern of national celebrations in Germany that went back to the commemoration on October 18–19, 1814, of the liberation of Germany from Napoleon at the Battle of Leipzig. The format was repeated later in such national celebrations as that in 1817 at Wartburg Castle, where three centuries earlier Martin Luther translated the Bible into German; in the 1857 festivals for the poet Friedrich Schiller; in the numerous celebrations of patriotic gymnastic associations, sharpshooters' associations, and singing societies;

in Sedan Day celebrations during the years of empire (1871–1918) commemorating the victory over France on September 2, 1870; in unveiling of
local monuments for fallen soldiers of the First World War; and in many
other local and national celebrations.[39]

Local variations of national celebrations existed and changes were
introduced over time, but as a whole Germans shared a common tradition
of national celebration performed on the local level, a sort of celebratory
manual of how to commemorate the nation. The Nazi burning of the
books in 1933 was part of this tradition. Interestingly, the descriptions of
the book-burnings, which are so rich, are silent about why the Nazis chose
this form of celebration to honor their revolution. But this accords with
sources of similar national ceremonies since the nineteenth century; significantly, they, too, are silent. It seems plausible that organizers never
questioned this form of ceremony to articulate German national identity.
One important aspect of the Nazi ceremony, therefore, was the emphasis
on continuity with a German tradition of national identity.

There was also continuity in the social profile of the celebrants. In
the nineteenth and early twentieth centuries the initiative to celebrate the
nation often came from local notables, university-educated citizens, and
students who combined nationalism and middle-class sociability. Local
associations organized the celebrations and mobilized the public. The
social composition of the 1933 burning ceremonies was similar.

By adopting the common tradition of national festivals to celebrate
the Nazi revolution, the participants placed the new Reich within German
history. Precisely because the Reich presented radical new elements and
the burning of the books was an extraordinary deed, it was important to
link the new era to the German past, thus giving the new regime the legitimacy that comes with the pedigree of historical roots. The book-burnings
were a way to internalize the new Reich through an old and familiar form
of national celebration as well as to appropriate the authority of a national
tradition in the service of the Reich. Nazis and other Germans understood
their own experience as building a revolutionary society that, at one and
the same time, commingled with cultural continuities.

The events were festive, public celebrations, carnivalesque rituals that
were meant to be seen and heard. The processions, torches, flags, pyre,

crowds, and incantations while throwing books into the fire made these special occasions. In Berlin celebrants used a truck decorated with posters of the confiscated books written in letters imitating Hebrew, in Frankfurt they rode on a wagon pulled by two oxen, while the students of the veterinarian institute in Hanover used a cattle truck featuring a poster that read, "Collection point for filth and trash." The Mannheim students were creative: a wagon pulled by two horses was decorated with Weimar flags, an anti-Semitic poster, and a second poster reading, "I am an ox who has read all these books." Youth and students rode jubilantly on the wagon.

The mood was joyous. Children participated, often via the Hitler Youth, providing a familial, community atmosphere. In Trier, the students of the Friedrich-Wilhelm Gymnasium were invited to participate by the regional school authorities. In Talar, the university provost, deans, and professors all took part in the event. The procession in Berlin, with torches, music bands, a wagon loaded with books, and lively participants, was three miles long, going through Brandenburg Gate and Unter den Linden until it reached the crowded Opera Square.[40] "Vendors were going around," wrote Arnold Zweig, the German-Jewish antiwar author. " 'Bonbons, chocolate, cigarettes!'—'Warm sausages, warm sausages!' . . . such entertainment, we could not have found any better, people giggle and titter, make jokes and laugh, passing comfortably the time until the burning."[41]

Not only books were burned, but also torched were left-wing insignia and flags, as well as socialist and communist paraphernalia, such as posters announcing ironically, "We greet the Soviet Union." Atop the pyre in Göttingen hung the sign "Lenin" (a postcard was later sold in local souvenir shops), and the Königsberg pyre was covered with Weimar's black, red, and gold flag. In Berlin, the students carried a bust of Magnus Hirschfeld, the director of the Institute for Sexual Science, and threw it into the flames. Music also played an important role. In Mannheim there were no fewer than eight bands. In Frankfurt, celebrants displayed dark humor: a band played a funeral march.[42] Chanting accompanied the throwing of books onto the funeral pyre. Goebbels, as always, was not at a loss for words:

> Against class struggle and materialism, for national community and idealistic outlook: I give the fire Marx and Kautsky.

Against decadence and moral decay, for discipline and morality in family and state: I give the fire Heinrich Mann, Ernst
Glaeser, Erich Kästner. Against literary betrayal of the soldiers
of the World War, for education of the people in the spirit of
truthfulness: I give the fire Erich Maria Remarque. Against
arrogance and presumption, for respect and awe in front of the
eternal German spirit: I give the fire Kurt Tucholsky and Carl
von Ossietzky.[43]

The significance of the ceremonies was not simply in what was said as
in what was done, seen, and imagined. Most participants had not read
most, if any, of the books that were burned or had ever heard the names
of some of the authors. In Heidelberg, books slated for burning were
defined casually as being of "Jewish, Marxist, and similar origins."[44] Some
students misspelled the names of authors on posters. In Berlin, wrote
Zweig, between the bonbons and the sausages, "the public was possessed
by satisfied passion, like animals, dull, passive, and with no idea [of the
goings-on]. 'What do they actually burn?' 'You know, Jewish books!' 'No,
un-German, indecent books.' 'One should throw them all to the Spree.'
'Well, this will contaminate the river.' "[45] Participants made a general idea
of the celebrations that was much more important than precise literary
knowledge. Zweig's protagonists got the point of the ceremony very well:
it was against Jews and other "un-Germans" who contaminated the social
environment.

Others made more careful sense of the events. Ernst Bertram, professor of literature at the University of Cologne, gave a lecture on May 3
entitled "A German Beginning," denouncing "the ideas of [the French
Revolution in] 1789" as anti-German. A friend of Thomas Mann and of
the literary scholar Friedrich Gundolf, he described in two letters of
May 7 and 8 his involvement in the burning ceremony: "On Wednesday
is the big, celebratory burning of un-German literature in front of the
monument of the fallen soldiers at the university. Many are of the view
that I should not be missing. To my chagrin also Thomas Mann will
be burned. With great effort I prevented having Gundolf on the list. . . .
So, I believe, the unavoidable manifestation will now take place with
dignity. . . . I have been successful . . . in preventing the absurd plan to

burn Gundolf and Thomas Mann. . . . I can therefore attend the solemn
'Auto-da Fe.' "⁴⁶ Mann responded to him several months later: "Dear
Bertram, live well in your national glass house protected from the truth
through brutality."⁴⁷

Bertram convinced himself that he could maintain his personal and
professional dignity while supporting book-burnings. Many German literati shared his view. The burnings were acted out in public by the finest
academics and the cream of German culture. For them the burning of the
books was a "symbolic act of purification," a cleansing rite of passage from
Weimar to the Third Reich.⁴⁸ The justification of burning the books was
not in question. But participants understood the transgression embedded
in their act. That is one reason speakers often presented the burning as an
act of renewal through destruction. Goebbels used this rhetoric, as did
Gerhard Fricke in Göttingen, who claimed that "this symbolic act is not
one of rejection and destruction but one of reconstruction."⁴⁹

It should not be surprising that refined intellectuals and well-
educated Germans supported the Nazis and burned books. We like to
think of Nazi Germany as an aberration. But, in truth, this is a partial view
of Western culture. We prefer to remember the positives and disregard the
negatives: to recall with pride, for example, Thomas Jefferson's poetic
words that all men are born equal but to ignore that his ownership of
slaves was equally a part of his heritage. For the Nazis, Germany was part
of Western culture. They staged the book-burning ceremonies in order to
promote and safeguard their idea of that culture. They were part of it,
much as the ideals of democracy and the pursuit of happiness have been.
And this is why Goebbels, Bertram, Fricke, and Behringer found meaning
in burning books.

Other Germans could also see only virtues in Hitler and his new regime.
From Gernsheim, a town on the Rhine, on June 26, 1933:

> Dear Mr Reich Chancellor! I am enclosing, Mr Reich
> Chancellor, a framed picture for you. I intended to send it to
> you for your birthday, but that was not possible because I
> designed and produced it myself as an amateur. I am 22 years
> old and the son of an ordinary railway worker. . . . Given my

financial difficulties it was not easy for me to make this picture. But for your sake Mr Reich Chancellor, I have saved every penny in order to give you a pleasure, and sign with the most devoted esteem, Peter Kissel, Hail Victory [*Sieg Heil*]![50]

Hitler received thousands of fan letters every month that attest to his popularity and adoration. Expressions of support began in 1925 when the Nazi Party began its rise to power, but after January 1933 the flood of mail was so intense that Hitler's office had to hire four employees to handle it. The letters contained expressions of gratitude and admiration, professions of loyalty, private petitions and political requests, and statements of dissent. In the following prewar years, every economic, political, diplomatic, or other improvement was acknowledged by gushing letters and presents. In the first few weeks and months of his chancellorship, for example, Hitler received countless saints' pictures, embroidered handkerchiefs, and other gifts. When the Soviets conquered Berlin in 1945, they found thousands of these letters in the chancellor's office and took them, together with other documents, to Moscow, where they are kept in the Russian State Military Archive. After 1989 they became open for scholars to examine.[51]

Typical of the letters is this note from Düsseldorf, on April 20, 1934: "My Führer! After I was ordained a priest on April 15, 1934, it was my sincere desire to offer my first mass as well as today's to God with a prayer for his richest blessing on your noble work. This is for you, my Führer, on your birthday today! Hail! Albert Spelter, Priest of the Free Catholic Church in Germany."[52]

The burning of the books linked the persecution of the Jews to the political reconstitution of the Reich and to the Nazis' fight against their enemies. The Nazis' list of modern enemies was long (they always had a long list of enemies and a short list of friends), but the events had internal coherence: we celebrate, Gerhard Fricke in Göttingen put it succinctly, against "democracy and liberalism, individualism and humanism, capitalism and communism."[53] There was room for improvisation, as well as for different speakers to add or remove certain ideas as they pleased. Thus some mentioned atheism, some pacifism, others sexual freedom, while others, as in Bonn, protested against decadent music and dancing in cafés.[54] But this diversity had a common general thrust. "The notion of 'un-German' spirit is not at all clear," admitted the leader of the Göttingen Students' Body. "But this is unnecessary. One cannot invalidate this initiative simply by asking what is actually the meaning of 'un-German.' This is sophistry, for ultimately we all had experienced fourteen years of this Jewish" influence during the Weimar Republic.[55]

The Jews gave meaning to the different "un-German" spirits of modernity, and yet the Jews were symbolically different. Goebbels mentioned the Jews in his Opera Square speech only twice, but the first time came in the opening sentence: "The age of inflated Jewish intellectualism is now finished, and the breakthrough of the German revolution" is under way.[56] *The Twelve Theses* of the students articulated clearly the persecution of the Jews as giving meaning to the greater reconstitution of the Reich. It discussed the general renewal of the German spirit but no fewer than four theses were dedicated to the Jew, including the following: "Our most dangerous opponent is the Jew and anyone who submits to him." The Zionist newspaper *Jüdische Rundschau* noted tersely on May 10: "The big spotlight at the Opera Square (in Berlin) shone also into our tangled experience and our fate. Not only Jews were accused, but also men of pure German blood. They will be judged individually according to their actions. For Jews, however, there is no need for a specific reason; the old saying applies: 'The Jew will be burned.' "[57]

The Reich began with massive anti-Jewish laws and decrees at the local, regional, and state levels, extending all the way from the Reich government in Berlin to small-town civic associations. Precisely 316 such measures were enacted in 1933, and 637 by the time of the Nuremberg Race Laws in September 1935. An additional 582 measures were enacted in the next three years leading to Kristallnacht, and 229 more by August 31, 1939. Altogether from January 31, 1933, to August 31, 1939, Nazis and other Germans comprehensively removed Jews from all aspects of social, political, economic, and cultural life via 1,448 legal measures.[58] We shall follow some of them as we go along. The first wave of anti-Jewish legislation, from January 31 to December 31, 1933, reads like a breathless whirlwind.

Berlin: Jewish physicians are excluded from the list of doctors approved to receive patients under welfare and health insurance plans. Prussia: Jewish judges and lawyers working at courts are immediately removed from office; the percentage of licensed Jewish lawyers should be equal to the percentage of Jews in the population; Jewish lawyers cannot represent the state. Cologne: Jews cannot use the city's sport facilities. Frankfurt: Jews must submit their passports for verification. Cologne: Jews cannot be employed in the city public administration. The German Boxing Association expels its Jewish members and will not work with Jewish entrepreneurs to organize events. The Law for the Reestablishment of the Professional Civil Service removes Jews from government service. The Law on the Admission to the Legal Profession forbids the admission of Jews to the bar. The Law Against Overcrowding in Schools and Universities limits the number of Jewish students in public schools. Bavaria: Jews cannot be admitted to medical school. Palatinate: Jews who are arrested for political reasons can be released from jail only when one of their guarantors or a physician who attests to their poor health will replace them. Baden: Yiddish cannot be spoken in cattle markets. The Law on Editors bans Jews from editorial posts. When sending a telegram by phone, it is prohibited to use Jewish names for spelling. Zweibrücken: Jewish businesses are forbidden to participate in the next annual market. Jews cannot own land sold by peasants. District of Bütow: Peasants are prohibited from selling their products to Jewish merchants. The following organizations expel their Jewish members: German teachers' associations, gymnastic and sport associations, the Association of German Blind Academics, the German Chess League, the Reich League of German Authors, and singing associations. Jewish newspapers from abroad are prohibited. Jewish students must have a yellow card instead of the regular brown student card. Jews are prohibited from practicing pharmaceutics. Jews are prohibited from visiting the following beaches: Berlin-Wannsee, Fulda, Beuthen, Speyer, and others. Jews cannot be part of the lottery sector. Jews cannot be jockeys. The mentioning of Jewish holidays in official and business calendars is prohibited. Jewish businesses are prohibited from displaying Christian symbols at Christmas.[59]

These measures put into law the ideas expressed in the burning of the books about purifying Germany of the Jewish spirit. In the burning ceremonies Germans told a story of the nation's recent decline and present-day resurrection. Goebbels was always articulate about the Jews:

"In this midnight hour, the evil spirit of the past is entrusted to the flames. This is a strong, great, and symbolic act . . . : here sinks the spiritual foundation of the November Republic [the Weimar Republic was created in November 1918], and from these ruins will rise victorious the phoenix of a new spirit."[60] The story emphasized foreign occupation and native resistance: "We are shaking off the yoke of a foreign power [namely, of Jewish influences], we are raising against an occupation. We wish to free ourselves from an occupation of the German spirit," declared professor Hans Naumann in the Bonn ceremony.[61] In this respect the burning of the books proposed values that were not only Nazi but agreed with general conservative views in society on how to redeem Germany.

A national redemption, not a racial revolution, was on participants' minds, to be celebrated within the tradition of German national festivals. The notion of race almost never appeared in these speeches and declarations. This is quite different from the picture painted by recent scholarship of the omnipresent notion of race in the Third Reich from the beginning. In fact, however, this absence makes sense. The burning of the books was about national redemption and the making of a new modern Germany by rejecting the ideas presented by the catchwords *Weimar* and *the Jew*. It is inconceivable to think that barely four months after January 30, 1933, Germans started to articulate their identity in terms of race, a notion that was present but not dominant beforehand. No one could articulate a clear idea of a racial Third Reich at that period. Only over time would it become a prominent part of Nazi rhetoric.

Arnold Zweig came to the Opera Square to watch his own books burned at the stake. Born in 1887, he joined the army in 1914 with a fervent belief in Germany and the war. He served at Verdun, one of the bloodiest battles of the First World War. This patriotic national feeling characterized German Jews; 80 percent who served were on the front lines.[62] By 1916 three thousand Jews had been killed in battle and more than seven thousand decorated. Still a persistent prejudice spread in German society that Jews avoided the front lines and served in the rear to enrich themselves at the expense of "good" Germans who shed their blood. In October 1916 the war minister legitimized this prejudice by ordering a "Jew census" in the army to determine the numbers of Jews in the front and at the rear.

The Reichstag and the press protested. The census was never published, and its findings disproved the accusation, although doubtless it would have not changed the view of any anti-Semite. The event had deep impact on Zweig, who vowed never to fight for Germany again. He wrote a macabre short story, "Census in Verdun," and became an antiwar activist.

Now, on May 10, 1933, he stood from nine in the evening until midnight squeezed among thousands of cheering, joyful spectators to watch the "witch-style burning of the books." Throughout the evening, "mystic, somber music in minor key" intoned from hidden loudspeakers. After several hours of watching flames devour books, the crowd grew tired. The evening ended with the singing of the Nazi anthem "Horst Wessel." "I was the only one among thousands who did not sing or raise his arm when the swastika flags passed by. I thought, I don't give a damn, and even if they lynch me, I am not raising my arm and I am not singing. It now became absolutely clear to me that there can be no more thoughts about staying [in Germany]. We have to leave. For better or worse." A disquieting thought pierced his mind: "They would have stared as happily into the flames if live humans were burning."[63]

The burning of the books involved a breaking of a moral taboo, an act of irreverence, and the total erasure of the opponents. The banned authors often possessed a keen sense of the moment that eluded the participants. When Freud was told by an outraged friend about the burning, he is said to have responded calmly: "Only our books? What a progress! In earlier periods they would have burned us as well."[64] Alfred Döblin, the celebrated author of *Berlin Alexanderplatz,* one of the masterpieces that emerged from Weimar culture, observed: "On May 10 there will be an auto-da-fé, I think, the Jewish part of my name is also there, fortunately only in paper form."[65] The antifascist authors of the *Brown Book on the Reichstag Fire and the Hitler Terror* had a sense of foreboding: "The burning was not meant as a symbolic act: the reactionary act of the German fascists is meant to burn the printed word that opposes it, in truth, not in a symbolic manner, as much as it wants the physical destruction of those who circulate and write this antifascist literature."[66] Oskar Loerke, the editor of Fischer publishing house, noted in his diary on April 27, "On May 10 books will be publicly burned, symbolically their authors."[67] "Oh, century!

Oh, science!" cried Goebbels at the Opera Square as the flames rose, "It is a joy to live!"[68]

The connection between Jews and burning books brought to mind images of historical origins and one other book, the Bible. Joseph Roth was born in 1894 to a Jewish family in Brody in the region of Galicia in the Austro-Hungarian Empire. A journalist and novelist, he traced in his work the decline of the Empire and of European culture. Following the burning of the books he wrote passionately that Hitler's aim was

> to burn the books, to murder the Jews, and to revise Christianity. . . . God is with the vanquished, not with the victors! At the time when His Holiness, the infallible Pope of Christendom, is concluding a peace agreement, a Concordat, with the enemies of Christ [Hitler and the pope signed a concordat on July 20, 1933], when the Protestants are establishing a 'German Church' and censoring the Bible, we descendants of the old Jews, the forefathers of European cultures, are the only legitimate German representatives of that culture. . . . This Third Reich is only the beginning of the end! By destroying the Jews they are persecuting Christ. For the first time the Jews are not being murdered for crucifying Christ but for having produced him from their midst. If the books of Jewish or supposed Jewish authors are burned, what is really set fire to is the Book of Books: the Bible.[69]

For Arnold Zweig, too, the burning of the books was linked to the Hebrew Bible. He wrote that "one who burns books, burns also libraries, bombs open cities, shoots down with cannons and airplanes temples and churches. The threat of the torch flying into the stack of books applies not to the Jews Freud, Marx, or Einstein but to European culture."[70] Perhaps Roth and Zweig arrived at their conclusions because, unlike other Germans and Europeans in 1933, as Jews they felt they were the most vulnerable victims, those, as Roth observed, that were, "thank God, safe from any temptation to take the side of the barbarians in any way. . . . Even if there were in our ranks a traitor, who . . . wanted to conclude a shameful peace with the destroyers of Europe—he couldn't do it!" for the Nazis would not accept him.[71] Roth and Zweig viewed the Nazi revolution as an attack on a certain European culture whose essence they believed to be the Jews. And precisely this belief was shared by the celebrants of the burning of the books, too, only with the morality inversed.

In Breslau, a German city and cultural center in the east, during the night following the burning of the books, someone stuck a small, subversive note on the poster announcing the burning ceremony at the university: "In delivering and burning books, one should not forget the Bible."[72] In May 1933, Nazis and other Germans did not dare to burn the Hebrew Bible. Would they?

T · W · O

Origins, Eternal and Local

T he flames of the burning books ultimately died down, but the
real terror against the Jews had only begun. Even if the burning
of the books was linked to the specific political and ideological
foundation of the Third Reich, from the beginning Germans
imagined the Jews in terms that cannot be reduced to politics, ideology,
economics, or definite historical events. *The Twelve Theses* manifesto of
the students who organized the burning celebrations stated: "The Jew can
only think in a Jewish way. When he writes in German, he lies. We want to
eradicate the lie. Jewish works should be published only in Hebrew. If they
appear in German, they should be identified as translations. German writing should be available for use only to Germans."[1] The students demanded
that Jews be banned from writing in German because any contact between
the German spirit and a Jew contaminated and endangered the German
source itself. Such anti-Jewish arguments linking the Jews to an abstract,
all-encompassing evil became more prevalent. After 1933 and the victory
over socialism and liberalism, the persecution of the Jews was reimagined
in ways that surpassed definable political and artistic movements.

Along this journey, which we will now follow, the Nazis perceived
the Jews somewhat differently from their other enemies. They had gone
to great lengths since the 1920s to show from experience and presumed
evidence the "crimes" of socialists, communists, and left-leaning liberals.

But the Jews soiled the German spirit, regardless of their intentions, simply by writing a word in German: their crimes needed no evidence and proof from experience. To be a Jew was a crime in itself.

Officer Kuh was very excited: he was to join the SS. There was just one small problem. He needed an official document showing that his great-grandmother had converted from Judaism to Christianity, and this had happened a long time ago, when Napoleon ruled Europe. He therefore made the long trip to Breslau, where he sought the help of Rabbi Bernhard Brilling, the archivist of the Jewish community, in finding the proof of conversion. The new German identity in the Third Reich required Aryans to document the purity of their lineage.

Following the recent Nazi attacks, the Jewish community in Breslau was very active. Jews who had been expelled from local civic associations formed new ones, and youngsters were thinking of leaving, many for Palestine. But one institution flourished surprisingly and unexpectedly: the archive. Its activity increased substantially because of inquiries from Nazi officials and aspirants to army, party, and government positions who had to prove their Aryan ancestry. Luckily for Officer Kuh, Rabbi Brilling found the appropriate documents. Kuh's career in the SS shone on the horizon. Yet an obstacle still remained: it turned out that his great-grandmother had converted in 1802. This was two years too late for the SS authorities, who set 1800 as the cutoff date. And so Kuh, considering his exciting future career and in appreciation of the good work of the archivist, asked Brilling to change the date to 1798.[2]

Officer Kuh got something absolutely right: even though the Nazis craved this all-too-human, though impossible dream of a fixed identity for all eternity, their idea of race was in fact unstable, open-ended, and, as "science," full of holes. People often conceive of race as a rigid marker of identity that, via biology and blood, clearly separates groups of people. But in reality things are very different. The idea of race in the Third Reich was the ideological bedrock of Nazi civilization, but it was also flexible; it called for documentation, but more important, it summoned the imagination. The Nazi idea of race sent Germans individually and collectively in search of their origins, transmuting the notion of race into *the* metaphor of origins in the Third Reich.

By making race into the principal idea in Germany, the Nazis transformed the notion of origins into the fundamental aspect of their policies
and beliefs. Race, as Nazi propaganda declared day and night, was "the
eternal source, from which the people draw its power."[3] The *German
National Catechism*, published in 1934 to instruct the new generation, was
clear: "What is the meaning of 'race'? The word 'race' derives probably
from the Latin radix = root. So is race for every person the root and the
origin of the inner essence and physical appearance."[4] The Nazis based
their racial ideas on a biological worldview that claimed that the history of
humankind is a story of racial conflict (as opposed to a story of class
struggle for Karl Marx and of individual liberty for Thomas Jefferson) and
that the characteristics of racial groups and their members were predetermined and could not be fundamentally changed. Racial experts did leave
some room for evolution and transformation, but they asserted that basic
racial traits of groups, such as Aryans and Jews, could not be changed
because their creation at the genesis of human history forever defined
their positive or negative distinctiveness.

In the Third Reich individual and collective proof of origin became
an issue of everyday life and death. In 1936 the Nazis introduced the
Ahnenpass, or racial passport, that notarized the births, marriages, and
deaths of members of the family in order to confirm Aryan ancestry.[5]
Genealogy became a small cottage industry. Germans traced their origins
in church and state registries, in state archives and libraries, in guild
records and even telephone books, forming family archives and recon-
structing family origins in order to certify the individual pure blood
origins that would ensure their inclusion in the national community. Jews,
in contradistinction, were not to hide their origins: one of the first anti-
Jewish laws of April 3, 1933, ordered that requests by Jews to change
their names were to be submitted to the Justice Ministry to prevent the
covering up of origins. On May 13, a new law forbade the change of name
altogether. And that is also the meaning of the Nazi legislation in the
following years about Jewish records and archives: court records concerning questions of racial origins and genealogy had to be preserved (1935);
material from the Prussian state archive about the history of Judaism
in the nineteenth and twentieth centuries could be consulted only by
authorization of Prussia's head of government (1936); all documents

about the influence of Jews in society, state, and culture had to be preserved (1937); all communities and institutions in the Reich had to report their holdings of books on Jews and Jewish research (1938); and, in Bavaria, Jews could not take materials from Jewish archives out of the state, while all Jewish archival material had to be handed over to the regional archive authorities (1938).[6]

The Nazis used the idea of race to tell a story of national origins, and Officer Kuh had the story clearly in his mind. The main point was not whether he was 100 percent Aryan according to the rules of the SS, for these rules could be bent and by none other than a rabbi: the main point was that the Nazi idea of race, consisting of a German past from time immemorial, explained and justified a certain German national existence without Jews (as well as without other groups). This was the ultimate consequence of the Third Reich's anti-Jewish racial ideas, whether Kuh's great-grandmother had converted in 1798 or in 1802.

The heady year 1933 came and went, and the Nazi seizure of power gave way to 1934 and 1935, years of Nazi consolidation and enlargement of power. Sebastian Haffner was preparing to leave Berlin in the summer of 1933: "For my part, I half felt as if I had already left. A few more months and I would be in Paris—I never considered the possibility of return. This was just a waiting period. It did not count anymore." He described the public mood as settling into the Third Reich: "Emotions became less intense in the course of the summer, the tension dropped, even the feeling of disgust weakened. It was all covered by a narcotic cloud. For many, who had to remain in Germany, it was a time of acclimatisation, with all its dangers." Years later, he would return.[7]

Christopher Isherwood had been preparing to end his memorable stay in Berlin, and on his last day in the spring of 1933 he wrote:

> Today the sun is brilliantly shining; it is quite mild and warm. I go for my last morning walk, without an overcoat or hat. The sun shines, and Hitler is master of this city. The sun shines, and dozens of my friends . . . are in prison, possibly dead. . . . I catch sight of my face in the mirror of a shop, and am horrified to see that I am smiling. You can't help smiling, in such beautiful

weather. The trams are going up and down the Kleiststrasse, just as usual. They, and the people on the pavement . . . have an air of curious familiarity, of striking resemblance to something one remembers as normal and pleasant in the past—like a very good photograph. No. Even now I can't altogether believe that any of this has really happened.[8]

It was difficult to believe because Nazi reality set in so firmly so quickly. On August 2, 1934, President Hindenburg died. Hitler used the occasion to combine the offices of president and chancellor as well as to take personal command of the armed forces. He assumed the title Führer (Leader) and Reich Chancellor, and army and public officials now had to swear personal oaths of obedience to him. A few weeks earlier, on June 30, Hitler had secured the support of the army behind the Third Reich. On the Night of Long Knives elite SS forces killed Ernst Röhm and the leadership of the SA, which had become a massive, unruly organization that clamored both for a second, social revolution of left-wing characteristics and for the abolition of the privileged officer corps in favor of a popular militia headed by the SA commanders themselves. Hitler had no patience for a second revolution because he sought domestic stability and the support of the army for his future war. Some one hundred SA leaders and several other regime opponents died in the purge, and in return the conservative army leadership agreed to Hitler's becoming the armed forces' commander-in-chief.

At the same time, the German economy, together with other economies in Europe and North America, started slowly to emerge from the Depression. Hitler's massive rearmament program, already evident in 1934, created plentiful jobs, and the number of unemployed went down. To the average German who was not a member of a persecuted group things looked to be improving. Political stability replaced the chaotic final years of the Weimar Republic, the alleged threat of a communist revolution was averted, and the economy was picking up. In addition, Hitler's piecemeal dissolution of the hated Versailles Treaty, which imposed harsh terms on Germany after the First World War, bolstered the regime's popularity and national feeling. In January 1935, following a plebiscite, the Saar territory between Germany and France returned to German jurisdiction.

Two months later, in March, the rearmament program, a blatant violation of the Versailles Treaty, was made public. A year later, in March 1936, German troops crossed the Rhine to occupy the demilitarized left bank, again in clear defiance of Versailles. These unilateral actions caused only limited criticism abroad. The regime's popularity skyrocketed. Hitler was venerated. "The first thing my German correspondent did when we showed her to her bedroom," recounted one writer in England in 1936, "was to pin a picture of Adolf Hitler over her bed."[9]

Things may have been improving, but the policies against the Jews only intensified. Anti-Jewish street and popular violence were daily occurrences in German localities. A barrage of laws discriminated against Jews and quickly made it almost impossible for them to take part in ordinary social life. Together, popular sentiments from below and policies of the regime from above coalesced, making it possible to imagine a Germany without Jews.

Officer Kuh got right something else, equally important: although the Nazi idea of race was based on a biological worldview claiming that racial groups have predetermined characteristics, the idea contained a strong religious component. On August 18, 1935, a group of Bamberg stormtroopers engaged in a propaganda contest in order to win the honor of participating in the upcoming annual Nazi Party rally in Nuremberg. A photograph shows them displaying on one truck a banner that read: "What the Jew believes is irrelevant, for in his race lies his rascal character." Race was about biology and immutable character.

But in a similar competition in Recklinghausen, also captured on camera, held on that same day, another banner read, "Knowing the Jew is knowing the Devil."[10] It is precisely this mixture of racial and religious metaphors of origins that gave resonance to anti-Semitism in the Third Reich, as we have already seen in the writing of Keller and Andersen in their book, *The Jew as a Criminal*. In principle, racial anti-Semitism contradicted religious doctrine because the aim of Christianity was ultimately to convert Jews, not to kill them, whereas Nazism rejected the possibility of redemption for Jews. But there is always a difference between abstract doctrines, be they racial or religious or any other, and how they are experienced in real life. Creeds are often presented in clear-cut fashion, whereas

the vicissitudes of everyday life usually impose a set of compromises and adjustments. In truth, racial identity in the Third Reich was a conglomeration of various identities that created a whole bigger than the sum of its parts.

The Jews were represented in terms of the present and the past, as race and the devil commingled quite well. Wide street banners declared that "knowing the Jew is knowing the Devil," while at the entrance to one village, next to a figure of Christ in a small, roadside Catholic shrine was a sign that epitomized Nazi racial exclusion: "Jews are not welcome here" (page 89). The approach that views racial ideology as hegemonic to Nazi beliefs understands these slogans merely as an attempt to "appeal to religious sentiments," thus assuming that the Nazis were not religious or that they used religion only as a vehicle of manipulation or that religious beliefs expressed by Nazis were not authentic.[11] All these arguments exclude the possibility that many Nazis did not simply "appeal" to religious beliefs but viewed Nazism as commingling race and Christianity as elements of German national identity.

When, following the stabilization of the regime, the leadership set out to define racial categories in the notorious September 1935 Nuremberg Race Laws, religious and historical origins, not science, came to identify who was an Aryan. Germans were classified according to one of four groups: Germans, with four Aryan grandparents; Jews, with three or more Jewish grandparents; half-Jews first degree, with two Jewish grandparents; and half-Jews second degree, with one Jewish grandparent. Aryans could be described only by the absence of Jewish blood, a negative definition. It is a mistake to see this definition as absurd and a travesty of Nazi claims that biological categories unrelated to religion defined Jewishness because this view is too narrow an understanding of racial as well as Nazi identity. The historian Richard Evans, while discussing the issue of race and religion in the Nuremberg Laws, defines the laws as "arbitrary" and making "nonsense of scientific claims about the importance of race and blood in determining Jewish or German identity."[12] This assumes that Nazi racism had a single, even fixed meaning, whereas in fact it combined scientific presumption with national and religious anti-Jewish traditions in order to say something that was fundamentally not about biology and race but about identity.

The Nazi racial idea included not only elements of religious origins but also of national ones. Since the unification in 1871, the idea of *Heimat,* or homeland, had become the ultimate metaphor for roots in German society, for feeling at home wherever the German Heimat was—the homeland, the region, or one's own hometown.[13] The commingling of racial and Heimat ideas in the Third Reich is an excellent illustration of the way the Nazis were part of, and placed themselves within, German tradition while building something new. The word *Heimat* is not easily translatable into English; it denotes one's emotional attachment to a territory conceived as home, be it a small locality or large, abstract homeland. It represented the ultimate German community of people who had a particular relationship to one another, sharing a past and a future, and projected the idea of German immemorial origins. By calling Heimat their community, region, and the nation as a whole, Germans took the intimate and immediate feelings associated with the community and projected them to the larger areas of region and nation. The Heimat idea thus made the nation into an intimate, cozy idea, replete with tender feelings.

The Heimat idea consisted of three elements—history, nature, and folklore, or ethnography—that were disseminated through diverse cultural creations. Some of the most important were Heimat books, published by communities to publicize their singularity in national and local history; Heimat studies, which entered the school curriculums in the 1890s; Heimat museums, founded across Germany from the metropolis of Berlin to small provincial towns; and a host of associations that cultivated and propagated the Heimat idea, such as local beautification societies and historical associations, regional Heimat associations, and, from 1904, the national German League for Heimat Protection, which thus added social continuity and regularity to the idea. Heimat knowledge combining history, nature, and folklore was called *Kunde,* a commingling of knowledge and sensibilities. The Heimat idea was always about feelings more than facts.

By mixing facts and literary narratives the Heimat idea gave Germans local and national roots in an ever-changing world. Heimat stories represented the nation as a three-tiered construction of local, regional, and national ways of life. Take, for example, the region of Württemberg in southern Germany and its people, the Swabians. A classic example of the three-tiered way of thinking was the study of the Swabian dialect. Language embodied Swabian distinctiveness, according to a Heimat book published in Württemberg: "The language of our people offers one of the most important means to know its peculiarity. . . . [Our language] still streams in the localities of our Heimat with its blend of power, originality, nativeness, and simplicity."[14] The first volume of the Swabian dictionary, published in 1904, symbolized this uniqueness. At the same time, language embodied Germanness. The editor of the dictionary, Hermann Fischer, declared in the introduction that the history of Swabian dialect was part of the history of German philology.[15] The nation resembled the Russian matryoshka doll, as it accommodated and integrated smaller versions of itself: areas in Württemberg had different dialects; together they formed the Swabian dialect; and all the regional dialects constituted the German language. Similar constructions occurred with regard to food, dance, and the like. Heimat folklore linked generations by emphasizing the longevity of traditions, real or invented, thus connecting past and present. In times of technological change, finding one's roots meant making sense of modernity.

A key institution for visualizing local and national origins was the Heimat museum. More than 350 such museums were founded in the decades before and after 1900 in cities, towns, and small towns across Germany. They embodied, first of all, the uniqueness of each locality. The past of even the smallest community was worthy of collection and exhibition, as museum activists in Oettingen, Bavaria, explained in 1908: "Although some may think that in the Ries there are no historical objects to collect, we are nonetheless convinced that even here there are plenty of interesting historical objects to find and to preserve."[16] As Heimat museums became the symbol of local identity, how could a community live without one? Heimat museums displayed the past in its entirety, from prehistory to the present, as a story of origins and everyday life experience. The museum activists in Oettingen were true to their words and collected "plenty of interesting historical objects": heraldic figures, documents, drawings, guild objects, pottery and kitchenware, furniture, genealogical albums, and "miscellaneous [items] such as" locks, shoe buckles, spoons, knives, and rings.[17] These objects, which filled Heimat museums everywhere in Germany, emanated from people's lives in the community—the private and the public spheres, home, work, and family.

Still, the aim of Heimat museums was not simply to tell the history of local communities but also to give meaning to the nation as a whole. Museum activists claimed that national identity sprang from local identity. The Heimat museum in Jever, in Friesland, founded in 1887, was established in order to "advance the local archaeology and through this activity the love for Heimat and for the German fatherland."[18] By founding Heimat museums that represented the local German pasts, *Heimatlers* constructed a typology of the national past. Although every local history was particular, that story was displayed by means of similar objects. Together Heimat museums across Germany reflected a national narrative that depicted "small people" instead of the elites, everyday life instead of major historical events, and the locality as the site of the nation's origins. As a national phenomenon, Heimat museums thus endowed the abstract nation the tangibility of local experience.

The Heimat idea transformed localness into a concept of nationhood. By allowing localities and regions to emphasize their historical, natural, and ethnographical uniqueness and at the same time integrating them all, the Heimat idea was a common denominator of variousness. It balanced the plurality of local identities and the restrictions imposed by the imperatives of a single national identity. It gave the German nation-state, recently unified in 1871, the halo and consecration of immemorial origins.

By 1933, the Heimat idea was perceived as an essence of Germanness. To lay claim to represent the "true Germany," the Nazis, like all modern German regimes, had to appropriate it. The Nazis linked the ideas of racial and Heimat origins. They maintained the notion of the German community of shared past, present, and future, only they now defined Heimat in terms of race, blood, and soil, as stated by a member of the Nazi Association of Teachers: "Yes, blood is a substance, but not in the false, materialist sense, rather in the sense of Heimat, soil, and racial property."[19] A vast literature disseminated in poems, novels, and plays the idea of the racially pure Heimat. Heimat history and Heimat studies blended "Heimat, kin, race, Volk, and Führer" in a mixture of fact and fiction about the history of the German racial community. For when it came to questions of ideology, the Nazis, like other Heimat believers before and after them, never let themselves be confused by facts. Heimat studies in schools thus began with Hitler as "Führer and master" and continued with the "Nordic race" as "creator and carrier of mankind's culture." Ultimately, Heimat education aimed, as one Heimat textbook put it in 1936, to make "every German youth . . . a follower of the Führer."[20]

The Nazis used the Heimat idea not because it was a Nazi concept *avant la lettre* but because it existed in German society as the most familiar icon to represent national identity. In this way they made the Third Reich amenable, familiar, and part of German tradition. Indeed, the 1938 edition of the *Catechism* book mentioned above was renamed *Small National Knowledge*, in which the word *Knowledge (Kunde)* stood for the mixture of knowledge and sensibilities in the tradition of the Heimat idea. By linking the Kunde of the idea of race with the Kunde of the idea of Heimat, the Nazis linked the new Nazi Germany to the most celebrated idea of origins in German culture and gave the Third Reich an intimate aura.[21]

The power of racial ideas in Nazi Germany was precisely their ability to combine different ways of thinking, as race became a metaphor of origin commingling racial, religious, and national attributes. This explains why Germans accepted the Nazi worldview, and accepted themselves as Aryans, in an incredibly short time.

Race, then, was a fantasy about eternal origins. The commonplace argument by scholars has been that Nazi racism was about biology and that the Nazis viewed racism as scientifically grounded. This is correct, of course, but there was more to Nazi racism than biology and science. Nazi racism was not primarily about biology but about the menace created by the body to the spirit. Biology, the body, was the raw material, but the essential issue was how the raw material affected the spirit. It was not the Jewish body per se that posed a danger but the Jewish spirit produced by this body. Biology and the spirit cannot be separated, yet by focusing on scientific biology we limit our understanding of the meaning of Nazi ideas. For Germans biology was fundamentally a moral category of right and wrong because, they believed, of the way it determined their spirit or, to use current terminology, their culture.

The Nazis threw the moral category of biology into sharp relief in their elaborate plans for the racial reorganization of German and European societies. Nazi racial ideology was arranged in three concentric circles. A memorandum circulated by the Ministry of Interior on July 18, 1940, gives an idea of the radical plans envisioned by the Nazis. While written in the early months of the war, it included ideas that were already common in the prewar years. According to this document, the inner circle concerned the transformation of German society by eradicating those regarded as "alien" or "unfit." It called for the rearrangement of German society based on racial fitness and social and economic performance. Society was divided into several groups that ranged from healthy to sick. The lowest group consisted of "asocial" elements who would be denied any social assistance; they would be treated according to "measures of negative population policy," namely starvation, deportation, forced labor, and ultimately extermination. The second lowest category consisted of those deemed "bearable"; for them, the possibility of sterilization was considered.[22] The memorandum did not simply chart plans for the future but reflected existing policies: 70,273 institutionalized mentally and physically disabled Germans had been murdered at six gassing facilities between January 1940 and August 1941.

A wider circle encompassed Nazi ambitions to restructure Europe, and especially eastern Europe, along racial lines. A war of racial domination meant creating whole groups of people without rights who would exist in function to their utility to German economy and production. Societies such as Poland and Russia would not be allowed to have any form of cultural, artistic, and creative life. Deportation, forced labor, and starvation were standard policies, as eastern Europe was to be prepared for a massive resettlement of Germans. Finally, a wider circle still on a universal scale included the struggle against the Jews, humanity's eternal enemy, as an essence and goal of Nazi racial ideology.

This elaborate plan of action was based not on hard, scientific evidence but on moral beliefs. Beyond that, the idea of race was flexible enough. No one held a copyright on it, and that is why it could be used by such different hands to mean such different things, whether by theologians, scientists, political leaders, or just about anyone, and at times also to mean different things to the same people. Hitler himself defined the Jews in *Mein Kampf*, written in the mid-1920s, as "a people with definite racial characteristics" and described them some twenty years later as "a community of intellect," a "spiritual race," not quite a natural-science definition.[23] Significantly, although some Nazis were interested in the physical look of Jews allegedly determined by the natural sciences, most Germans who had prejudices against Jews, including Nazis, were more concerned with the "Jewish spirit" and "Jewish mind."

This view was shared by natural scientists. Johannes Stark, a Nobel Prize–winning physicist who advocated for an Aryan physics and championed racist principles in the natural sciences, explained in a 1937 essay published in the official SS paper, *Das Schwarze Korps*, that the victory of "racial anti-Semitism" will come when "[we will] destroy the Jewish mind, which today can flourish more serenely than ever as long as its host can show the most impeccable proof of Aryan ancestry."[24] Without difficulty Stark linked the ideas of race, historical origins, and the Jewish mind. Hitler articulated a similar idea when he combined, in a speech to Berlin students on February 7, 1934, the notions of Aryan, racial, spiritual, and historical origins, talking about the "fruits of that Aryan spirit that, providing the roots of culture . . . , has bestowed upon the entire world the general foundation of our culture, our truly human foundations in the millenniums, upon which history has shed light."[25]

There were two kinds of science in the Third Reich, connected but not identical.[26] One legitimately sought verification based on evidence and measurements and guided by informed standards of the field. German scientists during the Third Reich were thus the first to discover the causal link between smoking and lung cancer and to recognize the danger of secondhand smoking as well as to document the dangerous effects of asbestos.[27] But another branch of science sought to prove Nazi racial ideas, conforming to its ideological imperatives. Racial experts read into the "evidence" what they had already determined before their research had begun. At research institutions they invested enormous resources and intellectual energy to determine scientifically who was a Jew and who an Aryan, a question that simply cannot be answered in biological, genetic terms.

Scientists were often frustrated by their inability to explain the purported biological mechanisms that undergirded racial difference between Jews and Aryans. Otmar von Verschuer was a distinguished pathologist and, beginning in 1935, the director of the newly founded Institute for Hereditary Biology and Racial Hygiene at the University of Frankfurt; Josef Mengele was one of his most favored students. In a lecture in 1938 on Jewish predisposition to diseases, he noted with dissatisfaction that the results were established via statistical data, not biological-genetic "evidence." Verschuer continued his research. In 1942 he became the director of the prestigious Kaiser Wilhelm Institute for Anthropology. Shortly thereafter, in the spring of 1943, Mengele received a new position at Auschwitz. The zeal to find genetic evidence to racial characteristics of Jews and Aryans led Verschuer to collaborate with Mengele's medical experiments. In March 1944, he wrote to the German Research Foundation, which funded his research: "My assistant Dr. Mengele . . . has joined me in this branch of research. He is at present assigned as SS-Hauptsturmführer and camp physician at the Auschwitz concentration camp. With the permission of the SS-Reichsführer [Heinrich Himmler], anthropological investigations of the most diverse racial groups are being conducted and the blood samples sent for processing to my lab."[28]

Racial experts usually finessed question of evidence with a powerful tool: narrative. Verschuer's mentor was the prominent racial anthropologist Eugen Fischer, who in 1927 founded the Kaiser Wilhelm Institute for Anthropology. In 1933 Hitler appointed him rector of the Friedrich

Wilhelm University in Berlin, and he later joined the party. In 1942 Fischer wrote a long essay entitled "Ancient World Jewry," arguing that "world Jewry" was a cohesive, unified racial entity of unbroken continuity from ancient times and into the modern era whose aim had been to attain power over the world. This fascinating hypothesis was based on 198 portraits of Egyptian mummies from the second and third centuries C.E., some of which, according to Fischer, showed resemblances to Jews. He concluded that the mummy portraits showed a recognizable "physiognomy of the world Jew ... [that] remains to this day." He did admit that his essay had problems of evidence that called into question the scientific validity of his interpretation. But he claimed that such a daring explanation could serve to push scholars toward a broader and deeper understanding of Jewry.[29]

Ultimately, storytelling was more important than science. Nazis continued to believe in their fantasies about the Jews because these required no hard facts. They used racial science not as a vehicle to find truth but as a modern seal of approval to predetermined anti-Jewish views. This is why they had no problem, in enacting the Nuremberg Race Laws, in defining Jews using a historical argument of genealogical descent. The main issue with respect to race was not that it was based on science but that it represented German national origins.

Indeed, even if the terms *science* and *biology* often evoke rational, calculated, cerebral activity, the best science is always also made by elements of art because we formulate our hypothesis based on our cultural views and prejudices (the world is flat or round?) and because the ultimate product is but an understanding of reality, as we order the facts into a story about the natural world, a narrative. In fact, science is a poetic enterprise no less than a research discipline. It is driven by metaphors: think, for example, of such present-day terms as *genetic code, electron cloud, DNA map*, and *quantum leap*. One must have a poetic, intuitive inclination to follow and contribute to exact scientific research. If this is the condition of serious science, it was all the more so with Nazi racial "science."

The result of the Nazi notion of race as a malleable mix of racial, religious, and Heimat elements was that ultimately everyone had his or her own idea of race in a Third Reich that was obsessed with historical roots precisely because it was revolutionary: Nazism was a forward-looking world-view permeated by the notion of origins because the new world was to be built on the ruins of an old one. New regimes and political movements often look to the past as a source of legitimacy to their policies and ideas. The Nazis sought the comfort of historical roots in the idea of race. Their insistence, indeed fanaticism, in this regard was linked to the regime's overall insecurity about these roots, unable to hark back to any golden age, as in Mussolini's Fascist Italy, which built on the Roman Empire, but also unwilling to sever all links to the past, as in Lenin's Soviet Union.

The stories expressed by Germans in the burning of the books and in the idea of race belonged together. A new beginning set off a new reading of the nation's present and past. In the book-burning ceremonies Germans recounted the present political and social transformation of Germany from Weimar democracy to Nazi dictatorship. In the idea of race they recounted a story of national past from time immemorial. These views were complementary, giving the Third Reich a new national narrative. From the beginning the Nazis expressed the human desire to start over and to have a story that went along with this transformation.

In thinking about race, the Nazis desired a stable national identity, a fixed existence in time that would give coherence to a fast-changing world that became ever more complex. There was nothing unusual about this desire to have a steady sense of self and collectivity: it is human, and one of the essential characteristics of the modern condition, in which history moves forward at such a speed that the past of even twenty years ago seems distant and alien. Twenty years earlier, in 1913, Germans had lived in an empire ruled by a kaiser, in a world that seemed simpler and familiar. Since then they had experienced in rapid succession the First World War, the 1918 Revolution, the Weimar Republic, the hyperinflation of 1922–1923, the Depression, and the rise of the Nazis. In the final years of the Weimar Republic they felt uncertainty about the future and a sense of a constant onslaught of unpredictable events since 1914. The notion of race lent Germany an apparent coherence and continuity that extended back into the past of not only two or three decades but several millennia, indeed to the dawn of humanity.

But the Nazi desire for a steady national identity clashed with the essence of identity and modernity, both of which are always made of shifting meanings. The dream of a steady identity is always impossible, by anyone, under any ideology or worldview, and for any collectivity, because identities are by definition ever-changing and multifaceted. The more you attempt to build a fixed, uniform, and constant identity, the more you are at odds with reality. The result produced a Nazi regime of intense uncertainty and of a continuous and ever more radical search for fixing its identity, leading from persecutions to exterminations.

It is also important to point out that although the Nazis were absorbed with the idea of race, which was in theory transnational and not bounded by state borders, Nazism was a German national movement that viewed other European nations as subordinates, even those nations of putative similar racial descent, such as the Dutch. Hitler had no intention of forming an egalitarian, multiracial, multinational empire, a sort of racial European Union. His conquests were to serve the German national interest. Nazi racial ideology was a national ideology. The notion of race was one metaphor in the German national tradition with which Germans articulated their sense of nationhood, together with other metaphors of different political and cultural valence since the unification in 1871 such as class and liberal freedom.[30]

Everyone had an idea of race in the Third Reich, and yet one group elicited for the Nazis no uncertainties, no doubts, and no discounts, regardless of the definitions of race: the Jews. In 1934 and 1935 the process of social isolation and segregation of Jews continued at full speed. Laws enacted at the Reich level were important, but especially injurious for Jews were laws made by local communities. They tore the Jews from their everyday habits and security and turned them into outcasts overnight. Most hurtful of all was that local laws were at times decided by familiar neighbors and acquaintances who sat on town councils, chambers of commerce, and the like, as happened in Hamburg, where in 1934 Jews were expelled from all civil associations.

1934. Jews are prohibited from trading in National Socialist literature. The participation of Jewish actors in theater is prohibited. Radio programs should not mention economic businesses that are known as being Jewish. Hessen: The Old Testament is taken out of the curriculum of Protestant religious classes and the hours are added to the studying of the New Testament.

Bad Kissingen: Jews are prohibited to use the city swimming pools. Jews can-
not be admitted to schools that train dancing teachers. Mannheim: Schools
are ordered to set up special classes for Jewish pupils. Jews are not allowed to
study veterinary science. The Technical University in Darmstadt and the
University of Giessen can no longer confer the postdoctoral Habilitation title
on Jews. Jews are excluded from all sections of the book trade, apart from
cases when they sell only to Jews.

1935. Jews are prohibited from displaying the swastika in their apart-
ments and businesses. The Tax Law forbids Jews from serving as tax consul-
tants. Dortmund: Jews are forbidden from using the local sport facilities.
Franconia: Jews are not admitted to youth hostels. Giessen: Jews are prohib-
ited from visiting the autumn horse market. Army law expels Jewish officers
from the army. The selling of Jewish newspapers on the street is prohibited.
Jewish owners of cinemas have two months to sell their business to an Aryan.
Breslau: Only Germans can sell products in the local annual Christmas mar-
ket. Munich: It is prohibited to rent lecture and performance halls to Jews.
Judges are prohibited from citing Jewish lawyers, legal professionals, and
authors in their rulings.[31]

Not a day went by in the new Reich without some aspect of the
Jewish Question being addressed in one way or another, be it in legislation, propaganda, or policy. "[I] think that most Jews will have to
leave. Herr Goebbels pledged once again on the radio that he won't rest
until the last Jew has gone!" wrote Betty Scholem to her son, Gershom,
on July 4, 1933, with perhaps a sense of discovered self-awareness.[32] The
regime's intentions were clear enough. The Security Service of the SS
(Sicherheitsdienst, SD), always a sensitive barometer on the Jewish
Question in the Third Reich, wrote as early as May 1934 that, for the Jews,
Germany had become "a country without any future."[33] Some days and
months, such as April 1, 1933, when there was a nationwide boycott of
Jewish businesses, or September 1935, when Hitler passed the Nuremberg
Race Laws, were especially brutal. Others were quieter. But the overall tra-
jectory of the regime's policy was evident.

Just as everyone had his or her own idea of race in the Third Reich,
everyone also had his or her idea of how to solve the Jewish Question,
from Hitler down to the last German. Some wanted to remove Jews from
society but let them stay in Germany as a minority with no rights, others

wanted all Jews to emigrate. Some found the anti-Jewish campaign morally outrageous and a shocking stain on German culture, while others
thought that Jews were generally guilty (the list of possible crimes from
which to choose was long) apart from their own classmate, whom they
knew personally to be really a good guy.

Everyone looked for meanings in the anti-Jewish policies, for a
glimpse of days to come, of the future of Jewish-German relations, but
also for an image of the self. The range of views was so broad that some of
them seem almost fictional to us today. Nikolas Kahlke, a war veteran and
pensioner, sent Hitler birthday greetings on April 7, 1935, combining devotion for Nazism with a view that, though actions were necessary against
some Jews, not all Jews were beyond national redemption:

> Providence, who gave you to us,
> keep you with us many years.
> Hail to you, Führer.
> . . .
> You've blasted the rats [the "Red tide" of communism]
> the enemy hung on us,
> Hail to you, Führer.
> But you reach out to Jews
> To those who sincerely want
> Germany's prosperity
> and Resurrection.[34]

Fortunately, Hitler, a gift from "the Lord," had "reach[ed] out to Jews."
Heinrich Herz was a German Jew:

> Very esteemed Mr Reich Chancellor! . . . I am turning to you
> . . . since my intuition tells me that you . . . will not accept [the
> violence against Jews]. I look on the events of the last years full
> of admiration and trust, and I am inwardly a good German
> who cares about the welfare of his country with every fiber of
> his being. But with all this admiration a drop of wormwood
> has slipped into my heart . . . [namely] the one-sided treat-
> ment of thousands of my co-religionists, whose feeling and

thinking are just as German as mine. How much I should like
to help build up my beloved Fatherland, if only an opportunity
to do so were offered me. . . . Mr Reich Chancellor, use your
authority to give us hope that we can live again. I shall thank
you thousands and thousands of times for it.[35]

Herz, a master craftsman from Hamborn am Rhein, wrote this letter on
April 27, 1934. It is almost touching in its naïveté as it is troubling for its sense
of denial. Only a man who felt totally German could write such a letter,
showing how hard it was for German Jews to fathom their total rejection.
Many hoped against all odds for the "true" Germany to appear; others
lost hope but carried a deep longing for German culture. German-Jewish
intellectuals in exile adapted only with difficulty to their new countries and
were homesick. They maintained Germany's best cultural traditions
throughout these harrowing decades. When Erich Maria Remarque, the
exiled author of *All Quiet on the Western Front*, was asked if he missed
Germany, he answered: "Why should I? I am not Jewish."[36]

No one thought in those early years of the Reich about a metropolis of
death such as Auschwitz. We should not look for 1943 in 1933. But starting
from 1933 the Third Reich searched for ways to bring about a Germany
without Jews. To create this world, it was not enough to talk about it. It
had to be imagined and felt. This world was created at the university halls
of Nazi "science" and by speeches of Nazi ideologues, but it was also created by Germans from all walks of life in their neighborhood and localities, by their actions and their emotions. To throw Heinrich Herz out of
German society ultimately demanded a moral decision—for it was his
neighbors and coworkers who cast him out—and therefore an undertaking that required some kind of moral justification and, hence, of emotional commitment. The power of this fantasy was not its scientific value,
which was at any event obscure to most Germans, but its emotional resonance. For anti-Jewish beliefs and actions in the Third Reich were all
about emotions from racial science ideology itself down to the flesh-and-
blood messy brutality on the streets.

    And so the abstract idea of racial origins was realized in the tangible
streets of German communities that provided the immediate spaces to get

rid of the Jews. Recording in his diary anti-Jewish terror in Munich on March 9 and 10, 1933, the journalist and socialist Walter Gyssling wrote:

> So it goes for hours. One terrible news follows another. I cannot bear it any longer, and go out. But I should not think of finding peace. On the street it is worse. Before my eyes, storm-troopers, drooling like hysterical beasts, chase a man in bright daylight while whipping him. He wears neither shoes nor stockings, no jacket, no trousers, only a shirt and long underwear. On his neck hangs a poster with the inscription, "I, the Jew Siegel, will never again file a complaint against National Socialists."[37]

Michael Siegel was a prominent attorney who on March 10 went to police headquarters to intercede on behalf of a Jewish client. He somehow managed to flee the crowd, find a taxi, and get home. He and his wife left Germany for Peru in late August 1940; their children had left for England the year before.

Public, raw, visceral violence against Jews became a staple in the years following the seizure of power. Neighborly violence where perpetrators knew their victims was common. The presence of Jews provoked beating and spitting. Nazis cut the beards and shaved the heads of Orthodox Jews; they rioted in front of Jewish businesses. In Harpstedt, near Bremen, local grocery shops refused to sell food to the three local Jewish families, who were forced to travel to Bremen to get provisions.[38] The aim of these acts was to humiliate Jews in public for all to see. It would be a mistake to dismiss this violence as simply produced by ignorant, unruly mob or as ordered from above by the regime's leadership. Although public stances were shaped by pressures emanating from the regime, there was considerable space for individual choice and action. The violence also emanated from popular sentiments and was perpetrated by Germans from all walks of life. No one in the Third Reich was punished for failing to act brutally against his or her neighbor.

"On the street it is worse . . . [men] drooling like hysterical beasts": this short, intense statement points to the emotions embedded in anti-Jewish actions in those heady years.[39] What Germans communicated emotionally in these acts was just as significant as what they said in words, and often it was much more significant. Social actions have meanings that cannot quite be fully articulated in the words of their participants, meanings that do not begin and end with the contentions of participants and with their explicit line of reasoning. People do not always tell themselves why they do certain things, especially if these acts are morally transgressive, and they do not always know how to articulate why they do them either. This is the reason that the notion of racial ideology cannot be regarded as a sufficient explanation for the Nazi imagination. Precisely because the Nazis and other Germans did talk about their ideology, what they left unsaid but performed in violent actions is revealing.

Raw hatred and cruelty were the most visible emotions. They were expressed openly everywhere in Germany in those years, either figuratively, such as by burning books, or physically, as when an SA man, recounted by Gyssling in his diary, attacked a Jew, shouting, " 'We starved for fourteen years [during Weimar] while you filthy Jews had stashed the money' . . . literally yanking out his arm."[40]

Mockery was expressed in anti-Jewish actions that had a carnivalesque atmosphere, as when books were carried to the pyre in wagons pulled by oxen or when Siegel was forced to walk the streets barefoot and almost naked. Underlying the cruelty and mockery was an in-your-face attitude, a defiant and bold aggressiveness toward Jews and anyone who stood up for them. This attitude came not simply from a feeling of wickedness and self-confidence but, on the contrary, often from a mixture of conviction in the justification of the actions against the Jews and of a sense of unease, whether because of moral inhibitions, religious beliefs, education, or repulsion from violence.

One reason for the importance of the public element of the anti-Jewish actions is that to make an impact, to steer people to act, emotions had to be seen and made visible. Nazis and other Germans built an "emotional community" that claimed to link the individual to the collectivity based on anti-Jewish sentiments.[41] They made it visible in order to stake a claim to speak for national identity, to convince others, and to intimidate those left unconvinced. These actions represented the new power relations in post-1933 Germany: the Nazis excluded not only Jews but also Germans who refused to join in. For Jews such as Herz, the creation of a national, anti-Jewish emotional community hurt most because he had believed himself part of Germany. For other Germans, it set a clear warning about the boundaries of Nazi national identity.

Other emotions, too, were expressed in anti-Jewish actions. These were discreet, subterranean, and for that reason perhaps more significant. Fear is ubiquitous: the obsession with race revealed a sense of fear of contamination and of unstable identity in constant danger. The power attributed to the Jews as makers of liberalism, bolshevism, capitalism, and anything in between was a fantasy undergirded by anxiety.

Lying beneath the fear was a sense of envy that propelled much of the bitterness. Some Germans were motivated by class and status envy, as articulated by one speaker at a book-burning ceremony who resentfully attacked intellectuals who "claimed to be the German spirit, the German culture, the German present and the German future."[42] Others were motivated by envy of the Jews' success in universities and the liberal professions. Underlying the attacks was an envy of that power and authority ascribed to the Jews in the first place. The obsession with the Jews was a result not of a belief in the Jews as weak and insignificant but, on the contrary, of the belief in their awesome powers.

Hovering above it all was a sense of moral transgression and shame that accompanied much of the street violence against the Jews. From the beginning, the campaign against the Jews commingled extreme brutality and deep unease, reflecting Germans' sense that the persecution of the Jews was not quite the same as the persecution of other groups. That is why Germans acted publicly against the Jews: to strengthen the self and build an emotional community that defied this inner sense of transgression.

Nazis and other Germans were in awe at the rapid succession of events after 1933, and they looked for meaning. The Swiss psychiatrist and psychotherapist Carl Jung, who evaluated National Socialism positively in the early years of the regime, recounts that when he visited Germany, probably in the summer of 1933, he was "consulted by some leading Nazis who wanted to keep me there, one of them actually said he would arrest me so that I would be forced to remain. But why? I said, 'I am no politician, I am a psychologist, what have I to do with your enterprise?' And he replied: 'Exactly, you are a psychologist, you are outside of the whole thing, so you are the man who could tell us what we are doing.' "[43]

Germans were members of several emotional communities at one and the same time, and some were opposing and even contradictory. One could be, for example, a woman, of middle-class origins, a Bavarian Catholic, and an anti-Semite: each of these identities reflected a different emotional community. Similar to the overlapping of identities, emotions are multifaceted, shifting, and negotiated. The anti-Jewish emotional community was one among others in the early years of the Third Reich, though it was more important than most because it received the energetic support of the state, touched on every aspect of life, and was displayed regularly in public. But the persecution of the Jews produced competing emotions. The emotional exhilaration of Nazi achievements clashed with a sense of apprehension of the power of the Jews and the violence and general fanaticism of the Third Reich. Burning books at universities is not typically associated with noble culture, after all.

Of course, emotions are absolutely individual; social groups cannot feel or remember, much as they cannot eat or dance. And yet, one's emotions, like one's memory and most intimate dreams, originate from the symbols, landscape, practices, and language that are shared by a given society. Since the making of emotions, personal and collective, are embedded in a specific cultural, social, and political context, we can explore how people make sense of their emotions and use them. They have consequences, as when anti-Jewish emotions crafted a sense of belonging and boundaries.

In their anti-Jewish violent public actions Nazis created a vision of the world beyond how it really was. Violence liberated the imagination and made it possible to envision, however vaguely, new social possibilities, new ways of life, linking an imagined world without Jews with everyday occurrences on the ground.

At first glance the connection between the idea of origins embedded in race and the emotions displayed in public violence may not be evident: but whereas the idea of race was a fantasy about historical time, excising the evil Jews from history, public violence was a fantasy about space, excising the evil Jews from the Germans' midst, their neighborhoods, schools, and towns, and ultimately Germany itself. The idea of race brought to mind eternal origins, anti-Jewish public violence, local existence.

One particularly humiliating form of violence that removed Jews from local spaces was their forcible parading in public places, which became popular immediately and with fervor after January 30, 1933. Nathan Neuhaus, a cattle dealer, was forced from his apartment in Göttingen on the afternoon of March 28, 1933, and made to climb into one of his cattle trucks. He was soon joined by other Jews who had been dragged from their stores on Gronerstrasse. They were driven around downtown accompanied by rejoicing SS and SA men. It was the highlight of an afternoon of vandalism against Jews.[44]

Similar acts occurred all over Germany, as local streets became public stages to act out the removal of the Jews. On the sunny Saturday afternoon of August 19, 1933, a man in a dark suit was made to march over the Weidenhäser bridge in the lovely town of Marburg with a poster reading, "I have defiled a Christian woman." The language was not "I have defiled an Aryan woman" because Christian, German, and Aryan terms blended to represent the national community. The scene was enveloped by the intimate familiarity of a small town such as Marburg, which had almost thirty thousand inhabitants in the 1930s. People on this bridge probably knew

one another, and perhaps they knew the victim. Creating the Jew as a social outcast created at the same time an intimate German community.

A mixture of space, intimacy, and rejection of Jews also dominated in the following years of prewar Germany in towns and villages that celebrated Carnival (Shrove Tuesday) and local holidays such as Thanksgiving Day. Carnival was celebrated mainly in Catholic areas in the period preceding Lent. It was a merry festival of dressing up, ridiculing the establishment, playing the fool, and street activity. Thanksgiving Day was a harvest festival with religious significance celebrated mainly in rural areas. Both holidays typically included a locally organized procession consisting of decorated floats and carts and conveyed common, clearly understood topics that created a sense of shared community among spectators. They were not ordered from the Ministry of Propaganda in Berlin. Carnival, especially, mocked community norms in order ultimately to create a sense of togetherness.

Imaginings of the Jews as a mixture of modern and ancient, racial and religious, roots dominated anti-Jewish representations in these processions. In Nuremberg, a float pulled by Germans wearing nose masks represented a large caricature of a Jew reading the Talmud.[45] In Altenahr, in the

Rhineland, the 1937 Thanksgiving Day parade featured an Orthodox Jew at a counting table surrounded by enormous bags of money profited from the grape harvest at the expense of the locals, while two young boys marched behind the float with a banner that read, "The vintner's happy harvest is the Jew's payday."[46] It is difficult to know from photographs of the scene where traditional anti-Semitic representations ended and new racial ones began.

The Jews were depicted in these parades in the usual, even trivial anti-Semitic clichés. One may scoff at these clichés as insignificant compared to the modern language of racial science in the Third Reich. But this would be a mistake. These images were trivial, and they did represent clichés, and here precisely lay their power in the mid-1930s. Their meaning was familiar, clear, and shared by all viewers. They were important, to articulate this idea with an oxymoron, because they were trivial. The new talk about race apparently did not engender a wholly new representational language to depict a world without Jews, while common, trivial images successfully internalized the radical new anti-Jewish policy of the Nazis. In Carnival comic entertainment Germans revealed more about themselves than they might have wished.[47]

The locality was the center of making a space without Jews. In the prewar years, long before Germans could even think of a world without Jews, they made real their own small locality without Jews: it was made by an anti-Jewish sign on a street, at a community festival, or in a parade on the neighborhood bridge. Displaying Jews in parades only confirmed the popular, carnivalesque elements of acts of public humiliation that had existed since 1933. Children were an important part of the action, as was music. In Marburg joyful children accompanied the march by foot and on bicycle, and the SA fife and drum band led the procession. In Altenahr they carried the anti-Semitic banner. Participants were of all ages, including mothers with babies, and some are seen laughing, joking, and having a good time. Nazis and other Germans who persecuted the Jews thus made their point in public about the new identity underlying the Reich. Those Germans who did not understand received a clarification, as when German women married to Jewish men were derided in public. In Breslau, storm-troopers stood before their homes carrying signs identifying their names and addresses, which were also written on the sidewalk.[48] Anti-Jewishness was thus interwoven into the everyday.

Who participated in these actions? Certainly SA men, but many others, as in the parades, came from all walks of life. Spectators filled the streets. It is not easy to evaluate how spectators and participants received and understood the events before their eyes. Some individuals protested the immoral acts. The parade of Nathan Neuhaus in Göttingen was stopped by a certain Fräulein Biermann, who stood in front of the cattle truck and reproached the SA men: "What do you think you are doing? Let the man go." The men obeyed, deserted the scene, and thus was Neuhaus liberated.[49] It shows that moral resoluteness and firm conviction could make a difference. But this was an exception. Most people saw the persecution as at least partially justified because they harbored anti-Semitic sentiments; for others, fear and opportunism played an important role. Public pressure as well as the coercion of the Nazi Party and state authorities weighted as well.

But the meaning of the public actions against the Jews was not about consent. "Because no one could escape taking a position—and this was the essence of the public action," observes the historian Michael Wildt in reference to the photograph of the man who was forced to walk with a sign in Marburg. "All spectators that accompanied the parade, as well as those with inner reservations, took part in its staging. They did not become perpetrators, but they did become accomplices to the politics of anti-Semitism."[50] And this was the point of the public actions against the Jews: not to make everybody agree with the violence but to make all part of it. Indeed, not everyone in German society agreed with Nazis' anti-Jewish policies, and many had doubts about all or some of them. But placing the acts in familiar and recognizable local, religious, Heimat, and racial terms made it possible for many Germans to justify, accept, or just go along with the persecution.

When we look from 1933 to the mid-1930s we can see the progression of anti-Jewish thinking in the Third Reich. In 1933, the Nazis set out to eradicate modern phenomena attributed to Jews in tandem with their antisocialist and antiliberal refounding of the Reich. In the following years, as the victory over socialism and liberalism was solidified, the Nazis turned to imagine the Jews beyond the strict labels of political and artistic movements. Of course, Nazi propaganda continued to scream about Jewish Bolsheviks or deformed art (as in the 1937 Munich exhibition *Degenerate*

Art), but more significant is the firming up of an imagination of Jews as a menace that demanded no proof from experience.

If the regime made the Jews into a fearsome enemy, this was a truth that demanded no evidence. There were no legal or show trials in the Third Reich to prove Jewish hideous crimes. Unlike the witchcraft interrogations of early modern Europe or the Stalinist show trials of the 1930s, the Nazis did not attempt to extract confessions from Jews about their crimes. These confessions were useless as evidence for proving "real" fraternization with the devil or "real" crimes against Stalin, but they do tell us what their hearers believed happened or how they imagined the world. The semblance of evidence and truth confessed by victims was crucial for both witchcraft interrogators and Stalinist judges. "Immense judicial effort was expended in extracting a full confession from the accused witch," notes the historian Lyndal Roper. Indeed, "only through confession and execution" could the court first convict and then reconcile the witch with the Church.[51] For Stalin and his judges, too, it was crucial to extract from the party enemies on trial confessions of their imaginary crimes against him and the party.

But for the Nazis it was irrelevant whether Jews admitted to crimes. It is not simply that truth was manipulated by the regime. This is predictable in a dictatorship (and not only there). As Bernhard Rust, the education minister, told an assembly of professors in Munich in 1933: "From now on it is not up to you to decide whether or not something is true, but whether it is in the interests of the National Socialist Revolution."[52] The point, rather, is that not all fantasies are born equal: to believe in the reality of their fantasies, believers of witchcraft and of communist treason carved an important part for the victim whose (obviously coerced) "confession" provided the "evidence" without which the reality of the fantasy was questionable. Nazis did try to corroborate anti-Semitism in racial, scientific research, but this activity did not see the Jews as bearers of any truth. "What the Jew believes is irrelevant," announced the banner of the Bamberg stormtroopers. Nazi fantasies were thus, in a sense, irrefutable to their believers, for they were not determined by rules of cause and effect.

One common denominator among Nazi race experts, and prosecutors in witchcraft and Stalinist trials, is that all had a predetermined idea of the truth that could only be confirmed, not refuted. Witchcraft and anti-Jewish accusations shared an additional aspect. Witches, it was believed, "dined off gold and silver plate, they drank vast amounts of wine, they danced and made merry, and they fornicated with the Devil. They indulged in every imaginable pleasure, and would accept no limit to their gargantuan appetite for delight. They broke every rule. And they flew."[53] Did demonologists and interrogators really believe all this? To the historian of mentality and human psychology this is a good question, demanding an answer that is not reduced to "yes" or "no." Protestant and skeptical Catholic demonologists had many doubts about this list of activities. But there is more to it, as Roper puts it illuminatingly: "It may seem incredible that intellectuals could be skeptical about much of what witches supposedly did, could be interested in the power of imagination and ponder the mechanics of illusion, and still be firmly convinced of the reality of witchcraft. Yet they apparently found no difficulty in squaring this particular circle."[54]

The Jews, it was said time and again in Germany after 1933, were responsible for—and let us register one more time the long list of their crimes—bolshevism, communism, Marxism, socialism, liberalism, conservatism, pacifism, cosmopolitanism, materialism, atheism, democracy, sexual freedom, psychoanalysis, feminism, homosexuality, abortions, modernist art, and Germany's general misfortune, on top of being a dangerous virus, a microbe, a carrier of syphilis and criminality, the opposite of a human being, the destroyer of God and nature, and the devil incarnate. Only flying was missing. Did Germans really believe all this? Many were skeptical about much of what Jews supposedly did but still remained believers in the irrefutable reality of the otherness of and threat posed by the Jews. After 1933 Nazis and other Germans had no difficulty in squaring this circle.

"Everyone asks me why I am still here and why I didn't leave long ago to be with you," wrote Betty Scholem to Gershom on April 9, 1933.[55] Barely nine weeks had passed since Hitler had become chancellor, but normal life seemed already a distant memory. Now, in the mid-1930s, a few more years had passed since 1933. Was there at least one quiet place for Jews in Germany? Was there any place for Jews in Germans' imagination?

Imagining the Jews as
Everywhere and Already Gone

rete Nussbaum was twenty years old and living in Cologne
when she decided to travel with friends over Christmas 1935
to Upper Bavaria for a ski vacation and to get away from two
horrible years of Nazi persecution. "Perhaps it is the last
time," she thought, "and I loved the Bavarian mountains so much." The
group arrived at sunset, the place was beautiful. "Then we came to the
entrance of the resort, and saw a wide banner stretched across the main
street: 'Jews enter this place at their own risk.' . . . Here went my vacation
mood." In the hotel she was greeted by another sign, "No entrance to dogs
and Jews!" It was a familiar sight. In her Cologne apartment building, the
building superintendent had placed a sign at the entrance: "The Jews are
our misfortune." She returned home the next day, without skiing once,
and left Germany forever several weeks later, in January 1936.[1]

In the mid-1930s, Germans lived in a land where the public space
was inundated by the Jews and their spirit. No other National Socialist
enemy received such public, popular attention. The Jewish menace was
seen as extending to the four corners of the land. A visitor ignorant of
the real situation in the Third Reich could have been excused for thinking
that millions of dangerous Jews were roaming the country unchecked,
threatening Germans from East Prussia to the Rhine. They did, in the
imagination, for Germans perceived the Jews as everywhere and at the

same time—through their violent removal from local social life—as already gone.

In reality, at the end of 1935 there were fewer than 350,000 Jews in a country of 65 million inhabitants. When the Nazis came to power there were 437,000 Jews in Germany. Sixty thousand left in 1933–1934, and almost 70,000 joined them in 1935–1937. Because most Jews lived in concentrated urban centers, most Germans never saw any Jews.

Yet wherever one turned in Germany, there were the Jews and their spirit. Photographs capture this sensation. The Jews appeared in the sky ("The Jews are our misfortune"), on water ("Whoever buys from Jews is stealing the nation's assets"), and on the road, as on the spare-wheel cover of a car that read "Jews are our misfortune," used as a focal point for four young men from Mannheim posing for a souvenir photo.

In towns and cities wide banners stating that Jews were not desired lined the streets, such as that on top of Nürnberg Gate, one of the entrances to the University of Erlangen, or at a main thoroughfare in Bad Tölz, in Bavaria.[2]

Walking in their neighborhoods, Germans encountered the Jew on every corner: the Grüne Tanne Guest House in Halle hung a sign, "This house is and will remain free of Jews," while in a local street a man hanging in effigy attracted children's curiosity. Here Germans who had any contact with Jews were already threatened. The banner behind the effigy read: "This will be the end of any member of the national community who buys from Jews, and of any Jew who trespasses into this town!!"

In Werl in North Rhine Westphalia, a large poster pasted to a kiosk identified the exact addresses of the eleven houses in which Jews lived, while in Reichenberg, near Würzburg, a local anti-Jewish sign, "We have

three dozen Jews to give away," served as a good spot for a photo souvenir of local children.[3]

The Jews and their menacing spirit greeted visitors to town halls, as in Lauf, in Baden, where an anti-Jewish doorknocker was affixed to the old Town Hall (it was removed in 1954), and to telegraph offices, as in

Nuremberg. The mural in Nuremberg read, "Trust No Fox in the Green Meadow and No Jew on His Oath," building on a theme from a popular children's book, *Trust No Fox*, published by the anti-Semitic Stürmer Publishing House. The children's book *Trust No Jew on the Green Meadow:*

A *Picture Book for Adults and Children,* by Elvira Bauer, was a hit in the mid-1930s.[4]

A forest of anti-Jewish signs covered Germany. In hotels, restaurants, and train stations, in spas, at the beach, and on the road from here to there: on the Munich-Landsberg road anti-Semitic flyers and a hand-painted note covered a traffic sign, all declaring, "Jews are not welcome," and on the bank of the river Mainz, a sign directed Aryans to the "German beach" on the left, while Jews were pointed toward the beach "only at the Jordan River—1933 kilometers."

Anti-Jewish signs were placed in local roads and provincial routes. Germans encountered them when hiking for pleasure in the countryside. A group of German boys hiking near Rennweg am Neuhaus in Thuringia posed for a photo beneath a road sign that warned, "Trek further Jews, get out! We do not want you in Neuhaus!"[5]

Some slogans were ironic ("Our demands for Jews has been suffi-ciently supplied!"), others menacing ("Jews enter this locality at their own peril!"). Some signs mixed race with religion ("The Jew's Father Is the Devil").[6] The signs gave the Jews a tangibility and a spatial omnipresence. Even where no Jews lived and had probably never even been seen, com-munities placed signs that read, "Jews are not welcome," or "This or that locality is free of Jews."[7] The Jews were here, there, and everywhere.

It was each local community's decision to place a sign. "Jews are unwelcome here! The Town Council," announced the small Bavarian town of Hussingen.[8] Communities were ordered neither by the Reich Chancellery nor even by the regional Nazi Party leader. The regime gave its blessing, but even a totalitarian state could not force the myriad of small localities to place a sign against Jews. Signs reflected popular senti-ment, as did opposition to them. Wilhelm Diester, a driving instructor from Braunschweig, placed a sign on his car that read, "Without breaking the Jewish monopoly there will be no solution for mankind." The sign was repeatedly torn down, he reported. "I fixed this one to the inside of the back window, and from there it was torn out."[9] As a new national identity, anti-Jewishness was contested. Others just went along with the sign of the times, and still others did not much care either way. But as an identity in-the-making, anti-Jewishness in the Third Reich became substantially popular, expanding the Jewish menace from the locality to the nation as a whole, making it visible and ever present.

The forests of signs added to the story that Nazis had already been telling about Jews and Germany. By burning books, Nazis excised Jews from national culture; by having faith in the notion of race, they excised them from national history; by using public violence, they excised them from local life; and by seeing Jews everywhere, they excised them from the national space. The anti-Jewish signs marked every space in Germany, every locality, every site, every landscape, as a place that Jews could not trespass.

The period after the Nuremberg Race Laws of September 1935 brought a certain order and regularity to anti-Jewish policies. They codified in law the relations between Aryans and Jews, which had been characterized since 1933 by violence and intimidation toward Jews and toward Germans who sought to help them. Many Germans welcomed the laws as a legalization of the rather extemporized measures of discrimination. Even some Jews greeted them with relief. Many Germans thought in the mid-1930s that Hitler and the Nazis were on their way to solve the Jewish Problem. The exclusion of Jews since 1933 from all areas of German society was so rapid, massive, and successful that the cumulative impact of legal limits and Jewish emigration pointed to a probable end of this "problem" in German society.

Germans turned their attention to topics closer to home. On the economic front, they found many reasons to be satisfied and proud. The economy was recovering, and millions were back at work. A government program of public works produced a new and modern network of inter-state highways, the famous German *Autobahn*. Between 1933 and 1938, almost nineteen hundred miles were built.[10] The "Führer's roads," as they were popularly called, captured the enthusiasm of Germans for a forward-looking regime that promised prosperity for all. This sentiment was strengthened when in 1936 the regime launched the "people's car," or Volkswagen, which Hitler imagined would allow every German to own an affordable, mass-produced car. The idea of motorizing the masses was halted by the war and in effect very few cars were produced, but it galvanized Germans' imagination who perceived their material quality of life as improving under Nazism.

For most Germans life indeed seemed promising, a feeling epitomized by travel and tourism in the prewar years that opened new horizons of expectations. After 1933 German tourism flourished as a result of the cumulative effects of Nazi policies and the improved world economy. The Nazi tourist activities ranged broadly; more Germans traveled, an experience that stood in stark contradiction to the Depression years. The 1934 Oberammergau Passion Play, the famous staging in the Bavarian town of the Passion of Christ, attracted four hundred thousand tourists (including sixty thousand from abroad). The 1936 winter and summer Olympic Games in Garmisch-Partenkirchen and Berlin put Germany on the map and attracted, in Garmisch-Partenkirchen alone, more than a million tourists. Between the Depression and the early 1960s, 1937 was the best tourist year. The improvement of tourism between 1933 and 1939 reflected the Nazis' ability to improve social and material conditions. For ordinary Germans, "Strength Through Joy"—the regime's plan to give every worker a paid vacation—became the most popular program instituted by the regime.

Improving quality of life for most Germans simultaneously meant discrimination of Jews, but by the mid-1930s, this discrimination had become a way of life. In the Third Reich, traveling, like every other sphere of life, was an integral part of the anti-Jewish terror. The Nuremberg Laws forbade most hotels from accommodating Jewish guests. A decree announced by the Interior Ministry on July 24, 1937, set extreme restrictions on the presence of Jews in spas; an additional decree on June 16, 1939, made their participation impossible.[11] Grassroots activity, before the Nazi legislation, had already removed Jews from tourist sites and hotels, and massive discrimination started in the fall of 1934. In small Neustrelitz, the owners of the town's hotels and guesthouses, together with the local tourist and transportation bureau, agreed "to post everywhere the inscription: Jews are unwelcome." The sign was at one and the same time a statement about the discrimination of the present and about a vision of the future.

Many Germans thought in the mid-1930s that the domestic and international successes of the Nazi regime were a good basis for building a strong, prosperous Germany. But Hitler had very different plans. The Nazi preparations for a European war started in earnest in 1936. In that year, the

Four-Year Plan, presided over by Göring, was initiated with the aim of making Germany self-sufficient in foodstuffs and raw material in view of the long war ahead. The plan accelerated the pace of rearmament and tightened the state's intervention in and control of economic planning. Priorities were set by the regime, not industry. On the foreign policy front, Hitler shredded to pieces one by one the harsh conditions imposed on Germany by the Versailles Treaty. After resuming building the German army in 1935, in 1936 he announced the re-militarization of the Rhineland area that bordered France. By placing the German army at the French border, Hitler deprived France of a crucial strategic advantage. In March 1935, again in violation of Versailles, Germany introduced a one-year army conscription, raising it to two years in August 1936.

Hitler now moved more resolutely against France and Britain. The Spanish Civil War, which broke out in July 1936, forged close relations between Hitler and Benito Mussolini, the leader of Fascist Italy. Mussolini had already received Hitler's support when he invaded Abyssinia in the Horn of Africa in October 1935 in violation of international law and in defiance of the League of Nations. In Spain the two dictators supported the fascist leader Francisco Franco, who staged a rebellion against the legitimate government of the Spanish republic. The Rome-Berlin Axis of the two Fascist leaders was strengthened through repression at home and by fighting a war abroad to shift the balance of power on the Continent.

The realization that Germany was headed toward a major European war caused conflict between the increasingly radical regime and the old elites in the army and the foreign office. The elites, who made Hitler's appointment possible in January 1933, favored the dismantling of the Versailles Treaty and sought a powerful, hegemonic Germany that could dictate policy to its neighbors. But they understood with foreboding that the Nazis had something totally different in mind: a war of extermination against all the European powers. Hitler had already replaced the respected minister of economics Hjalmar Schacht in November 1937 because he disagreed with the unorthodox economic policies of the Four-Year Plan. But the clash with the army leaders in the winter of 1937–1938 was a more serious challenge to the regime. The contest ended with a clear victory for Hitler and marked a further step in the drive toward war. By February 1938, Hitler had purged the army of critics. Ousted were fourteen senior generals and the commander in chief of the army, Werner von Fritsch, in favor of General Walther von Brauchitsch, a Nazi supporter. The post of war minister was abolished, and Hitler, who was already supreme commander of the army as head of state since Hindenburg's death in August 1934, now also became commander-in-chief of the armed forces. In addition, in the Foreign Ministry, Joachim von Ribbentrop, the fanatic Nazi who opposed an alliance with Britain and pushed for the Axis with Italy and Japan, replaced the elderly Baron Konstantin von Neurath as foreign minister.

War or peace, by early 1938 it had become an article of faith in the Third Reich that the national community could no longer tolerate the presence of the Jews. The policies against the Jews intensified, and they included not only legal and economic measures but also the removal of Jews and, more important, of Judaism from all spheres of German identity, as for example from German history by rewriting the past and from the urban landscape by demolishing synagogues. This project of erasing Jews and Judaism from the present while also denying them the right to a past and a future, which began to evolve in the mid-1930s and into the summer of 1938, had potentially much more radical consequences than the persecution that removed Jews from defined social and economic spheres. Let us follow these changes.

Anti-Jewish legislation remained vigorous in 1936 and 1937 and continued to encompass all fields of life, none deemed too trivial. The creativity of the Nazis knew no bounds, and they began 1936 with a law prohibiting the instruction of English in Jewish schools. Other laws followed.

To avoid making a bad impression on foreign visitors to the Olympic Games, anti-Jewish signs with extreme language should be avoided: the sign "Jews are not welcome here" is enough. Bavaria: Schools are to set up special classes for Jewish pupils in elementary education. The Ministry of Education bans Jewish teachers from public schools. Important documents about the history of the National Socialist movement should not be destroyed: these include material about the influence of Jews in society, state, and culture. Aryans may change their Jewish family name. Jews who appear in court are not allowed to use the German Greeting (Hail Hitler).[12]

In economic terms, of the fifty thousand Jewish businesses in the Reich in 1933, only nine thousand remained in July 1938, and their number

decreased rapidly thereafter. Jews continued to leave Germany. By the end
of 1937, almost 130,000 Jews had left; by November 1938, just 300,000
remained in the old Reich (without Austria, annexed in March 1938, and
the Sudetenland region, annexed from Czechoslovakia in September
1938). In the meantime, the anti-Semitic exhibition *The Eternal Jew* was
viewed in Munich by four hundred thousand visitors in the short period
from December 1937 to January 1938.

The joining of Austria to the Reich in March 1938 was accompanied
by tremendous indigenous violence against Jews. Old and new rituals of
humiliation were practiced: Jewish books were burned in Salzburg on
April 30 while Viennese men and women were made to scrub the streets.[13]
Jews were prohibited from entering public parks and from walking on
beaches. When the Nazis marched in, there were about 200,000 Jews in
Austria, most in Vienna. By November 1938, 50,000 Jews had left Austria,
and by September 1939, some 130,000 were lucky enough to have fled.

But the Nazi ideas about the place of the Jews in the world were not
restricted to the present. When in the mid-1930s Rabbi Ernst Appel of
Dortmund took the occasion of a funeral to comfort his community in
the face of persecution, he was called after the ceremony to the Gestapo:
"How dare you, dirty Jew, tell your people that they should hope for a better time to come?"[14] If by 1938 Germans could imagine only with strenuous effort a Germany with Jews, there existed a porous line between
imagining a Germany without Jewish presence, here and now, and the
more radical view that Jews had no right at all to a promising future anywhere, as implied in the Gestapo's rebuke of Appel.

Even dead Jews had no right to exist in peace. The Department of
Anthropology at the University of Vienna was keenly interested in policies
to de-Judaize Vienna because this provided it the opportunity to acquire
invaluable material for research on the physical and cultural racial characteristics of the Jews. In October 1938, a letter was sent from the department
to the local authorities:

> I have learned through the local party leadership that there is a
> plan to turn the Eisenstädter cemetery into a park and there is,
> therefore, the upcoming opportunity to uncover valuable and
> useful Jewish skeletons. I beg your friendship in telling me as

soon as this plan is carried out, for I have a lively interest in this—as you will understand—out of pure scientific motivation, and the Anthropological Institute has a large involvement in the Jewish question. At the same time, I have written a letter to the mayor of Eisenstadt in which I expressed my interest. Hail Hitler, E. Geyer.[15]

For Geyer, the Jews were already relics, archaeological artifacts of a vanished world, lost and then unearthed only to be studied.

Such thinking led to unusual events, as when the Nazis invented stories that seemed to belong to the distant Middle Ages. In these stories they told more about themselves than about the Jews. On April 28, 1937, the Gestapo in Würzburg arrested eight Jewish men with the accusation of ritual murder. Eight years earlier, on March 17, 1929, a seven-year-old boy named Kesler had been found dead in Manau in Lower Franconia. Easter was approaching, and rumors spread quickly that Jews had used Kesler's blood to make matzos, the unleavened bread of Passover. But the blood libel had died down. Yet in 1937 the head of the regional government of Lower Franconia, a man named Hellmuth, revived the case. The eight Jews, who lived in communities around Manau in 1929, were promptly accused "of being on March 17 [1929] at 2 pm at the market square in Hofheim," the biggest town in the district and some forty minutes away from Manau. One of the Jews, Blumenthal, was soon released for lack of evidence. It is said that the Gestapo even apologized to him for the arrest, although it is not known whether this was a fact or a popular legend. The Gestapo did order Blumenthal to keep quiet about the whole affair lest he be prosecuted for spreading atrocity fables. In the meantime, the matter was referred to the regional courthouse in Bamberg for investigation into the Jews' possible crime. Months passed. Finally, after scrutiny of the evidence, the court dismissed the case. By then, two Jews had been jailed for six months and two others for eight months while waiting for acquittal.[16]

Some months later, in Frankenwinheim, also in Lower Franconia, a man told his friends at a local pub that he had bought the house of his Jewish neighbor who had left Germany. He mentioned that before leaving, the neighbor apparently threw a dead calf into an unused well on the property. After the incidents that followed, the man observed, "Had I known that my story would have such results, I would have never recounted it." A rumor spread that the Jews poisoned the water resources. From then on Jews "could not go in the village without being mistreated." On one Saturday, stormtroopers hauled young Jews from their homes to the local pub. The Jews were made to say, "I am a criminal, I have cheated people, so teaches me the Talmud." When three peasants present in the pub protested against the violence, saying, "Enough now, this goes too far!" they were forced to stand on chairs and shout, "We are servants of the Jews." Similar mistreatment happened elsewhere in the area. In the meantime the Jew who had sold the house, now in the United States, was informed of the events by local Jews. He wrote to the mayor of Frankenwinheim that he had indeed dispensed of one of his dead calves before leaving by burying it in his yard, and he gave the exact location. This information could have stopped the rumor. The mayor later explained that he had kept the content of the letter secret because the Jew broke the law by burying the calf in his yard and not outside the village. By then, Kristallnacht had come, and the poisoned well was forgotten.[17]

Anti-Jewish accusations of ritual murder and poisoning wells had been common in the Middle Ages as part of a culture that believed in magic. They declined over the centuries but even in the modern period did not disappear completely from the rich repertoire of Jewish accusations. As late as 1900 a ritual murder accusation accompanied by violent riots engulfed the town of Konitz, on the eastern edge of the German Empire, when a young boy was found murdered. Still, these accusations did not sit comfortably with many Germans in the Third Reich who saw themselves as modern and rational and who therefore turned to "scientific" racial anti-Semitism as providing "proofs" about Jewish degeneration.

The events in Manau and Frankenwinheim did not mean that Germans in the mid-1930s necessarily believed the preposterous accusations made against the Jews or that anti-Jewish beliefs had not changed since the Middle Ages in an unbroken anti-Semitic tradition. Indeed, the stories included specific details as well as hints that Germans did not believe in the accusations: rumor had it that the Gestapo apologized to one of the accused in Manau, and ultimately all were released; in Frankenwinheim, the buyer of the house distanced himself from the accusation, the SA men seemed to take advantage of the rumors to act violently against the Jews, while the three peasants at the pub tried to stop the violence. But it is precisely contemporaries' incredulity that makes the cases illuminating: fantastic stories were nonetheless a vehicle for violent social actions against Jews. In this sense, "scientific" racism was as much the stuff of fantasy and fable as these accusations of ritual murder and poisoning of wells: in 1937, a display on the Jew as a racial "alien body" set to destroy Germany was added to the permanent exhibition of the regional history museum in Braunschweig.[18] The point is that in the mid-1930s in Germany the Jews became the subject of wild stories, and any fable could be attached to their identity.

Many of the motifs of Nazi anti-Semitism revealed in these stories and in anti-Jewish laws were anything but original; the repertoire was almost banal and certainly predictable. The Jews as racially inferior, religiously deviant, physically deformed, sexually polluting, psychologically treacherous, makers of bolshevism and liberalism—all these themes had long featured in the accusations made against Jews in Germany and elsewhere in Europe, in Poland, France, and other countries. It might be argued that the Nazi fantasies about the Jews were old wine in new bottles, nothing more than the usual cocktail of modern anti-Semitism. But if motifs were familiar, this simply gave them added force, because the Nazis used recognizable anti-Jewish sentiments, which were shared among wide sections in German society, in order to forge a new German identity. By "used," I don't mean that the Nazis chose these sentiments with the primary intent to manipulate. This may also have happened, but it is less important. They used them because they were available as cultural idioms to imagine the Jews, even as they created with them something new.

Still, no one knew on January 1, 1938, what the year would bring. As it turned out, 1938 was a very good year for Hitler and the Nazi regime. Nazism was victorious on all fronts, and the regime enjoyed tremendous popularity at home. Germany's position in Europe was the strongest it had been since the defeat in 1918. After peacefully dismantling the Versailles Treaty, Hitler had his biggest successes in 1938. Born in Braunau am Inn, on the Austrian border with Germany, he had always dreamed of uniting his natal and adopted homelands into a Great German Reich. Since 1933 the Nazis had constantly intervened in Austrian domestic politics, and on March 12, 1938, after considerable pressure on the Austrian chancellor Kurt Schuschnigg, Germany invaded Austria and annexed it to the Reich. Hitler made a triumphant return to Vienna, the city where he first collected his mishmash of prejudices as a failed art student. Tens of thousands of Viennese cheered Hitler enthusiastically as the victory parade passed along the city's elegant streets.

The Anschluss, as the political union between Austria and Germany is known, dramatically changed the balance of power in Europe. Britain and France recognized this, but they did not intend to go to war to prevent it. Germany's position in central Europe improved, in particular with respect to Czechoslovakia. After 1918 the Czech democracy built a series of fortifications along its border with Germany, but these became irrelevant because the German army now took positions along the former Austrian border instead. In the summer of 1938, Hitler set his eyes on Czechoslovakia. Pretending to defend ethnic Germans in the border areas of the Sudetenland, he threatened war. A German military mobilization was followed by a Czech one, and for a week in August 1938, it seemed that war was about to break out. Diplomatic attempts at mediation brought Italy, France, Britain, and Germany to Munich in September. Czechoslovakia, whose fate was to be determined, was not invited. The result of the Munich conference was the ceding of the Sudetenland to Germany and the famous photograph of Neville Chamberlain, the British prime minister, waving the agreement with Hitler's signature and announcing "peace in our time." The agreement did buy Britain and France time to prepare for war, which many thought unavoidable at this point. It was too late for the Czech democracy, which, demoralized and betrayed by France and Britain, was now at the mercy of Hitler's expansionist plans. The year 1938 amounted to a revolution in the European balance of power—without a single shot having been fired.

The regime's anti-Jewish policies also seemed to have been particularly successful. Many Jews emigrated. The young left first, while those who remained were mostly old; some 25 percent were over the age of sixty-five. In barely five years the Nazis had reversed a history of German-Jewish coexistence that lasted for centuries. The deeply rooted Jewish community in Germany had no future. It would soon disappear. This was made clear by the continuous flood of anti-Jewish laws between January 1, 1938, and November 9, 1938, that further isolated and segregated the Jews and injured their sense of self and collectivity. Especially noteworthy in this regard was the law of August 17, 1938, stating that from January 1, 1939, Jews must have a first name from an officially approved list of Jewish names. In addition, it was compulsory for all Jews to add the name "Israel" or "Sarah" to their existing names. This law joined others in the period from January to early November 1938.

Jews are prohibited from using state archives. Tents used by youth in camping should bear the inscription "used by non-Jews." Jews are forbidden to attend university lectures as guests. The Law on the Profession of Auctioneer excludes Jews from this occupation. The Gun Law excludes Jewish gun merchants. Baden: All books by Jewish authors should be removed from school libraries. The Decree against the Camouflage of Jewish Firms forbids the changing of the names of Jewish-owned businesses. German identity cards and passports of Jews are invalid; new ones will be issued with a stamped "J."[19]

Would these successes in the fight against the Jews signal the end of the Nazi obsession with them?

In the summer of 1938, a new wave of anti-Jewish persecution swept Germany. On one level, it seemed to accord with Goebbels's note in his diary on November 29, 1937: "The Jews must get out of Germany, indeed out of Europe altogether. That will take some time yet, but it will and must happen."[20] The persecution came from the Nazi leadership. Jews were deprived of medical care; by July, only 709 of the remaining 3,152 Jewish doctors were allowed to practice, having been denied the right to call themselves doctors and being restricted to treating Jewish patients. In September the same principle applied to Jewish lawyers: only 172 were allowed to continue working, representing Jewish clients only. In January 1939, the measure was extended to Jewish dentists and apothecaries.

In the meantime, a committee set up by Goebbels recommended requiring Jews to wear special identifying marks and confining them in separate quarters of towns, their total removal from entire professions, and additional similar measures aimed to drive Jews completely from German life. By now these ideas were shared by large segments of German society, for the anti-Jewish measures from above had been accompanied by tremendous violence from below. In 1938, Jews were forcibly expelled from several communities, including small localities in the Hunsrück and in Bechhofen, Franconia. According to the Security Service reports, Jews were "dragged from their homes, beaten, spit upon, and kicked. Some were dragged barefoot through the town. After being instructed to do so, the children took part in this demonstration."[21] In various villages in southern Germany in the summer of 1938, mayors ordered the Jews to leave within a few weeks.[22] In Zeven, Jews had been expelled a year earlier.[23]

But on another level, the anti-Jewish measures took a new turn that accorded with Goebbels's sentiments articulated in the 1937 annual Nazi Party rally in Nuremberg: "Look, this is the enemy of the world, the destroyer of cultures, the parasite among the nation, the son of chaos, the incarnation of evil, the ferment of decomposition, the visible demon of the decay of humanity."[24] Flying was still missing. Any contact between something Jewish and German contaminated the latter. The idea that Jews represented evil across space and history was not new in itself, but it did point to a new direction in the Third Reich once adopted as Nazi policy. The period from the end of 1937 and into 1938 presented a new phase in the Nazi imagination of the Jews: the anti-Jewish fight for Nazi modernity had been won, and the Nazis now turned to tell a story about the past.

In truth, measures against the Jewish soiling of the German spirit had been taken early on. In December 1933, Jewish businesses were prohibited from displaying Christian symbols at Christmastime. In the following years, Jews were prohibited from trading in National Socialist literature, from acting in German theater, from displaying the swastika in their apartments and businesses, and, in Breslau, from selling products at the famous local annual Christmas market. In 1937, Jews who appeared in court were not allowed to use the Hail Hitler greeting, and a year later, Jews could not receive music lessons from Aryans.[25] In 1938, police arrested a Jew who sold swastikas in his Regensburg shop.[26] Jews in Austria were prohibited from dressing in the traditional German costume, or *Tracht*. After Kristallnacht, the Nazis, not wanting to risk the slightest possibility of contamination, decreed that Jews could not be members of the Hitler Youth.[27] In January 1939, the German spirit expanded to the animal kingdom as Jewish veterinarians were allowed to treat only pets owned by Jews; pets owned by Germans were now considered Aryan.

Taking the anti-Jewish measures a qualitative step further, not only Jews were targeted, but Judaism, and not simply as icons of modern times in, for example, the legal and medical professions but as symbols of historic traces that soiled the nation. Munich's Great Synagogue was torn down on June 9, 1938. It was located, together with the Jewish community building, next to the German Art House. When Hitler had visited Munich several weeks earlier, he had ordered that the buildings be demolished before German Art Day on July 8. A parking lot was created in their place. The Torah scrolls, about to be destroyed, were saved at the last minute.[28] The Munich municipality compensated the Jewish community for one-seventh of the value of the two buildings. The matter was not published in the press, for at that time there still existed some sense of transgression with regard to demolishing synagogues. But the destruction was nonetheless public and could not be kept a secret.

The demolition of the Munich synagogue was not an isolated event. In June 1938, three Berlin synagogues were razed to the ground. In Dortmund, the Jewish community was forced to sell the synagogue building on Hansastrasse (the Nazis later confiscated the money the Jewish community received for the sale). The demolition of the synagogue began in October 1938, and on October 19, the dome was destroyed. In Nuremberg, Jewish community leaders were told by local officials that the synagogue "spoils the look of the city" and would have to be destroyed. The Jews were allowed to hold one final Friday night service before the synagogue and the Jewish community building next door were demolished on August 10, 1938. The "Jewish stone," a remnant of the earlier medieval synagogue that was used as the base of the Holy Ark in the modern synagogue, was saved by a non-Jewish architect.[29] Following this, synagogues were destroyed in at least a dozen other towns, and possibly many more, as happened to the insides of the synagogues in Regensburg and Leuterhausen.[30] In Vienna, after Austria joined the Reich in March 1938, Torah scrolls were used as carpets.[31]

That Nazis chose to demolish synagogues is worth thinking about because this was not an obvious choice. Synagogues evoked a sense of tradition and history, and by demolishing them, the Nazis insisted that the connection between German and Jewish pasts had to be severed in order to free up German national history. It is significant that just as the Nazis started to demolish synagogues they founded a new discipline of studies on Jews, lending academic authority to a new history of German-Jewish relations. In 1935, Alfred Rosenberg founded in Berlin the Institute for the Study of the Jewish Question. Although he remained uninfluential among Nazi leaders, Rosenberg carved out an important place for himself in promoting anti-Jewish scholarship and building a network of institutions and organizations whose aim was to present a "true" history of the Jews in Germany and elsewhere in Europe. Shortly thereafter, the foundation in Munich in 1936 of the Department of Research on the Jewish Question at the Reich Institute for History of the New Germany created a key and productive site for Nazi "scholarly" work on Jewish and German history. The president of the Reich Institute, the historian Walter Frank, identified the institute as the center of a new history with a National Socialist orientation. The Jewish department was run by Wilhelm Grau, whose February 1933 dissertation had explored the end of the Jewish community in Regensburg in 1519, earning him a name as an authority on Jewish history. He articulated in the following words the mutual relations among German, European, and Jewish history: "It cannot be overemphasized that modern and contemporary German and European history must be written while taking the Jewish question into account." He did not mean any positive influence of Jews. Instead, in order to excise Jewish from German history, Grau argued, it was essential to understand how a history of the Jewish Problem influenced the roots of the nation going back to local and regional history that started with the German cities in the Middle Ages.[32]

According to this idea, Germans and Jews had to be separated because they were inextricably linked. The enormous Nazi effort to demonize the Jew appears a result not of the total disconnection of the two groups but on the contrary of their intertwined relations. This sheds light as to why mockery and humiliation were so central to German anti-Jewish violence: they were essential in order to overcome a sense of discomfort at the violation of an intimacy.

For these scholars, understanding Jewish history was a way to understand German history. Volkmar Eichstät, a librarian and bibliographer at the Reich Institute for History of the New Germany and at the Prussian State Library in Berlin, compiled a comprehensive *Bibliography on the History of the Jewish Question* in 1938 as a research tool for scholars.[33] His view was that "the history of anti-Semitism has not been written" yet because scholars had failed to understand the connections between Judaism and German identity. He explained these connections in a talk entitled "The Literature on the Jewish Question in German Libraries," delivered at the annual conference of German librarians in Graz in June 1939. This literature, according to Eichstät, meticulously collected by previous generations, was essential for the "life of the nation because by researching the hard and ultimately victorious battle between our German nation and the racially foreign element of Judaism we gain a closer understanding of our own German character. And by doing so we increase not only our knowledge but strengthen our commitment to national life."[34]

Nazi scholars of Jewish studies took this connection very seriously. Johannes Pohl, a Judaica specialist, based his career on his familiarity with Judaism, the Jewish community in Palestine, and modern Hebrew. He arrived to Nazism via his religious interests. At the beginning of his career Pohl took a degree in Catholic theology in 1926 from the University of Bonn and entered the priesthood. He then received a fellowship and spent two years (1932–1934) in Jerusalem, where he studied at the Hebrew University and completed his second doctorate at the city's Papal Bible Institute. When he returned from Jerusalem, he left the priesthood, got married, and joined the group of Nazi scholars around Rosenberg. He wrote a book about the Talmud and was a contributor to Julius Streicher's rabid anti-Semitic newspaper, *Der Stürmer*.[35]

By 1938, Nazi anti-Jewish policy makers had several options. The project of creating a Germany without Jews was by all accounts progressing well. A modern European state without Jews had long existed in the wild imaginations of many anti-Semites, though not as a political, official policy bolstered by moral justifications. But on January 30, 1933, Hitler and his regime opened for Germans the possibility of creating such a state, reversing decades of post-Enlightenment values and an established policy of Jewish emancipation. Imagining a Germany without Jews had been one fundamental cultural creation in the years 1933–1938. Imagining this did not equal agreeing with it, but it did mean a shared mental horizon. A threshold was breached and a new one set up: within a few short years, a Germany without Jews had been created in a complete, massive, participatory fashion, without opposition.

But in spite of the evident success of the anti-Jewish policies the Jews continued to be central to Nazi identity. The enormous mobilization against the Jews in 1938 was directed not at practical steps to exclude and banish Jews in the present—was there any field of life from which Jews had not been already totally excluded?—but at much broader claims about the need to sever the link between the German and Jewish past and identity. Perhaps even more, Grau, Eichstät, and Pohl were interested in the German and Jewish past with the aim of rewriting not only German history but also Jewish history. They proposed in effect to appropriate history from the Jews and to write a new German and European history without Jews and Judaism. This was an idea far more radical than removing Jews from economic, social, and cultural positions in German society. What would the Nazis do next?

PART II

1938–1941
The Jew as the Origins of Moral Past

F · O · U · R

Burning the Book of Books

As in my hometown the synagogue was set on fire, we Jews were arrested and forced to watch the synagogue burning, while becoming spectators to SS men playing soccer with a Bible. Then came an SS man to us and said . . . : "We are after all stronger than your Jehovah."

Willy Schiller, Hindenburg, Silesia

The Nazis burned the Hebrew Bible on November 9 and 10, 1938. Not one copy but thousands, not in one place but in hundreds of communities across the Reich, and not only in such metropolises as Berlin, Stettin, Vienna, Dresden, Stuttgart, and Cologne but in such small communities as Sulzburg, a Protestant village in Baden with 1,070 inhabitants where the stone tablets of the Ten Commandments were thrown from the roof of the synagogue and the Nazis marched mockingly up and down the main street with Torah scrolls before destroying them.[1] By fire and other means, the destruction of the Book of Books was at the center of Kristallnacht, when fourteen hundred synagogues were set on fire.[2]

In Berlin, Germans burned the Torah scrolls of the Hebrew Bible in front of the Levetzowstrasse synagogue, while others carried the scrolls from the Fasanenstrasse synagogue to Wittenberg Square and burned them there.[3] The scrolls that were saved from Wittenberg Square were later buried by the

community in Weissensee according to Jewish tradition. In Pestalozzistrasse shredded Torah scrolls and prayer books as well as religious objects from the altar littered the area near the synagogue. Children were mockingly marching on the shredded Torah with top hats on.[4] In the Jewish quarter of Leopoldgasse in Vienna, the Arks and Torah scrolls from four synagogues were piled up in the street and set on fire. In Mosbach, in Baden, a community of five thousand souls, a photograph captured local inhabitants watching as the interior of the synagogue was burned on the morning of November 10.[5]

Destroying the Hebrew Bible in small communities was a public event no one could ignore, one in which children often participated. In Fritzlar, a small town in Hessen where in the year 919 the Reichstag gave birth to the Holy Roman German Empire, Torah scrolls were rolled along the Nikolausstrasse as Hitler Youth rode their bicycles over them.[6] Children played with the Torah on the street in Hirschberg, in Silesia, while in Herford, a small town in western Germany, they shredded it to pieces to a general bellowing and laughing.[7] In the village of Kippenheim, Baden (1,821 inhabitants), youth threw the Torah scrolls into the local brook, while in one quarter of Vienna, schoolchildren were taken to watch the Torah set on fire.[8] Jewish children conjured their own image of the Bible on that day. Batya Emanuael, thirteen years old, watched with her brother the destruction of a small synagogue that stood next to their house in Frankfurt: "A window was pushed open, a chair flew out.... It was followed by another chair and yet another. And then there was silence.... A white snake jumped down from the windowsill and slithered down, down to the ground below, it seemed unending. 'Scrolls of the Law, Torah Scrolls,' we gasped, not wanting to believe our eyes."[9]

In Aachen, Nazis tore the Torah in front of the synagogue and put scraps in their pockets, claiming it would bring them good luck (an old belief of unknown origins).[10] In Vienna, Siegfried Merecki, a fifty-one-year-old lawyer with three children, lived near one of the city's synagogues. That night he saw "packages being carried away.... Shadowy figures were moving toward the bridge over the Danube. Then I understood. The Torah scrolls were being taken to the bridge and thrown into the river. I watched and counted six [scrolls] and heard hideous laughter."[11]

Also in Vienna, Jews were dressed in the robes and decorations of the Ark and then marched and chased through the streets with torn Torah scrolls tied to their backs, while in Frankfurt Jews were forced to tear up the Torah and burn it.[12] In small Schmieheim, a Protestant community of 752 souls in Baden, Nazis rolled the synagogue's seven Torah scrolls down the street like a carpet. Some rolls were later hung in the train station of the nearby village of Dinglingen bei Lahr.[13] A Jewish woman who attempted to save the scrolls and ritual objects in Lichtenfeld, Bavaria, was stopped by children. A scuffle ensued, and the woman was killed. The children later played football with the prayer books.[14] In Altdorf, a Catholic village of 1,112 souls in Baden, a German man mimicked the Jewish prayer in front of the synagogue using the *talith*, the Jewish prayer shawl, as toilet paper, and then read from the prayer book, spitting invective against Jews.[15] And in Wittlich, in western Germany, "a shouting SA man climbed to the roof, waving the rolls of the Torah: 'Wipe your asses with it, Jews,' he screamed while he hurled them like bands of confetti on Carnival."[16]

In Württemberg, a man who picked up Jewish prayer books in the street, presumably as an act of respect toward the holy objects, was later hanged publicly on a tree on the road from Steinach to Hall. In Euskirchen in the Rhineland, the Torah was rolled open and hung from the adorned roof of the synagogue at Annaturmstrasse, visible to the crowd who

gathered before the building as well as to those who viewed the smoking temple from a distance.

As Torah scrolls burned in a synagogue's yard in Düsseldorf, German men, some wearing the robes of the rabbis and cantors, danced around the fire.[17]

Accounts of Kristallnacht and of the Third Reich have overlooked the burning of the Bible. The scholarship of Kristallnacht has focused on two main topics. One concentrates on the interactions among Hitler, his closest party leaders (mainly Goebbels), party organizations, and down to all levels of German society in setting off and undertaking the violence. The main concern has been to find out who gave the orders and whether the violence was commanded from above, a reflection of grassroots sentiments, or both.[18] The second focuses on the reactions of the German population and international public opinion.[19] But one surely must see the gap between these topics and the profound issues raised by destroying one of the most sacred symbols of European-Christian civilization, including the relations of race and religion, the symbol of origins associated with the ancient text, and the Nazi emotions and imagination that made these attacks possible. Why did the violence of Kristallnacht consume the book that had dominated Christian imagination for millennia, adorning such cultural icons as Palermo's Cathedral of Monreale, the Sistine Chapel, and the Kremlin's Cathedral of the Annunciation?

The silence of scholars is interesting because the sources I have used to reconstruct the events, based on local and eyewitness accounts assembled shortly after Kristallnacht, are accessible. Some scholars have not "seen" these sources is the explanation of Kristallnacht via impersonal arguments that stress state structure and policies. Scholars thus interpret Kristallnacht by avoiding the Jews altogether, arguing that it was not anti-Semitism that caused the violence but the "domination structure of the Nazi regime's decision-making process," as if history is made by structures and not by human beings.[20] Others have understood the event in terms of Nazi policies to speed up the emigration of the Jews from the Reich.[21] But certainly the Nazis could have found other means to speed up emigration than burning the Bible. This act cannot be reduced to an issue of policy decision-making, ordered from above and diligently executed from below, for this view tells us nothing about why the people of Schwinzingen burned the Torah. These interpretations of Kristallnacht are ultimately revealing in what they ignore in the historical record.

The difficulty of historians in accounting for Kristallnacht within a broader view of Nazism is reflected in the work of Saul Friedländer, who otherwise has been successful in drawing out the psychological aspects of Nazi worldview. When he recounts Nazi anti-Semitism in the prewar years he reached an impasse when discussing Kristallnacht and ultimately forgoes an explanation. He first rejects the idea that Kristallnacht was a step in the Nazi plans to hasten Jewish emigration, a view that comports with his interpretation of Nazi anti-Semitism as dominated by a racial, redemptive ideology that saw the battle against the Jew in apocalyptic terms. But in his book *The Years of Persecution* he does not attempt to place Kristallnacht within this argument. Instead he writes: "At that moment [November 9], abysmal hatred appears as the be-all and end-all of the onslaught." This is a surprising assessment because it intimates that, with respect to Nazi brutality, Friedländer has arrived here at the limit of his historical, reasoning power. It is revealing that he ends his narrative of Kristallnacht with the following story of despair in the face of the unexplainable. Herr Marks, who owned a butcher shop, was arrested. "The SA men were laughing at Frau Marks who stood in front of her smashed plate-glass window [with] both hands raised in bewildered despair. 'Why are you people doing this to us?' She wailed at the circle of silent faces in the windows, her lifelong neighbors. 'What have we ever done to you?' "[22]

We have already encountered one reason recent scholars have not "seen" the sources about the burning of the Bible, namely the largely unquestioned belief that racial ideology was the ultimate source of motivations and beliefs in the Third Reich. Indubitably, racial ideology, however important, cannot adequately account for the cultural meaning of destroying synagogues and the Bible. Instead, our story so far makes it possible to ask a new question that challenges our understanding of the Holocaust: Why did the Nazis, set on constructing a *racial* civilization, burn the Bible and synagogues, which are *holy, religious* symbols? The event becomes meaningful when we place it within the Nazi tale about Germans, Jews, and roots. The burning of the Bible was about covenants: old, new, and newer still.

Burning the Bible, and by extension Kristallnacht, was part of the Nazi tale about the Jews as inheritors of a tradition, of historical origins, that threatened the Third Reich. Kristallnacht was not simply a dramatic enactment of the idea that "Jews are not welcome" or that "this or that locality is free of Jews" because burning the Bible was targeted not at Jews as individuals, liberals, Bolsheviks, or racial enemies but at Judaism as a whole; it was not about fixing the present but about fixing the past; it was not primarily about emigration policies or uncontrollable hatred but about building a racial civilization by extinguishing the authority of the Jews over a moral, ancient past embedded in the Bible. I do not argue that this was the only meaning of the burning of the Torah, but I do advance the claim that it was the most fundamental one.

The Bible was destroyed because it was disturbingly important for the Nazis. In burning it, the Nazis expanded on the idea of eternal racial origins by adding the desire for a clean slate of religious origins. While racial ideology provided a modern, scientific proof of the Jews' eternal guilt, in Kristallnacht the Nazis created at the same time a German national and Christian community that was independent of Jewish roots. The idea of race gave proof of Jewish immemorial crimes for a national community that set out to liberate itself from the authority of Judaism represented in the immemorial Book of Books. In this way, for the Nazis, Jewish modern and ancient vices linked and complemented each other. The Jews were excised from Germany because they epitomized both the rootlessness of modern times *and* the ultimate historical origins embedded in the Bible. Rootlessness and roots commingled in crafting the Nazi idea of origins. The Nazis persecuted the Jews because as rootless cosmopolitans they did not belong with German identity and they also persecuted them because as the people of the Book they did belong in German, Christian identity.

Burning the Bible was a way to visualize Judaism, to make tangible the enemy that was being destroyed. Some of the Germans who participated knew that the Torah scrolls included the five books of Pentateuch, from Genesis to Deuteronomy, that were read in temple. Others may have had only a vague idea of the scrolls' contents, while still others may have had no idea at all but joined their friends in the act of vandalism. The point was not whether they had precise knowledge of Jewish religious practices and rituals or of the exact biblical books included in the scrolls. Participants knew that the Torah scroll was the holiest and most sacred object in the synagogue. This was enough. The scroll was an image of Judaism, and the scroll on fire provided a symbolic destruction of authors, cantors, and readers. The burning continued a practice familiar from May 1933, when the meaning of the burning of the books was not determined by the precise literary knowledge of the participants and the audience. The burning was the meaning.

The scrolls were touched, carried, rolled out, trampled on, biked and walked over, tied to the backs of Jews, thrown into rivers, torn apart, set ablaze: Germans intimately engaged the physicality and materiality of the Torah. The destruction called forth the five senses at once. It was a tactile act of palpable contact, replete with the sensuality and excitement that comes with destroying dangerous objects. Dangerous—because by burning the Torah Germans also acknowledged the power of the object, much as they acknowledged the power of Judaism in burning fourteen hundred synagogues. The scrolls had to be vanquished with bare hands and demonstratively, publicly, for all to see. Germans destroyed the Bible not sheepishly in secret but in a stirring theatrical performance with actors and audience, be it applauding, bellowing, or in shocked silence. By burning the Bible in public, the Nazis made everyone complicit in the act of transgression, and in this sense as well Kristallnacht was similar to the public carnivalesque rituals of humiliation of previous years.

Burning the Bible was an awesome display of superiority over the Jews, so massive, brutal, and transgressive that it was as if the Nazis were effectively saying to the Jews and other Europeans that they and not the Jews were now the chosen people. The act of destruction was also an act of appropriation of the authority of the Hebrew Bible and a sort of overcoming an original sin of origins—namely, that the roots of Christianity (and therefore also of German Christianity) were Jewish. In their actions the Nazis conveyed that the new master race had been replacing the old chosen people. In Regensburg Jews heading the parade of humiliation were made to carry a banner that read, "Exodus of the Jews." In exorcizing any religious past that linked Judaism and German identity, the Nazis created a new past for the Third Reich and for German Christianity.

In small Baden-Baden, Kristallnacht brought an end to the local Jewish community, which was first mentioned in the historical record in the year 1267. In 1584 the local Jews, except for the two richest families, were expelled. Permanent residency was allowed only in 1862 following the emancipation of the Jews in the state of Baden. After Germany was unified in 1871, the community grew apace, and a beautiful synagogue in the Roman revival style was built in 1897–1898 at Stephanienstrasse 5. A cemetery was consecrated in 1921. The community remained small: in 1925, 425 Jews lived in a town of 25,692 inhabitants. Anti-Semitism, Zionism, and the lure of the big city and of foreign lands reduced the Jewish population to 260 by 1933. After Hitler's rise to power the community dwindled rapidly; 65 Jews left between 1933 and 1938.

Arthur Flehinger, who was a teacher at the local gymnasium in the 1930s, recalled how Jewish men in the community were arrested on the morning of November 10 and brought to the police headquarters. A policeman showed up at his flat at 7:00 a.m. and took him to the station. At this early morning hour the streets were largely deserted, apart from fellow Jews, about fifty local men and community leaders in all, who were also rounded up and taken to the station.

Toward noon a forced march to the synagogue began. The distance between the police headquarters and the synagogue was quite short, but the march intentionally went through the town's main streets, via Leopold Square, Augustus Square, and Ludwig-Wilhelm Square. At the head of the march walked two elderly community members holding a Star of David with the inscription "God, do not abandon us!" The irony required no explanation. The parade evoked religious associations. "One of the many decent citizens is reported to have said," remembered Flehinger, " 'What I saw was not one Christ, but a whole column of Christ figures, who were marching along with heads high and unbowed by any feeling of guilt.'" A large crowd was waiting outside the synagogue at Stephanienstrasse. The Jews went up the stairs to the temple through the hostile gauntlet. In the sanctuary they were forced to remove their hats,

sing the "Horst Wessel" anthem, and listen to anti-Semitic lectures. Flehinger was then told to come up to the lectern from which the Torah was usually read and to recite selections from Hitler's *Mein Kampf* to the congregation. The Nazis were not pleased by his reading because he did not show enough conviction. He was duly beaten. Other community members were asked to read from the book and were beaten as well. After these ceremonies, which took some time, the men were allowed to relieve themselves in the yard against the synagogue's walls. Fifty-two of them were then loaded onto trucks and taken to Dachau. And now the synagogue was set on fire. It is said that the crowd attempted to throw the synagogue's cantor into the flames, but he was saved by a fireman. "If it had been my decision," said one of the Nazis to the Jews, "you [all] would have perished in that fire."[23]

The synagogue was razed to the ground. The remaining stones were used to pave a road, and a city park was built where the synagogue once stood.

The brutality of November 9 sprung precisely from the strenuous attempt to remove any link between German and Jewish identity. Of course, sadism, hate, drunkenness, peer pressure, and incessant anti-Jewish propaganda were present, but these elements alone are insufficient to explain the gleeful desire to injure and insult and the pleasure to humiliate. A mix of intimacy and repulsion drove the persecution.

And so Jews, tied to one another in ropes, were marched through Trebniz, near Breslau, to watch the burning synagogue. All Jews in Emden, in East Friesland, including those living in the local retirement home, were paraded through town to participate in setting the synagogue on fire. There, before the flames, they were forced to sing. Rabbi Jacob Horovitz of Frankfurt, who earlier had suffered a nervous breakdown because of Gestapo mistreatment, was forced to leave the hospital on November 9 to watch the burning of his synagogue, where his father, Marcus Horovitz, had been a rabbi before him. He had a second breakdown in front of the synagogue and died in early 1939. At the end of Harscampstrasse in Aachen, Nazis burned the synagogue and then pelted the Jews with burning embers.[24] In Emmerich, Jews were forced to set fire to their own synagogue.[25] And again in Emden a Jew by the name of Mindus was forced by the Nazis to declare before his fellow Jews, all standing before the smoldering synagogue, that he was the one who had set the building on fire.[26]

The American consul in Leipzig, David Buffum, sent the following report to Washington:

> Having demolished dwellings and hurled most of the movable effects to the streets, the insatiably sadistic perpetrators threw away many of the trembling inmates into a small stream that flows through the Zoological Park, commanding the horrified spectators to spit on them, defile them with mud and jeer at their plight. . . . The slightest manifestation of sympathy evoked a positive fury on the part of the perpetrators, and the crowd was powerless to do anything but turn horror-stricken eyes from the scene of abuse, or leave the vicinity. These tactics were carried out the entire morning of November 10 without police intervention and they were applied to men, women, and children.[27]

The orgy of violence was to Germans both shocking and familiar. On one level, Kristallnacht was not a dramatic rupture in Nazi policies but a magnification of what had been going on since 1933. In burning the Bible Germans reached straight to the Torah Ark to apply what many in German society, such as the scholars who studied the Jews, had been advocating for some years—namely, to sever any connection between Judaism and German identity. The intimate brutality continued a pattern of violence that had been present since January 1933 because synagogues were burned and razed to the ground, and Jews were expelled from German communities, before November 1938.

But on a different level, Kristallnacht was shocking. In Regensburg, a regional high official reported to Munich that although the population supported legal measures against the Jews, the Kristallnacht vandalism was opposed and indeed raised sympathy for the Jews.[28] As the Jews were forced to march through Regensburg's streets, some residents had tears in their eyes.[29] A man in Württemberg wrote in a letter: "Terrible, what happened here. This is after all a house of God. Do not fool yourself, God does not let his people be ridiculed."[30] What shocked Germans in 1938 was the transgression against symbols of religion and morality—that is, the unsettling realization that by burning synagogues and the Bible the Third Reich had been attempting to change not only the centuries-old history of Germans and Jews but also the role of Jews in Christian civilization.

By burning synagogues and the Bible the Nazis placed unavoidably at center stage the relations of Nazism and Christianity. Scientific racism was a relatively novel set of images with which to imagine Jews; it had to negotiate with Christian anti-Semitic images as well as with religious images of the Jews as the people of the Bible, of the Ten Commandments, of the Law, and therefore, for some, of morality. Scientific racism's depiction of Jews as vermin and microbes after 1933 did not simply conquer overnight the imagination of Nazis and other Germans, no matter how diffuse was Nazi propaganda. Old and new ideas commingled.

This process of negotiation gave meaning to Nazi anti-Semitic ideas: whatever the Nazis said about the Jews as racial enemies, they still had to imagine them also within past religious tradition of the Jews as the people of the Bible. Modern, racial anti-Semitism was closely connected to the tradition of Christian anti-Judaism. The two were different but not separate because modern, racial anti-Semitism took shape within the context of memories, habits, and beliefs inherited from Christian anti-Judaism, and in circumstances before 1933. Of course, some Nazis were anti-Christian, particularly anti-Catholic, but their anti-Semitic imagination was nonetheless a jumble of Christian and racial images. We need to acknowledge the persistence of a Christian imaginary tradition about the Jews in order to understand the transformation of anti-Jewish imagination in the Third Reich.

Nazism did not and could not reject Christianity. Religious sensibilities in German society during the Third Reich were profound. By the count in 1939, over 95 percent of Germans were registered, baptized, taxpaying members of the Protestant and Catholic churches.[31] Hitler himself never left the Catholic Church. Many Germans did not regularly observe religious practices, but more important was that they shared a sense of Christian tradition that was connected to their national identity. The Nazis were part of this tradition. The broad popular support enjoyed by the Third Reich owed much to the regime's preservation of religion, along with private property and mass consumption. The Nazi revolutionary attempt to construct a new racial society acknowledged that even the most radical transformation was maintained by links to the past. In contrast, in the 1920s and 1930s the Bolsheviks attacked Christianity, demolishing church buildings and turning them into barns for storing grain and housing cows when they did not blow them up altogether. They saw religious practice as a dangerous, treacherous activity and were determined to break the grip of the past by proposing a worldview that had no place for Christianity.[32] Being Bolshevik and practicing Christianity was, ideologically at least, a contradiction. But in the Third Reich many Nazis were openly and proudly Christian, and the Nazis never seriously considered adopting Bolshevik-style religious policies. Their aim was not to eradicate Christianity but to eradicate Christianity's Jewish roots; not to replace Christianity with racism but to blend the two.

Traditional Christian anti-Jewish motifs found their way into Nazi racism. Jews were routinely linked with the devil. Children's literature, using familiar and easy-to-grasp themes to produce the Germans of tomorrow, particularly emphasized this link. The 1938 book *A German Mother* inculcated: "Children, look here! The man who hangs on the Cross was one of the greatest enemies of the Jews of all time. . . . He said further to the Jews: Your father is the Devil! Do you know, children, what that means? It means that the Jews descend from the Devil."[33] The idea of the Jew as a portent of disease and epidemics had also been commonplace for centuries in Christian Europe. The Nazis' fear of racial contamination was linked to this idea, as well as its metaphoric counterpart. As Hitler wrote in *Mein Kampf,* the Jew is "a pestilence, a moral pestilence, with which the public was infected . . . worse than the [fourteenth-century medieval] Black Plague."[34]

There were more direct applications of the age-old idea that Jews carried disease. In April 1933, Jewish scientists at the Kaiser Wilhelm Institute in Berlin were denied access to stocks of typhus, cholera, and other diseases lest they poison the water supply. Shortly after the invasion of Poland in September 1939 the Nazi organ *Völkischer Beobachter* reported that Jews had poisoned water supplies used by German troops. The *New York Times* reported from Berlin on November 20, 1939, that Germans planned to confine Warsaw Jews into a ghetto because, according to the

Germans, "they are dangerous carriers of sickness and pestilence."[35] The Nazi depiction of Jews as ugly and smelly also had a long tradition.

The Jewish badge was a medieval invention (the first one, featuring the Tablets of the Law, was introduced in 1218), as was the use of Hebrew or pseudo-Hebrew lettering to connote Jewish evilness and to accuse Jews of crimes against Christ and Christians.[36] In 1941 the Nazis introduced the yellow badge, a star with the pseudo-Hebrew lettering of the word *Jude* (Jew) in the middle. Jews had long been reputed to have supernatural powers in European culture; the Nazis articulated this idea anew after 1933 and with special vigor during the war when they argued that world Jewry had instigated the conflict in order to eliminate Germany.

Christians in the Middle Ages greatly coveted Jewish amulets with Hebrew inscriptions as bringing good luck.[37] Had the Nazis in Aachen who kept scraps of the Torah for luck ever heard of this precedent? Probably not. There is no direct genealogical link from Nazism all the way back to medieval society; Nazism did not start in the Middle Ages. The Nazis were aware of some historical precedents in the European anti-Semitic repertoire of images and symbols, but they often unintentionally and not quite consciously used this repertoire while giving it a new, modern meaning. Certain kinds of symbols appear again and again over long periods of history because they come to be identified with a particular object. They make a certain archetypal symbolic manual that is available for use, though the meaning changes from one historical period to the next. Nazi anti-Jewish imagination mixed racial "science," which gave it the legitimacy of modern rationality, with Christian elements, which gave it the familiarity of tradition.

In their aim to eradicate Christianity's Jewish roots the Nazis found support in the German churches. The German Christian movement was an enthusiastic pro-Nazi group within the German Protestant church that during the Third Reich slowly gained control of most of the regional Protestant churches in the country, attracting between a quarter and a third of church members. The Confessing Church, a minority group within the Protestant church that attracted some 20 percent of church members, opposed what it viewed as the efforts of the German Christian movement to undermine basic Christian doctrine but did not contest

Hitler or the Nazi regime. The Catholic Church had the most complex relations with Nazism over political and religious power. Since national unification in 1871, German Protestants identified Protestantism with national identity. Two-thirds of Germans were Protestants, including the emperor, who ruled until 1918. Anti-Catholic feelings among Protestants and a suspicion that Catholics owed primary allegiance to the pope in Rome at the expense of the German nation led to heightened tensions. Otto von Bismarck, the Protestant chancellor who unified Germany, launched a vicious campaign against political Catholicism in the 1870s, which had lasting impact on the relations between the state and Catholicism. Catholics were patriots but wished to preserve the autonomy of their church and schools from encroachment by the state, whatever regime was in power. These factors also played a role in the Third Reich, during which the relations of the Catholic Church and the regime were often tense. But most important for our topic is that during the Third Reich the three churches were overall united in the idea of the Jews as a degenerate moral and spiritual influence on German Christians that should be removed, in one way or another. None of the churches defended the Jews after 1933.

Although the Nazi regime tried to weaken the political power and moral authority of the institutional churches, especially of the Catholic Church, on another level there was a fundamental affinity between Christianity and Nazism. The single most persistent aspect of Nazism was anti-Semitism, just as Christianity provided Nazism with the richest tradition of anti-Judaism. At the same time, in the decades before 1933, German Protestant theologians and clergymen (and also some Catholics) came to appreciate the potential of racism as a vehicle to rid Christianity of everything Jewish while shaping a German national Christianity. Racism made it possible to argue that Jesus was not a Jew and that Christianity owed nothing to the Old Testament. The argument was that Jesus was Aryan, and since Aryans and Jews were opposing races, so Jesus and Christianity had nothing in common with Judaism. In the Third Reich, Catholics also shared the idea of dejudaizing German Christianity. Cardinal von Faulhaber of Munich argued in his Advent sermons in 1933 against eliminating the Old Testament as a Jewish book, as demanded by the German Christian movement. His argument, though, was not in favor of the Jews: instead he claimed that the Old Testament was in fact an anti-Jewish text that proved the sinful ways of the Jewish people.[38] At least von Faulhaber argued for keeping the Old Testament as part of the Christian liturgy. Others in the Christian establishment were more radical. The Synod of Saxony stated in 1933 that "we recognize . . . in the Old Testament the apostasy of the Jews from God, and therein their sin. This sin is made manifest throughout the world in the Crucifixion of Jesus. From henceforth until the present day, the curse of God rests upon this people."[39]

The burning of the Bible, however extreme, fit within a broader history of the Bible in Europe in the decades before 1933 and within theological debates about separating Christianity from Judaism, especially among Protestant theologians. Already in the late nineteenth century several leading German liberal Protestants called for a full separation of Christianity from Judaism. Some argued that Jewish stubborn resistance to acknowledge Jesus as the Messiah was attributable to an immutable Jewish racial character. Adolf von Harnack, one of the leading Protestant theologians of the twentieth century, proposed to separate the Old Testament from Christianity. In 1920 he published his study on Marcion of Sinope, the second-century preacher who taught that the God of mercy of the New Testament had nothing to do with the flawed, angry God of the Old Testament and that Christianity and Judaism must be totally disconnected. In his book Harnack did not attack contemporary Jewry in the name of political anti-Semitism. His critique was theological, but quite clear at that: "To preserve [the Old Testament] in Protestantism as a canonical document [nowadays] is the consequence of a religious and ecclesiastical crippling."[40]

Expunging the Old Testament from Christianity was therefore not simply a Nazi idea or a crude Nazification of Christianity: these ideas were discussed and debated by serious Protestant (and some Catholic) theologians in the decades before the Nazi movement gained any significant power.[41] It is on this ground that Nazism and aspects of German Christianity found a common denominator in the Third Reich: they proposed a project of national identity based on the physical removal of the Jews from Germany and on the cultural removal of any (real or perceived) trace of Jewish origins. Race and this version of German Christianity were corresponding more than opposing ideas, two worldviews that met in their desire to create a German national identity that owed nothing to the Jews, thus erasing any symbolic dependence on Jews as the origins of modernity, the German past, and Christianity.

But removing the Jews was tantamount to uprooting Christianity's own origins, for the Christian claim that Jesus was the Messiah was based on a belief in fulfilling the Old Testament promise for a messianic figure. Whatever the Nazis thought of the inferiority of the Jews, they operated within their own civilization that shared with Jews history, culture, and religious aspects, and they were aware of it. The Jews may have been sub-humans, but they still stood at the origins of Jesus and the New Testament, and therefore of any notion of German Christianity. Here we find a fundamental element in the persecution and extermination of the Jews. The Nazis persecuted the Jews because these were a key element that came from within their own German and European-Christian civilization; to rebuild this civilization anew, they had to destroy a central part of their own culture.

In this respect, Jews, as an inferior race, were unlike colonial subjects, for European colonialism posited different relations to roots and persecutions in the colonies. Germans and other Europeans did not view the cultures of colonized peoples in Africa, Asia, and the Middle East as part of their own. Colonial empires set out to conquer cultures and societies viewed as distinctly outside their own European civilization, which gave justification to genocides in the colonies. But Nazis and other Germans treated the persecution and extermination of the Jews with conviction mixed with a sense of transgression precisely because victims and perpetrators shared historical and cultural common denominators.

The problem the Nazis faced was how to justify the violent uprooting of one's own heritage. Siegfried Leffler, a pro-Nazi German Christian leader and official in the Thuringian ministry of education, explained in February 1936 at a meeting of theologians:

> In a Christian life, the heart always has to be disposed toward the Jew, and that's how it has to be. As a Christian, I can, I must, and I ought always to have or to find a bridge to the Jew in my heart. But as a Christian, I also have to follow the laws of my nation [Volk], which are often presented in a very cruel way, so

> that again I am brought into the harshest of conflicts with the
> Jew. Even if I know "thou shall not kill" is a commandment of
> God or "thou shall love the Jew" because he too is a child of the
> eternal father, I am able to know as well that I have to kill him,
> I have to shoot him, and I can only do that if I am permitted to
> say: Christ.[42]

Leffler was not perturbed by his call to kill the Jews, and there is no indication that his audience reacted to or discussed these remarks. Apparently,
the idea did not sound shocking or original. What disturbed him was how
to reconcile his aim to create a Germany without Jews and Judaism with
his acknowledgment of the historic position of Jews in Christianity. His
words make clear that he had already decided that the link between
Judaism, on the one hand, and German Christianity and national identity,
on the other, had to be violently severed. He and his audience were beyond
this mental threshold. Two years later, Germans burned the Bible as part
of this Nazi imagination, and not at all as an aberration.

For many Nazis and Germans this project of a Germany without
Judaism was not anti-Christian because it meant a refoundation of
German Christianity. For other Germans the burning of the Bible was
abominable. A difference can also be discerned between Protestants and
Catholics because Protestant theology was much more open to the idea of
refounding Christianity without Jews. The complexity of the relations
between Nazism and Christianity should be kept in mind and cannot be
fully discussed here. At the same time, a pattern emerges of an imagination of a Germany without Jews shared by Nazis and the Christian
churches. The Protestant and Catholic churches in the Third Reich supported the Nazi policy of severing Judaism from Christianity. They did
not criticize Kristallnacht publicly, a stance that was determined only in
part by political calculations. The pogrom did create some tension between
the German Catholic Church and the regime. But the actions and statements of the churches, which detached themselves from Jews and their
plight, in effect began to create a new Christianity with no Jewish roots.
On November 10 the National Socialist Association of Teachers decided to
expel all remaining Jewish pupils from German schools, and forbade giving them Christian religious education, claiming that "a glorification of

the Jewish murderers' nation could no longer be tolerated in German schools." Shortly thereafter Cardinal Bertram made clear the position of the Catholic Church when he protested to Reich education minister Rust that everyone knows that "the assertion [that the Christian religion glorified the Jews] is false and that the contrary is true." In February 1939, the Evangelical Church of Thuringia banned its own baptized Jews from its churches. The measure soon spread to Saxony, Anhalt, Mecklenburg, and Lübeck. Not long thereafter all pastors of non-Aryan ancestry were dismissed.

In April 1939 the Evangelical Church Leaders' Conference signed an agreement with the Ministry of Religious Affairs settling the relations between the Protestant churches and the state. The Godesberg Declaration of the same month articulated the new principles: "What is the relation between Judaism and Christianity? Is Christianity derived from Judaism and has therefore become its continuation and completion, or does Christianity stand in opposition to Judaism? We answer: Christianity is in irreconcilable opposition to Judaism."[43]

And yet, the charred, deflagrated Torah scrolls and synagogues did transgress a tangible boundary. This must have been the meaning of an incident in Gablonz in Bohemia (Sudetenland) that left the community speechless. As the synagogue was set on fire, people pushed a Jew named Robitschek into the flames. Suddenly, the synagogue's organ started to play. Terror and "an uncanny sentiment" gripped the community. The Jew was left alone and nothing further happened to him.[44]

The silence of the Gablonz community poses an interpretative challenge for the historian because Germans did not quite know how to articulate their transgression. When we look for explicit mentions by Germans of the burning of the Bible, the sources on Kristallnacht, which are so rich on other matters, are silent. The sources I have used to reconstruct the event come from testimonies given by Jews shortly after Kristallnacht and kept since in the Wiener Library in London. The stormtrooper who yelled from the roof of the synagogue—"Wipe your asses with [the Torah], Jews"—did not elaborate on the motivation for his action. Nazis and other Germans did not go around articulating publicly and privately their motivations for burning the Bible and the synagogues. More broadly, only here and there do we find in the sources expressions of Nazi racial ideas as motivations for Kristallnacht, and these sound like the reiteration of contemporary platitudes. For an event that destroyed a holy object at the core of German and European culture, it is precisely the silence that is revealing. The evidence we seek, therefore, goes beyond what was explicit and conscious, beyond expressions of beliefs in formal ideology propagated by the regime, into that which was inexplicit and unconscious—sensibilities, emotions, and sentiments revealed in public actions—but therefore potentially more fundamental. For human beings do not always say what they think and do not always know how to explain why they do certain things. Kristallnacht is a case in which that which the actors actually articulated as the meaning of the event is less significant than what they kept silent about.

But not everyone kept silent. Some voices pierced the wall of taciturnity, and they articulated what happened in moral terms linked to the Christian-Jewish past. Julius Streicher, the notorious Nazi anti-Semite and editor of *Der Stürmer*, gave a speech on November 10 to a crowd of almost a hundred thousand at Adolf Hitler Square at the center of Nuremberg: "Do not forget that this murderer is a Jew. The Jew has the murder of Golgotha on his conscience. This people cannot be a 'chosen' people. Nuremberg's teachers have decided that, in the future, they will teach children only those words that come from Christ's mouth. They refuse to teach the children any longer about a holy people of God."[45] The audience was left to imagine who the chosen people were now. In Munich, a priest told his congregation that the meaning of recent events is that the Jews would ultimately have to pay for the blood of Christ. It was not clear when this would happen, but "what happened with the Jews [on November 9] is God's will."[46]

A diametrically opposite opinion was voiced exactly a week after Kristallnacht on Wednesday, November 16, the Day of Prayer and Repentance, a Protestant holiday in Germany. Helmut Gollwitzer, a Confessing Church priest who was close to the anti-Nazi theologian Martin Niemöller, began his sermon in Dahlem, an affluent neighborhood in Berlin, by asking: "What should one preach today? Isn't our mouth chockfull? Can we do anything else today but be silent?" He wrote down later that day: "According to the old Prussian liturgy of the Day I read the Ten Commandments. In the dead silence of the shocked community they sounded like hammer blows. The questions that began the sermon were anything but rhetorical."[47] Gollwitzer, born in 1908, was at the time a young priest barely thirty years old. He arrived in Berlin after having been expelled in 1937 from Thuringia by the Gestapo. After Niemöller's arrest, Gollwitzer took his place in the pulpit of the prominent parish of Dahlem. In 1940, when he was expelled also from Berlin and banned from preaching, he volunteered as a medical orderly in the army and was sent to the Eastern Front. In May 1945, in the last throes of the war, he was taken prisoner by the Red Army. He returned home on December 31, 1949, and wrote a book on his experiences that made him famous in Germany and beyond.

Priest Julius von Jan held a holiday sermon in Oberlenningen near Stuttgart in southern Germany on Jeremiah 22:29: "The prophet calls: 'O land, land, land, hear the word of the Lord.' . . . We have today really all the reasons to hold a Repentance Day, a day of mourning for our sins as well as for the sins of our people."[48] Von Jan was later arrested, mistreated by a crowd of people who saw him as a traitor, put on trial, and imprisoned. Prelate Bernhard Lichtenberg of Berlin's Saint Hedwig Cathedral ended his sermon on November 10: "What was yesterday, we know, what will come tomorrow, we don't. But what happened today, this we have experienced: outside burned the temple—this is also a house of God!"[49] He was later murdered by the Nazis for his public prayers for the Jews deported to the east.

Of course, Streicher, on the one hand, and Gollwitzer, von Jan, and Lichtenberg, on the other, had entirely different evaluations of Kristallnacht. But this is precisely the point. In spite of their differences they all significantly viewed its meaning as embedded not in the idea of race, emigration policies, or uncontrolled hatred but in the relations among Nazism, Christianity, and Judaism, in the nexus of morality, trans- gression, and the Third Reich. It may be argued that these individuals were exceptional and do not represent most Germans in 1938. Streicher was not a mainstream leader of the Nazi Party, and his anti-Semitism distin- guished itself even among the Nazis, while these pastors had moral cour- age to speak up against the Nazis. But sometimes extraordinary individuals express what ordinary individuals cannot articulate out of fear, opportunism, repression, guilt, or emotional difficulty. They embody "the exceptional normal," when a dissonance, such as speaking after November 9 about burning the Bible, indicates in fact a general, deeper meaning.[50]

It is often the case with momentous events that years later they resurface in people's memory in a different context, as people suddenly come to "recall" their importance, to understand their meaning, and to acknowledge their own experience in a different light. Would Germans remember Kristallnacht during the war with a renewed, altered sense of urgency, even guilt?

But Germans did articulate their inner thoughts in Kristallnacht by acting out their emotions, which speak even when people keep silent, conveying them in two public rituals: in extinguishing Judaism by fire and in humiliating Jews in parades through the streets of their communities, outward and away from the neighborhood, town, region, and country.[51]

Shortly after 10 a.m. on Thursday, November 10, forty-nine Jews of the Regensburg community were forced to march through town. By this time, the synagogue had been burned, all Jewish men were arrested and twenty-one were transported to Dachau, while the remaining group had been subject to hours of violent and mocking abuse. Heading the march was a banner that read "Exodus of the Jews," carried by two youngsters, one of whom was Paul Hettinger, the sixteen-year-old son of lawyer and community leader Fritz Hettinger. Other young Jews were dressed in ceremonial robes the Nazis had found in the synagogue the night before. Sixty-six-year-old tobacco seller Joel Lilienthal, who was sick, was placed in a cart drawn by his son, Kurt. So moved the parade from Saint-Georgen Square, via Unter den Schwibbögen and Goliathstrasse to the old town hall and from there to Wahlenstrasse and Residenzstrasse, via the chapel and Maximilianstrasse to the train station.[52] Someone took a photo of the parade on Maximilianstrasse.

And so it went with local variations all over Germany. In Dinslaken, the Jewish parade consisted of children from the local Jewish orphanage who were put on a wagon pulled by four Jewish teenage boys. Other children were led around town with cords tied to their necks.[53] In Kippenheim, a small community in Baden where seventy Jews lived in 1938, the principal, a man named Gallus, canceled school on the morning of November 10 to allow pupils to be present as the Jews were marched out of town.[54] In Zeven, a community of 3,079 souls in Lower Saxony, the town's 21 remaining Jews were forced to climb onto a truckbed and driven around town to the sounds of honking and people banging on tin plates. The driver often

braked hard, causing the Jews to fall off the truck to general jubilation. In the afternoon, the men were led to the Gestapo headquarters and from there to Sachsenhausen concentration camp. The women and children were set free. In the meantime, a pyre was set up at the central square. The *Zevener Zeitung* reported that the modest synagogue, consisting of a room in a house, "was cleaned up and all its stuff was brought to the new market square, where it was publicly burned as a symbol that the tolerance toward the Jews has come to an end."[55]

Via the raw emotions of hatred, anger, mockery, fear, transgression, and guilt, Germans conveyed a sentiment, perhaps even an understanding, that a Germany without Jews and Judaism was becoming a reality and, consequently, that a threshold leading to a new idea of morality had been crossed. One approach diminishes the importance of emotions in history and in understanding the persecution and extermination of the Jews. There is a common view of Nazism as the progression from raw to emotionless anti-Semitism, from the brutal street scenes of the prewar years and Kristallnacht to the cold extermination of the gas chambers during the war. One scholar has described the brutality of Kristallnacht as the barbaric methods of the SA and the mob before the turning point, shortly thereafter, to the "emotionless 'modern' anti-Semitism executed by the state administration vested in the law."[56] But by viewing Kristallnacht as a turning point from raw emotion to the cold, administrative process of extermination we disconnect Kristallnacht from the genocide during the war. This view assumes that anti-Semitic emotions are part of premodern, traditional society, while modern anti-Semitism is restrained and devoid of feelings. It sees modernity as rational (and by implication secular), as if emotions are not part of it as well; most important, it sees emotions and the prewar years as somehow separated from the genocide of the Jews in the war. But one wonders when anti-Semitism can ever not be a product of emotions and imagination.

By expressing emotions, Germans made sense of Kristallnacht whether they participated in, approved of, or opposed the violence. Some took pride in the destruction and took souvenir photos in front of destroyed synagogues, as did a group of SA men in Münster who posed for a photo amid the ruins of the local synagogue. Some smile at the camera, but others are serious, feeling perhaps the weight of the moment or a sense of unease. In Dortmund locals had their photo snapped in front of the ruined Hörder synagogue, smiling and laughing.[57]

People from all walks of life participated in the violence. Young males, enrolled in the SA and the SS, were overrepresented. But all sections of German society were involved. Teachers dismissed children from school to take part in the goings on, as in Schweinfurt, Franconia, where children

were sent to ransack the apartment of an eighty-year-old woman. Civil servants and educated liberal professionals were also present. In Würzburg, the rector of the university, Ernst Seifert, was one of the leaders of the group that burned the synagogue. One Jewish woman elsewhere recognized among the vandals the landscape architect who set up her garden some years before.[58] The participation of university-educated professionals calls into question the artificial distinction between the rowdy anti-Semitism of the mob and the alleged emotionless, cold, reasoned anti-Semitism of educated professional Nazis. This distinction assumes that riffraff have uncontrolled emotions, whereas bourgeois educated professionals are self-composed rationalists. But it may simply be a self-projection of scholars, who are educated professionals.

Beneath the veneer of gleeful destruction there lurked contradictory coexisting emotions, including guilt. The councillor at the British embassy in Berlin, Sir George Ogilvie Forbes, reported his first impressions: "I especially noted the demeanor of the groups which followed each band of marauders. I heard no expression of shame or disgust, but in spite of the complete passiveness of the onlookers I did notice the inane grin which often inadvertently betrays the guilty conscience."[59] It is not that mockery and brutality simply accompanied Kristallnacht everywhere. Instead, these emotions created the meaning of the event: they were essential to exorcizing Jews and Judaism from German soil, while at the same time, the terrific violence that reduced Jews to nonbeing was essential to defend against a sense of moral unease.

Shame and fear often accompanied a sense of foreboding. "Everyone felt at the depth of his soul: this was an unconscionable crime," recalled a Catholic priest in his commemorative speech of November 1948.[60] In Aachen, one man murmured in front of the burning synagogue, "Hopefully, this will have no consequences."[61] In Cologne, a woman said to a policeman who tried to disperse a crowd standing in front of the burned synagogue on the morning of November 10: "Are we not allowed to think about what we're supposed to have done?"[62] Germans in Regensburg watched with teary eyes and others kept silent as the humiliated Jews passed in the streets. Shame also led many in Dinslaken to watch the Jewish parade in silence.[63]

Many Germans disliked the violence of Kristallnacht but still accepted it and did nothing to stop it. "Setting the synagogue on fire was, I believe, viewed by many inhabitants in Aachen as a crime," said an eyewitness. "Other actions, such as the destruction of shops, had a different quality and were perceived differently. It did not involve those poor, less well-off" Jews.[64] In Regensburg one man who watched the Jewish parade commented that in principle he agreed with the expulsion of the Jews from town, but "Hirschfeld," meaning Max Hirschfeld, the owner of a local business and an acquaintance, really did not deserve such treatment.[65] This man stood for many in avoiding the issue at the heart of Kristallnacht—namely, the destruction of Judaism on German soil—while projecting what happened onto the Jews' alleged crimes: Jews were guilty unless they looked poor or were my acquaintance Hirschfeld.

Even though clearly not all Germans agreed with the anti-Jewish measures on Kristallnacht, the event made possible and available a new imaginary horizon. For all intents and purposes, Germany was after

November 1938 a land without Jews and Judaism. A fundamental historical bond had been broken. In five years and ten months, German society
had brought about one of the most fundamental changes in the history of
European civilization and the most fundamental change in the modern
history of Jews and Christians in Europe. Jews had been expelled from
European countries before, though not for centuries, but even so, Judaism
as the predecessor of Christianity had never before been erased.

The character of Nazism as a German national movement comes
here into sharp focus. In burning the Bible the Nazis laid the foundation
for a revolutionary idea of time that could legitimize their expansionist
and genocidal plans of the future: by destroying a key part of European
civilization, they ushered in the making of a new one. The eradication of
Jews and the Bible was a Nazi transgressive act against a key symbol of
European culture, transgressive yet also liberating: the new national identity owed nothing to the Jews but also owed nothing to previous moral
and cultural constraints in treating other Christian Europeans. The
enslavement of Europeans, which would soon follow to the amazement of
the people of the Continent, went through the destruction of the Jews.
The Nazi empire of destruction was made possible first by imagining a
new Nazi empire of time.

In local communities, in the meantime, burning the Bible was celebrated
as a new German identity. The small, disbanded Jewish community in
Rätzenburg, Pomerania, sold the local synagogue before November 1938,
and it was made into an egg market. As Kristallnacht came, and hundreds
of localities across Germany burned synagogues, some inhabitants in
Rätzenburg protested. They also wanted a synagogue to burn, for what
was a locality without a burned synagogue? This was akin to not taking
part in the new national history. The local Jewish community was thus
forced to annul the sale and return the money. The eggs were removed, the
synagogue was restored, and Rätzenburgers set their synagogue on fire.[66]

The Coming of the Flood

In Talheim bei Hilbronn, a small town in Württemberg, the mayor's office announced on November 11, 1938: "Relations with Jews . . . 1) He who still has relations with Jews, in spite of all the warnings, will be publicly beaten on the Jewish pillory; 2) Any public presence of Jews in streets, squares or in their vicinity is from now on forbidden."[1] The order was revoked a week later after Jews who could not buy food went starving. In big cities and small towns, only rarely did one now see a Jew on the street. Jews did not go out, but for the most urgent business; when they did, they took a taxi in order not to be seen in public. They spoke in whispers and walked on tiptoe.[2] In Garmisch-Partenkirchen, a local official reported that "the population welcomes the disappearance of all the Jews from the area."[3] After the Torah was burned, the synagogues were destroyed, and the Jews were brutalized, "it was as quiet as an execution," according to the American journalist Frederick Oechsner, reporting from Berlin. A silence of Jewish presence descended on the land, as Germans imagined Jews vanishing from existence.[4]

In Berlin, many Jews "are wandering about in the streets and parks afraid to go to their homes. . . . People [are] about to rot away in starvation," telegraphed Sir George Ogilvie Forbes to London. There was a new rush immediately after November 9 across all German communities to post more signs barring Jews. In Munich, reported a British journalist on

November 13, "cowering from every lighted corner, creep the Jews. They are searching for food. Every shop in this fourth biggest city in Germany today bears the inscription 'NO JEW ADMITTED.' Food stores, cafes and restaurants, pharmacists, fruiterers and banks—in all of them hang the same sign. And the Jews may buy their bread, their milk, only after nightfall, at back doors—if they happen to know a friendly shopkeeper."⁵

The months after Kristallnacht and into 1939 presented a new, European context to the persecution of the Jews in Germany because everyone in Europe now knew that sooner or later war would come. First, the Nazis, between November 1938 and August 1939, brought to an end any remaining viable Jewish life in Germany. Then on September 1, 1939, came the war, and with it the jolting changes for people on the Continent, as well as for the persecution of the Jews. But however different from the prewar period was the persecution of the Jews between September 1939 and June 1941, when Nazi Germany invaded the Soviet Union, the two periods shared a common denominator in the Nazi imagination of the Jews crafted between 1933 and 1939. The war brought changes undergirded by continuities. Let us trace this period from November 1938 to June 1941.

Nazi measures between November 1938 and January 1939 terminated whatever sources of livelihood still existed for Jews. On November 12, Hermann Göring decreed the cessation of all Jewish economic activity as of January 1, 1939. Jews were prohibited from almost all existing options for employment apart from certain services done by and for Jews. Employed Jews were fired without the right to claim pension or compensation. Jews had to sell everything, according to the decree: "their enterprises, as well as any land, stocks, jewels, and art works." All Jewish shops "will gradually be taken over into Aryan hands," and shops that had not been sold by the beginning of 1939 would be taken over by the state.⁶

Also on November 12, Göring convened a high-level conference on the Jewish Question in the Reich that was attended by, among others, Joseph Goebbels and Reinhardt Heydrich, head of the Security Service of the SS. The discussion focused on further economic measures against the Jews and on the urgent problem of compensation for the damage caused to Jewish property during the violence of the preceding days. The insurance costs for the broken windowpanes of Jewish shops alone were valued at six million US dollars. Two days earlier, however, Hitler had already given a secret order that Jews would bear all the costs of repairing their businesses.

The meeting is most interesting for the participants' discussions on topics beyond practical measures against the Jews. These were characterized by phantasmagoric ideas about how to extinguish Jews from German life and had a tone that oscillated between sadistic mockery and obsession, with various ideas betraying anxiety over the presence of Jews in Germany.

> GOEBBELS: "It might . . . become necessary to forbid the Jews to enter German forests. In the Grünewald whole herds of them are running around . . ."
>
> GÖRING: "We shall give the Jews a certain part of the forest . . . [and make sure] various animals that look damned much like Jews—the elk has such a crooked nose—get there also and become acclimated."[7]

Some ideas were by now familiar. When Goebbels declared, "I consider it as out of the question that my son be seated next to a Jew in a German school and [that the Jew] be given a history lesson," he merely expressed the idea just put into practice in Kristallnacht that any link established between Judaism and German identity, even one made in the mind of a Jew who thinks of German history, contaminated German culture.[8] But more ideas were soon suggested. Heydrich reminded the participants that emigration from the Reich would not solve all the problems because the government would still have to administer the relations with the remaining Jews, and the talk turned to ghettos and branding the Jews with a special sign. Heydrich and Göring had the following exchange:

> HEYDRICH: "Who is Jewish according to the Nuremberg Laws shall have to wear a certain insignia . . ."
>
> GÖRING: "A uniform."
>
> HEYDRICH: "An insignia . . ."
>
> GÖRING: "But, my dear Heydrich, you won't be able to avoid the creation of ghettos on a very large scale, in all the cities. This shall have to be created."

HEYDRICH: "... The control of the Jew through the watchful eyes of the whole population is better ..."

GÖRING: "We'd only have to forbid long-distance calls ... and in towns all their own."

...

HEYDRICH: "... As some additional measures I'd propose to withdraw from the Jews all personal papers such as permits and driver's licenses ... By not being permitted to live in certain districts he should be furthermore restricted to move about freely ... The same would go for ... exclusion of Jews from public theaters, movie houses ..."

GÖRING: "[... from] health spas ..."

HEYDRICH: "Well, then I'd like to propose the same thing for hospitals."[9]

For Heydrich and Göring the existence of the Jews that would remain in Germany already meant confined neighborhoods, branding signs, and deathly isolation. They were not thinking of the special circumstances of a war but of regular peacetime conditions. Indeed, a confined area for Jews had been suggested earlier, in mid-1938. A "Memorandum on Treatment of Jews in the Capital in All Areas of Public Life," written for Julius Lippert, mayor and municipal president of Berlin, discussed the influx of Jews from the provinces and rural areas to Berlin and noted that, "while it appeared impractical at the moment to concentrate Berlin Jews in a ghetto," their existence should be restricted to specific neighborhoods with no permission of employment.[10] In the November 12 meeting neither the sartorial differences of opinion between Göring and Heydrich on marking the Jews nor the differences on their spatial isolation was resolved. Three weeks later Hitler decided against ghettos and insignia for the time being. But on December 28 the first decree was issued to concentrate all Jews in "Jews' Houses."

For Germans, their country did become in the months after Kristallnacht a land without Jews. Between January 1933 to September 1939, 282,000 Jews had left Germany, and around half of them had left in 1938–1939. By May 1939, only 188,000 Germans of Jewish faith remained in

Germany. Of those, more than a third lived in Berlin, a result of inner-migration to the big Jewish community to find employment and the security that came with the anonymity of the metropolis. Seventy percent of Jews lived in a total of twenty-four cities, a fraction of German communities in 1939: a third of the Jews still lived in smaller localities, and their numbers were dwindling daily. The Jewish population was aged (21.3 percent were over sixty-five), scared, and profoundly isolated.[11] For most Germans there were simply no Jews and Jewish markers to be seen in Germany anymore apart from the signs that everywhere read, "Jews are not welcome." Slowly also the signs were taken down, a recognition that the Jews had disappeared. Jews did continue to exert malevolent influence in Moscow, London, and Washington, but not in Germany: here they existed now only in the imagination as a relic of the past extinguished in public in a terribly short time through violence and fire.

A Germany without Jews and Judaism was for all Germans a novelty that called for meaning, for new stories and storytellers. The Institute for the Study and Eradication of Jewish Influence on German Church Life was opened on May 6, 1939, in the castle of Wartburg, where Martin Luther in 1521 translated the New Testament into German and where German students in 1817 burned objectionable books. Appropriately, the final organizational push for the institute was made several days after Kristallnacht; the aim of the institute was to create a dejudaized German church and to formulate new biblical interpretations and liturgical substance. Walter Grundmann, professor of the New Testament at the University of Jena and the academic director of the institute, explained in his keynote address that the present era was similar to the Reformation: Protestants today had to overcome Judaism just as Luther had to overcome Catholicism, for just as Christians in the sixteenth century could not imagine Christianity without the pope, contemporary Christians could not imagine salvation without the Old Testament. But this task could be achieved: the Bible would be purified and its ultimate truth reinstated—namely, that Jesus sought the destruction of Judaism. "The elimination of Jewish influence on German life is the urgent and fundamental question of the present German religious situation." The new, present-day Reformation would thus complete the work started by Luther.[12]

Building on works of theologians and scholars before and after 1933, the institute thrived with conferences, lectures, and publications. Its appeal was extraordinary not only among scholars and students of Protestant theology but also among geographers, linguists, archaeologists, anthropologists, and historians in a veritable interdisciplinary spirit. The headquarters in Eisenach, not far from Wartburg, were housed rent-free in a building owned by the Evangelical Lutheran Church in Thuringia (additional offices were located in Romania and Scandinavia). Many institute members came from this strongly Protestant region, and it received support from state and church institutions as well as local pastors. Funding came from the pro-Nazi German Christian movement, donations from regional churches, and the sale of publications. Staff members received their salaries from their church and university positions, thus enabling the institute to run on a modest budget, most of which went to organizing conferences. The scholarly side was divided among three groups charged with scholarly projects, conferences of scholars and clergy, and publications. These publications, a combination of scholarly books and popular pamphlets, made the institute's greatest impact on German society, especially those publications aimed at laypeople: a dejudaized New Testament, hymnal, and catechism that made it possible to begin worshiping a Christianity without Judaism.[13]

A look at the history of the institute is important to identify trends in the Third Reich with respect to the relations among race, Christianity, and Nazi anti-Semitism. The institute reflected the popular appeal of the German Christian movement among Protestants in the Third Reich and of the idea of a Germany without Judaism. It commingled Nazi ideas about the Aryan race with Christianity, while pastors, scholars, and church and state institutions lent its message support and legitimacy. Of course, there were other, very different ideas on these matters in the Third Reich. The German Christians were not a majority movement. Many Catholic and Protestant clergy and laypeople saw Nazism as an adversary of Christianity and, especially as the crimes of the regime became more evident, viewed it as a moral stain on Christian Germany. We shall later encounter some of them. But the institute does provide an important indication as to how some Germans in key theological and pastoral roles began to understand the end of Judaism in Germany and how they told anew the story of the testaments.

Siegfried Leffler, who in 1936 called for Germans to love Christ by killing Jews, was one of the institute's leaders. Members and associates, many of them comprising a younger generation of theologians and scholars of early Christianity trained by Germany's leading professors in the finest universities, viewed the aim of the institute as both theological and national: to eradicate Judaism in order to purify Christianity and Germany. The result, as Susannah Heschel has observed, was to frame "Nazism as the very fulfillment of Christianity . . . [and] Christ [as] a prefiguration for Nazi Germany's fight against the Jews."[14] Their work after May 1939—describing Jesus' goal as the destruction of Judaism, removing all positive Jewish references from Christian texts, and eliminating the Old Testament from church liturgies—contributed on the level of textual exegesis and academic research to a situation that already existed in every German town: Jews and Judaism had already been destroyed in November 1938.

Different interpreters in small, provincial communities acted out on the local level what Grundmann and his fellow scholars set out to accomplish on the national, theological one. They placed the local history of Kristallnacht within the new Nazi anti-Jewish story, as happened on February 19, 1939, the first Carnival after Kristallnacht. Catholic German localities continued a Third Reich tradition of including in parades floats and groups of actors featuring anti-Semitic themes. In Neustadt an der Weinstrasse, in the Rhineland-Palatinate, there was the usual representation of the Jew as a cattle dealer carrying a pile of money in his pocket.[15] A float in Mainz showed a huge caricature of the ugly head of a crooked-nosed Jew wearing a cap with a large visor with the label "pure Aryan." It portrayed the Jews as concealing their identity in order to pry on innocent Germans.[16] These floats represented the usual stereotype of Jews as racially inferior, economic manipulators, and treacherous folk who seek to harm Germans.

But a new float was added to the parade in Neustadt an der Weinstrasse, a locality of about 22,000 inhabitants in 1933. Of the 266 Jews who lived there that year, 65 remained by the end of January 1939, most of them elderly and trying to flee. By September, the number had declined to 41. The local coverage of Kristallnacht was typical. The newspaper *Pfälzer Anzeiger* reported on November 11 that "the overwhelming majority of

the Jews left the town yesterday." About November 9 it said this: "In addition to the synagogue, the Jewish retirement home on Karolinenstrasse was also set on fire on Thursday evening. Otherwise, all was quiet yesterday in Neustadt."[17]

The new float featured a burning synagogue, while an actor representing Moses held the Tablets of the Law also destined for destruction. It showed the Jews not only as an ancient people of the Bible but also as people who already belonged to the past and had no place in the present. Mocking Kristallnacht in a city that had almost no Jews was not about mocking the present (as, for example, in mocking the mayor) but about remembering an event that made the Jews themselves a past. Neustadters thus made sense of an important event by placing their local experience within recent German history in the making.

In the meantime, anti-Jewish legislation in the few short weeks between November 10, 1938, and January 30, 1939, drastically curbed Jewish existence. The list of laws accelerated for Jews an impending total social suffocation, while for Germans it brought the reality of a local and national life without Jews.

Jews are excluded from the general welfare system; there are no more hospitals or medical services offered for them. Jewish children cannot attend regular schools; there will be establishing of schools for Jews only. The minister of the interior decrees that Jews' access to public places be limited to a few hours a day. Berlin bans Jews from all theaters, cinemas, cabarets, concert and conference halls, museums, fairs, exhibition halls, and sports facilities, as well as from districts with government offices, major monuments, and cultural institutions. All unemployed Jews fit for work must register for compulsory labor. Jews are deprived of their driving license and must sell their cars to Aryans. The Law on Midwives bans all Jews from this occupation. Jews are prohibited from keeping carrier pigeons. Jews are forbidden from having a phone line.[18]

Then, on Monday, January 30, 1939, Germany's most important interpreter of the Jewish Question made public his own vision. Hitler commanded quasi-religious authority, explaining the past, fixing the present, and setting out the course of the future. And so it may come as a surprise that he said little in public about the Jews from January 1933 to January 1939 when we consider the massive anti-Jewish policy orchestrated by him and his regime. After the seizure of power and throughout his 1933 speeches transmitted to more than twenty million radio listeners, he barely mentioned them. Hitler authorized the April 1, 1933, national boycott against Jewish businesses, in which stormtroopers harassed Jewish shopkeepers, marked their shops with the Star of David, and prevented Germans from buying there. But he distanced himself from being publicly associated with the action by leaving Berlin. He then said nothing about Jewish policy in public until he announced the Nuremberg Race Laws in September 1935.[19]

In the early years of the regime Hitler took care to preserve a public image of a statesman and to distance himself from the public, violent anti-Semitism. This was left to Goebbels and the Germans who acted it out on the streets. Hitler needed a respectable image abroad to negotiate with leaders of other countries as well as at home. Many Germans were not against the measures discriminating communists, socialists, and Jews but wanted them to be implemented in an orderly and legal fashion and without the disrupting consequences of public violence. In addition, conservative elites in the army, industry, and foreign office distrusted the SA, which was a main agent of the public violence, and Hitler was determined in the early years of the regime to keep the loyalty of these elites to lend stability to the dictatorship with an eye to the future war.

Hitler, of course, continued to harbor extreme anti-Jewish phobias, but he kept his utterances to private meetings and dinner table conversations. Now on January 30, in his annual speech to the Reichstag on the anniversary of the seizure of power, Hitler interpreted for himself and for the German public the post-Kristallnacht relations of Germans and Judaism:

> I have often been a prophet in my life and I was mostly laughed at. In the time of my struggle for power it was in the first place the Jewish people who received with nothing but laughter my prophecy that one day I would take over the leadership of the state and with it the whole people and then among many other things bring the Jewish problem to its solution. I believe that the roars of laughter of those days may well have suffocated in the throats of the Jews in the meantime.
>
> I want to be a prophet again today: if international finance Jewry in Europe and beyond should succeed once more in plunging the peoples into a world war, then the result will be not the Bolshevization of the earth and thus the victory of Jewry, but the annihilation of the Jewish race in Europe.

For the first time since 1933, Hitler addressed publicly upfront the future of the Jews in unveiled threats. The context of the speech has been convincingly reconstructed.[20] It was a stage in Hitler's preparation for war, and it aimed, in his paranoid mind, to neutralize the Jewish threat to Germany's power. Jewish international finance and communism were plotting to broaden the European war into a world war in order to prevent German victory. The murderous threats would convince Jews in European and American public life to moderate their anti-German propaganda and warmongering at a time when Germany and the United States were negotiating over the issue of Jewish refugees. This reading is correct, but the speech also had an important place within the anti-Jewish imagination that had solidified in Germany in early 1939.

Hitler the orator was highly sensitive to his audience. For years since 1933 he sensed, one can assume, that it was too early for his German (and certainly international) audience to hear such an announcement, and perhaps more important, it was too early for Hitler himself to hear himself uttering these words as chancellor in public. But the attack on Judaism in November 1938 shaped a new mental horizon and opened new destructive possibilities. In his speech Hitler reiterated what had been, in a sense, taking place in Germany already and then only broadening the scope to Europe as a whole. He used the word "annihilation" without providing details, as a vague metaphor. Yet by now Jews and Judaism had been obliterated from sight in Germany for several months. The novelty of his speech lay in that, for the first time, Germany's chancellor, as a head of state, voiced public, official approval of a policy of "annihilation." Hitler could utter these words officially only because "annihilation" had already become a shared social practice and part of the cultural imagination. For his audience—both in the Reichstag hall and across Germany, where the speech was transmitted over the radio—Hitler merely described an existing reality. The words reflected an imaginary bond between speaker and audience. Hitler's listeners in the hall, on hearing the words, did not react with shock, disbelief, or astonished silence but immediately burst into the resounding applause of instinctive understanding.

In fact, the notion of annihilating the Jews had become in the period before January 1939 a shared expression and a respectable topic of discussion in polite society. Hitler mentioned it several times to foreign dignitaries between September 1938 and January 1939.[21] Public discussions about solutions to the Jewish Question by professionals such as race experts, scholars who studied Jews, and SS officials always included the option of extermination, even if in these early years it was usually discarded.[22] The talk of annihilation was common immediately before and after Kristallnacht. On November 8, Himmler addressed a top-echelon group of SS officials. In the case of war, he predicted, the Jews knew that "if Germany and Italy were not annihilated, they themselves would be annihilated. . . . In Germany, the Jew will not be able to maintain himself; it is only a matter of years." But if the Jew should win—Himmler let his imagination run wild—he would exterminate Germany: "Everybody will be included, the enthusiastic supporters of the Third Reich and the others; speaking German and having had a German mother would suffice."[23] Himmler was imagining the future extermination of the Jews by projecting onto Germany a fantasy of annihilation. Several weeks after Kristallnacht, on November 24, the official SS newspaper, *Das Schwarze Korps,* published an article with the sardonic title "Jews, What Now?": "This stage of development [of the Jews] will impose on us the vital necessity to exterminate the Jewish subhumanity as we exterminate all criminals in our law-abiding state: with fire and sword! The outcome will be the actual and final end to Jewry in Germany, its total annihilation."[24]

Fire and sword had just been used by Germans against Jews, and an end to Jewry in Germany just been accomplished. What did "annihilation" mean in January 1939—for Germans but also for Hitler—because Hitler, too, was the creation of social, cultural horizons of his society bounded by space and time? He, too, could have uttered and imagined certain things only at a particular historical time. "Annihilation" did not mean Auschwitz; no one in Germany knew exactly what the word meant or how this meta-phor of "annihilation" would come to pass. Instead, the image of annihila-tion drew from the very recent past. When Hitler, Himmler, and *Das Schwarze Korps* talked about annihilation they at one and the same time reproduced, confirmed, interpreted, and opened up for new destructive possibilities the present conditions whereby Germans smothered in six short years all traces of Jewish life. Hitler did not go out on the street and burn synagogues, but throngs of Germans did (or assisted, watched, or supported the actions). When Hitler talked about annihilation in the abstract, they thought of their lived experience of annihilation in their locality. Hitler's words articulated an anti-Jewish social practice and cul-tural imagination that had become a way of life, a sensibility shared by the Führer and his audience.

But how can we know and document that shared sensibility between Hitler and his audience? By looking at those emotional connections and relationships that existed but are not directly documented in the historical sources. The emotions revealed in Hitler's speech were very similar to the emotions that had been revealed in public actions against the Jews since 1933. Hitler expressed, first, mockery. Foreign countries, he said, criticize Germany for treating harshly such highly cultured people as the Jews. Why then do these countries not take advantage of Germany's gift and take in these "magnificent people"? Other emotions were articulated: resentment—"I was mostly laughed at"; vengeance with sarcasm—"the roars of laughter of those days may well have suffocated in the throats of the Jews in the meantime"; and brutal hatred—"the result will be . . . the annihilation of the Jewish race."

The whole passage is couched in a tone of enraged violence. These were precisely the emotions exhibited by Germans who had acted against Jews and understood by those who did not act. Nazis and other Germans could connect emotionally to the mockery, resentment, and violence expressed in Hitler's speech because they communicated these emotions themselves in anti-Jewish actions. The meaning of the speech was not revealed primarily in deciphering what Hitler meant by "annihilation" and what the German public really understood by it. Hitler himself did not know exactly what "annihilation" meant on the evening of January 30, 1939. The primary meaning of the speech is that it reflected, as well as shaped, an existing sensibility. On January 30, Hitler did not so much express a groundbreaking idea as give an official voice to a reality that had already been created.

This understanding of the speech is important for two reasons. First, it restores to Hitler his place as an individual influenced by the culture of his time, even when he single-handedly drove anti-Jewish policies forward. Many biographies see Hitler as shaping Nazi Germany but never as being shaped by it in return. Yet Hitler was part of the anti-Jewish emotional sensibilities in the Third Reich; he shaped them and was in turn shaped by them. The meaning of the speech is not so much that it was a radical departure that paved the way from persecution to extermination as it was a reflection of anti-Jewish sensibility, in which Hitler is revealed not simply as a shaper of German culture but as its product as well.

Second, it is a corrective to the common understanding among laypersons and scholars that the Holocaust was unimaginable and that the total removal of the Jews had not been anticipated. Of course, Germans could not imagine in 1939 the mass shooting in just two days in September 1941 of 33,771 Jews in Babi Yar and the gas chambers of Auschwitz. But Hitler could utter his words only because he and Germans could imagine a world in which extreme violence was applied to get rid of Jews and eliminate Judaism.

Indeed, looking back over the first six years of the regime, we can observe with certainty that many Germans participated in the persecution of the Jews while many others, indeed German society as a whole, did not oppose the regime's anti-Jewish initiatives. No group in German society firmly rejected the Nazi assault on Jews and Judaism. What did Germans create and enable by these stances of participation and nonopposition? The problem is not to what degree Germans *really* believed in Nazi ideology. Nazi ideology and intentions were not fixed things that existed out there asking people to really believe in them or not, for the Nazis changed them with time. Instead, what Germans created was a culture that made available the imagining of a Germany without Jews and Judaism as a recognizable, internalized idea. In 1939 Germans could imagine this idea, and here lies the anti-Jewish revolutionary achievement of the Nazis in the prewar years.

Everyone in Europe shared the impending expectation of war as the months of 1939 went by. The pace of Nazi aggression quickened. In March, Hitler tore up the Munich Agreement, signed less than six months earlier, guaranteeing the sovereignty of Czechoslovakia. During the night of March 14–15, the Wehrmacht marched into Czechoslovakia, meeting no military resistance. On March 16, a victorious Hitler entered Prague and announced from Prague Castle the incorporation of Bohemia and Moravia (the two regions of the Czech Republic) into the Reich as a protectorate. Germany had now added the substantial Czech armament industry to its military war machine. In May, Germany signed the Pact of Steel with Italy, laying the foundation of the wartime alliance of Mussolini and Hitler. And in August came the crowning diplomatic achievement of Hitler's preparation for war with the signing of the German-Soviet Nonaggression Pact, better known as the Ribbentrop-Molotov agreement. Revealed to a stunned world on August 23, the pact included a public section including protestations of friendship between the archrival communist and Nazi powers. This was shocking enough. The secret section divided eastern Europe between German and Soviet spheres of interest and established a line in the middle of Poland as the border. Hitler was preparing for an imminent attack on Poland. His generals, who had misgivings about his expansionist policies, were now in no position to contradict him. The agreement with the Soviet

Union assured that he would avoid a war on two fronts if France and Britain should declare war on Germany. War was a matter of days away.

With respect to the Jews, by September 1939 there remained according to one estimate 185,000 in Germany. Some 115,000 had left Germany in the ten months between November 1938 and September 1, 1939, the largest emigration of Jews from prewar Nazi Germany in one year. Altogether, 400,000 Jews had left the Reich (Germany and Austria) since January 1933. Most went to the United States, Palestine, and Great Britain, but Jews left for any country that would accept them, anywhere, to Brazil, Argentina, Australia, South Africa—even Japanese-occupied Shanghai, where 8,000 fled. Those who could not flee were old and impoverished. They were excluded from the general welfare system after Kristallnacht and had to apply to special offices in hopes of receiving help. Jewish welfare services aided as much as they could. In December 1938 the Reich Labor Exchange and Unemployment Insurance ordered all unemployed Jews fit for work to register for compulsory labor.[25] The Jews feared the Gestapo, but another anxiety consumed their daily life: they feared starvation because from 1939 the regime limited when and where Jews could shop. Ration cards for Jews were cut; they received less meat and butter and no cocoa or rice.

The rhythm of anti-Jewish legislation continued unabated between February and August 1939. For the Nazis, the Jews were still a formidable enemy.

Jews are not allowed to buy flowers. Jews must surrender their jewels, diamonds, and precious metals. The cost for the disposal of the ruins of Jewish synagogues will be levied on the Jewish communities; the synagogues will not be rebuilt. Law on Renting to Jews: A Jew cannot have recourse to protection if the landlord offers him or her substitute accommodations, naturally inferior in quality. Jews are disbarred from hunting grounds and cannot receive a hunting permit. In reporting legal cases against Jews, newspapers are advised to mention the middle name Israel and Sarah so that the reader will know that the accused is Jewish. The president of the German Lottery forbids the sale of lottery tickets to Jews.[26]

An atmosphere of gloom engulfed the Jews who remained in Germany. Victor Klemperer was before 1933 a scholar of modern French literature at Dresden's University of Technology. Although his father was a rabbi, he converted to Protestantism in 1912 when he was thirty-one and felt German through and through. His home was German culture. The Nazis thought differently, of course. Together with all Jews who taught at German universities, Klemperer lost his position after the seizure of power. The tremendous blow came later as he slowly comprehended the total rejection of him by friends and acquaintances. He wrestled strenuously to explain how it had happened that German culture produced Nazism, and his answers swung according to his circumstances and those of the Reich. At the beginning, like Christopher Isherwood and many others, he thought that Nazism would not survive, but as the years went by he had to acknowledge the regime's popularity. Still, he wanted at all costs to hold onto his pure idea of German culture. So he oscillated between viewing Nazism as a non- and anti-German phenomenon and viewing it as reflecting popular sentiment. Meanwhile, he survived the Third Reich largely because his wife, Eva, was non-Jewish, which afforded a modicum of protection. From 1933 he kept a remarkable diary.

Klemperer's life became considerably more difficult after the seizure of power, but the dramatic shift, when any kind of normal life became impossible, came for him in the months after Kristallnacht, not during the war. The Klemperers lived in Döltzschen on the outskirts of Dresden, so they were spared the Kristallnacht violence. But new measures enacted in the following months made their life unbearable. As a Jew, Klemperer was not allowed to drive, which not only made life difficult but also deprived him of an activity he enjoyed. A more serious restriction came when he was no longer allowed to use or even enter the public library. The librarian cried as he issued Klemperer the ban. And the local authorities harassed the Klemperers over the most trivial details of the maintenance of their house and garden.

"We are completely isolated," wrote Klemperer two months before Kristallnacht, on August 10, 1938. Frau Lehman, a friend, planned to visit them. She arrived in an agitated state. She had waited for complete darkness to enter their house so that no one would see her visiting the couple. But when she arrived, someone was in the street, and now she was afraid. "She did not realize how terribly that depressed us," he wrote. A few weeks later, on September 2, he added: "I am gradually beginning to believe as firmly in the unshakability of the NSDAP as if I were a sworn supporter. . . . Thus are our hearts very dejected, each day a little more."[27]

June 20, 1939, was a beautiful summer day: "The garden blooms as it has never bloomed. Now roses and more roses, jasmine, carnations, sunflowers. . . . Absolute silence on the part of all relatives and friends. Absolute isolation. In the last two weeks only expensive taxi rides to the dentist."[28]

The summer was about to end, and the war was at the gate. What would happen to the idea of a Germany without Jews? Most Germans failed to think deeply on the eve of the war about the short- and long-term consequences of their new imagination. They avoided the long-term consequences of building a new humanity based on violently eradicating, on a European scale as promised by Hitler, a tradition and a book that inextricably belonged to their own culture. And they avoided the short-term consequences of their actions in a war that drew ever closer. For Germans had already mistreated, humiliated, profited from, brutalized, killed, and denied the legitimacy of existence (or consented to all this) to their "own" Jews, German citizens who looked and talked like them, distinguished members of society. How would they treat, then, east European Jews in the coming war? These Jews looked and talked differently, were viewed as primitive, filthy, Bolsheviks, if not subhuman, and were significantly more numerous than German Jews. At a minimum they would receive the treatment of "our" Jews. To obliterate these Jews from existence, what options had Germans left for themselves apart from exercising harsher violence? On what terms were these Jews to be allowed to live in the conquered territories, if at all?

"During the morning hours of the first of September, 1939, war broke out between Germany and Poland. . . . We are witnessing the dawn of a new era in the history of the world. . . . Wherever Hitler's foot treads there is no hope for the Jewish people."[29] Chaim Kaplan, a Zionist, Hebraist, educator, and principal of a Jewish school in Warsaw, described in his diary the beginning of the Second World War. From 1933, when he was fifty-three years old, Kaplan kept a diary in Hebrew, and he continued to write it during the war. What began as a diary recording personal matters turned into a document recording extraordinary times. His evaluation could have been shared by Germans as well: the war would be momentous and Jews had no place in the new Nazi empire. Kaplan felt a suffocating sense of foreboding when he wrote several weeks later, on October 28: "We move along the earth like men condemned to death. . . . In the eyes of the conquerors we are outside the category of human being. . . . We sense that we are caught in a net, doomed for destruction."[30]

Kaplan, like other Jewish diarists of the period, revealed a side of the Nazis that was difficult for them to express. The Jewish victims could at times sense meanings that the perpetrators were unaware of, did not want to understand, or preferred not to admit. They felt that they uniquely could illuminate what seemed to them an unprecedented period of persecution and sought strenuously to understand the conscious and unconscious motivations of the Nazis. Kaplan wrote as early as on February 3, 1940, just a few months into the war and before the extermination began, that "only the one who tasted the Nazi rule in all his being and essence . . . only this kind of an author, if he is a sensitive man and his pen flows, maybe will be able to give an accurate description" of Nazism.[31] We shall not take their words at face value but rather use them as a window to understand how they and Germans understood the persecution and extermination of the Jews during the war.

Seventeen months later Emanuel Ringelblum confirmed Kaplan's direst fears. Ringelblum was a promising young educator and historian of Polish Jewry who established the Oyneg Shabes archive to record in detail Jewish life in the Warsaw Ghetto. *Oyneg Shabes* is Yiddish for "Sabbath pleasure," referring to cultural gatherings taking place on the Sabbath. The archive expanded over the years to record all aspects of life and death in the ghetto, including documents, research projects, maps, drawings, diaries, and photos. In May 1941, Ringelblum described ghetto conditions in his diary:

> In the middle of May, hunger and mortality were at their peak. Recently, people have been dying at a rate of 150 a day . . . and the mortality keeps growing. The dead are buried at night between 1 and 5 A.M., in mass graves, without shrouds, but in white paper that is also later removed. At first they used to be buried in separate graves one next to the other; now they are all buried in one grave. There's a shortage of burial ground

now. . . . Consequently, the Germans and Polish health authorities are considering a special crematorium for the Jews.
Various groups of visitors come constantly to the cemetery,
military people and private visitors. Most do not show any
sympathy at all to the Jews, on the contrary, some think that
mortality is too low. Some take photographs. Of special interest [to these visitors] is the shed, where dozens of corpses lie
during the day waiting to be buried [at night].[32]

The war Kaplan and Ringelblum described began at 4:45 on the
morning of September 1, 1939, when Wehrmacht soldiers advanced into
Poland. France and Britain declared war on Germany on September 3,
although they did not immediately take part in military action. The rapid-
ity of the German advance was stunning, and by early October, Poland
surrendered. Several weeks after the German offensive, the Soviet Union
attacked Polish territory from the east, halting on the line established in
the Ribbentrop-Molotov agreement. The Germans divided their Polish
territory in two. The western part, including Danzig and Lodz, was
annexed to the Greater German Reich. The remaining part, which included
Warsaw, Kraków, and Lublin, was called the General Gouvernment and
was administered like a colony. The governor-general was the jurist Hans
Frank, a longtime companion of Hitler and a rabid anti-Semite.

The policies against Polish Jews after September 1939 were genocidal,
and they were for German soldiers both new and untried as well as intimate and decipherable. It was new because Germans did not treat German
Jews in such a way between 1933 and 1939, but it was intelligible because
they had already agreed on and gotten used to the idea that Jews and
Judaism had no place in the new Germany. I use the term *genocide,* building on the substantial scholarship of comparative genocides, to mean not
only the total physical annihilation of a certain group but, more broadly,
the strangling of the life opportunities of a group by starvation, deportation, and the creation of other conditions to destroy its life as a whole or
in part. The genocide embarked on by the Third Reich against the Polish
Jews from the autumn of 1939 to June 1941, when Germany invaded the
Soviet Union, was not a result of the Nazi war effort going awry or of perceptions of Nazi leadership that the Reich was in military danger. Germany

was winning on all fronts. From Berlin, the Reich ruled in this period over Vienna, Prague, Warsaw, Copenhagen, Oslo, Amsterdam, Brussels, and Paris. Rather, the genocide was a result of the shared experience and imagination of Germans constructed over six prewar years. The starting point of Germans' attitude toward Polish Jews was not the persecution of 1933 but the exorcizing of Jews and Judaism in 1938. Germans' threshold of expectation from the new world they were building was how, how soon, and to where the Jews would vanish.

Still, the war changed the prewar relations between Germans and Jews. Between 1933 and 1939 Germans shared an anti-Jewish experience across the national territory. Of course, every locality had its own particular experience, but the making of anti-Jewish culture happened all over the Reich in familiar, public patterns involving legal measures, propaganda, and street violence. The war broke up the uniformity of anti-Jewish experience. After September 1939, German officials and soldiers treated millions of non-German Jews in ways more brutal than had been practiced against Jews back home. In the prewar years actions against Jews were in the national sphere, whereas after September 1939 they took place mostly far from German civilians.

German soldiers during the Polish campaign first treated Jews according to anti-Jewish acts familiar from the prewar years. Previous experience is often the first guide for action. Synagogues were burned and Torah scrolls destroyed all over Poland. In Wloclawek, Wehrmacht soldiers burned down the two large synagogues on the Day of Atonement. They then arrested twenty-six Jews and forced them to sign a declaration that they had set fire to the buildings. Waving the declaration, the Germans now told the men they would be arrested for arson unless they paid 250,000 zloty. The Jewish community collected the sum, and the men were released.[33] The event's carnivalesque mockery and gleeful brutality continued prewar anti-Jewish behavior.

This continuity was common. Fritz Cuhorst, now the Nazi mayor of Lublin, wrote in December 1939 about a visit of German dignitaries to the city. "They were lucky: it was just Jewish Monday," meaning a day of public mistreating and humiliating the Jews. "These were scenes!!" he wrote. "I was there for two hours, and took a Torah scroll"—perhaps as a souvenir of a people on the way to extinction or as an amulet of good luck.

"Otherwise," summed up Cuhorst, "my fingers remained clean."[34] The use of excrement to humiliate Jews was common, as had happened on Kristallnacht. Ringelblum wrote in his diary of "a rabbi [who] was ordered to shit in his pants."[35] Wehrmacht soldiers in Wieruszów employed a familiar repertoire on September 3. All Jewish men aged seventeen to forty were assembled and, after passing through a gauntlet of severe beating, were loaded onto open army trucks that were adorned with writing in big letters: "Here are the Jewish swines who asked for the war and shot at German soldiers." The convoy crossed the border to the territory of the Reich, where the Jews were paraded in various German cities. Some Jews, severely wounded from the beatings, died on the trucks during the parades.[36]

But right from the beginning it was clear that anti-Jewish practices in prewar Nazi Germany constituted a minimum threshold of behavior toward Jews in Poland. That same day, the company of soldiers in Wieruszów, recounted a Jewish eyewitness later, led "twenty Jews into the market place and shot them. . . . Liebe Lewi, the daughter of Israel Lewi, ran over to her father to bid him farewell. The German brutes ordered her to open her mouth for this impudence, fired a bullet into it, and she fell dead on the spot."[37] Such a public execution of "our" German Jews had not taken place in the Third Reich. All moral restraints were now removed with respect to Polish Jews, who looked different than German Jews and seemed to confirm in the eyes of soldiers the anti-Semitic caricatures of *Der Stürmer*. The overwhelming majority practiced Judaism, many dressed differently and had beards and side locks. Eighty-five percent spoke Hebrew or Yiddish as their first language, not Polish and certainly not German. And most of all, there were many, many of them. In 1939 there were three and a half million Jews in Poland, and two million lived in areas seized by Germany in September 1939.

The policies toward the Jews can be understood only within the Nazis' overall plans for demographic changes in Poland and eastern Europe. Hitler told his generals shortly before the outbreak of the war about the forthcoming "extermination" of the Polish nation as a collectivity. On September 7, 1939, Heydrich ordered the special units of police and SS to destroy the leadership elite in Poland and expel all the Jews in areas under German control: "Nobility, clergy, and Jews must be killed." The

Poles were to be reduced to a people of slaves, and their right to live was tied to their usefulness to the German racial empire and economy. Germans banned activities that developed Polish education, art, and culture, seized businesses, and terrorized the population to prevent opposition. A network of concentration and labor camps interned Poles and Jews as slave laborers to build roads, dams, and other projects. It is important to emphasize that most of these measures concerned Polish gentiles and Jews alike.[38]

Himmler was the mastermind of the racial reorganization of Poland in 1939 and of eastern Europe as a whole during the war. His General Plan for the East in 1941–1942 envisioned eastern Europe thirty years after the war's end as a vast area populated by Germans. The plan set a target of the decrease of the local population by the following numbers: Poles, 85 percent; Belarusians, 75 percent; Ukrainians, 65 percent; Czechs, 50 percent. This tremendous diminution would be achieved from extermination through forced labor, disease, starvation, and reproduction control. The ultimate fate of surviving Slavs would be linguistic-cultural extinction. These policies qualify as genocide according to the 1948 United Nations convention, and we should understand the Nazi rule in eastern Europe between 1941 and 1945 as a series of interconnected genocides. The plan itself, which projected the most extreme result of Nazi rule in eastern Europe, could not be realized fully because of the demands of the war and the German defeat, and also because the Nazis viewed the Jews as their most dangerous and immediate enemy. Within the wartime universe of Nazi genocides, the Jews were a priority.[39]

And so the Nazis conceived of various plans in the months following the beginning of the war for how to get rid of the Jews. Already on September 21, 1939, Heydrich, by now chief of the SS Reich Security Main Office (Reichssicherheitshauptamt, or RSHA), ordered the commanders of the Einsatzgruppen, or Task Forces, to concentrate all of Poland's Jews in larger cities "as [a] first prerequisite for the final objective," which should be kept secret. By "final objective" he probably meant the deportation of the Jewish population from the various Polish regions and their concentration in a Lublin reservation.[40] Shortly thereafter the plan was not that secret anymore, showing how quickly mental barriers fell. A few days later, on September 27, Heydrich mentioned in a conference of the

RSHA another idea, approved by Hitler, namely, to expel all Jews across the demarcation line into the Soviet Union. Theodor Schieder, a historian from Königsberg in eastern Prussia, proposed a different, creative plan. In a memorandum submitted to Himmler, he suggested an energetic German settlement in Polish areas, the expulsion of Jews from German cities, and, overall, a "total de-Judaization of remaining Poland" with the aim of sending the entire Jewish population overseas.[41] Schieder would later become a key historian in postwar West Germany. The next plan picked up on this original idea. After the fall of France in May 1940, it was suggested that all the European Jews be sent to Madagascar, which as part of the French empire had now fallen into German hands. Hitler talked about it, and the RSHA wrote memos to that effect. Hans Frank, the governor-general of occupied Poland, was elated: the last thing he wanted was to have the Jews dropped in his Lublin backyard. We shall ship them, he said on July 12, 1940, to an exceedingly amused crowd in Lublin, "piece by piece, man by man, woman by woman, girl by girl."[42] And when the plans for invading the Soviet Union were in full swing in early 1941, Himmler raised the idea of expelling the Jews to Siberia after the victory.

Embedded in all these plans were two meanings, one expressed, the other hidden. On the level of policy, the Nazis planned the removal of Jews, possibly after the victorious war, to beyond the Urals, Madagascar, or wherever. But on a different level, they already imagined a world without Jews and had established that Jews did not deserve to live among humans (that is, themselves). The very making of different plans set the Jews as a "problem" that needed a "solution." The spectrum of possible solutions assumed that Jews had no right to meaningful life in a Nazi world: the Nazis' point of departure was with this or that plan in Lublin or beyond the Urals, but from there any solution was imaginable. It is not that the Nazis sought to manipulate others and conceal an existing intention to kill all the Jews. The two levels of meanings coexisted in various degrees of self-consciousness. Nazi policies were about the technicalities (how to remove the Jews and where to move them) of bringing about a world without Jews. They combined a policy to move the Jews within an imagination that denied their victims human existence. Some planners seriously thought of "only" moving the Jews spatially rather than killing them outright (as would happen two years later), but getting rid of the Jews physically once and for all was already on the spectrum of imaginable possibilities.

All these plans assumed that Jews did not deserve to live in the Nazi empire: contingent factors—such as the development of the war in 1940, the international situation, public opinion, or the plan to settle Germans in Poland—did not change this basic idea. The essence of the plans was the expectation that the Jews would ultimately perish by the combined measures of forced migration, starvation, overcrowding, diseases, hard labor, lack of sustainable economic development, and sheer violence, be it in Lublin, Madagascar, or somewhere beyond the Urals. In the meantime, the regime continued officially also to promote emigration. Holding on to various policies was not contradictory. All measures were useful to solve the Jewish Problem. In any event, no Nazi seriously thought that emigration to Madagascar was intended for Jewish prosperity. The Nazis had the Jews emigrate in order to die off far from their sight. The territorial solution was always a fiction, a Nazi fable about getting rid of the Jews.

One interpretation views these plans as evidence of Nazi experimentation to find solutions for the Jewish Problem and as showing the radicalization of Nazi thinking during the months from September 1939 to June 1941 when they did not yet have a blueprint for exterminating the Jews. There are elements to recommend in this view, such as the emphasis on the growing extremity of Nazi ideas and the contingent nature of Nazi policy in this period, but it also gets some things wrong. It is not sufficient to argue that the Nazis did not have a clear idea of what to do with the Jews in 1940. The question is, which ideas did they have? Which options for treating the Jews did the Nazis really view as possible, practical, and going hand in hand with their beliefs? The plans they devised show their search for ways to solve the Jewish Problem—but only insofar as they were different expressions of the will to destroy Jews through the forces of nature instead of with guns and gas. The Nazis proposed different plans but always within their basic idea that the Jews' right to live in this world was open to question.

This period of persecution was one of experimentation, but so was the period of extermination that followed. Every period is experimental in its own way. The months from September 1939 to June 1941 were not simply an antechamber to the main period of extermination. This view is based on our hindsight knowledge of the Final Solution to come, but Germans who lived during these months did not know that at the time. They gave meaning to their actions then and there by making sense of their new anti-Jewish actions in the occupied territories based on their experiences in the prewar and early war years. The period 1939–1941 makes sense within the anti-Jewish culture of a world without Jews.

This was understood by both Germans and Jews. Eduard Koenekamp, a member of the Stuttgart Institute for Foreign Countries, recorded in 1939 in a letter to a friend his impressions following a visit to several Jewish quarters in Poland: "The extermination of this subhumanity would be in the interest of the whole world. However, such extermination is one of the most difficult problems. Shooting would not suffice. Also one cannot allow the shooting of women and children. Here and there one expects losses during deportations. . . . All agencies which deal with the Jewish Question are aware of the insufficiency of all these measures. A solution of this complicated problem has not been found."[43] Koenekamp's sentiments remind one of those of Siegfried Leffler. Neither was perturbed by his call to exterminate the Jews, but each was disturbed by how to reconcile this with his own sense of self, Christian in the case of Leffler, and of moral dignity in the case of Koenekamp. It is fine to exterminate the Jews, Koenekamp seems to be telling himself, but we have to find a way to do it that won't offend our sensibilities.

Imaginary plans such as the Lublin reservation and the Madagascar project, as well as the actual ghettoization of Polish Jews, was a way to "exterminate the subhumanity" while keeping German moral sensibilities intact. It was a genocide perpetrated via the strangling of the life avenues of the community, as the German actions of concentrating Polish Jews in ghettos sealed from the wider world made clear. On November 23, 1939, all Jews over the age of ten were required to wear on their right sleeve a white armband at least four inches wide bearing a blue Star of David.[44] A host of restrictions followed on Jewish movement, occupation, and owning property. Ghettoization started in October 1939, a drawn-out process that lasted months. Jews from the countryside were forced into big cities, losing of course all their property in the process; the Jews of the Warthegau region, annexed to the Reich and destined for Germanization, were also expelled to large urban ghettos.

The Lodz ghetto was established in April 1940, and on May 1, the Germans hermetically sealed the ghetto and its 163,000 inhabitants from the world. Warsaw's Jews were also ordered to move and live in one part of town. "At a funeral for the small children from the Wolska Street orphanage," described Ringelblum of the conditions in early September 1940, "the children from the home placed a wreath at the monument with the inscription: 'To the Children Who Have Died from Hunger—From the Children Who Are Hungry.'" On November 16, the Warsaw ghetto was sealed. "A wave of evil rolled over the whole city, as if in response to a nod from above," Ringelblum wrote three days later.[45] Some 338,000 Jews were now separated from the world. A third of the city's inhabitants were crammed into 2.4 percent of its territory, an area of just under a thousand acres. In early 1941 the ghetto's population swelled to some 445,000 people as a result of the influx of Jews from the surrounding areas. The death rate among Jews in Warsaw rose from 1 per 1,000 in 1939 to 10.7 in 1941. In Lodz, the rate was 43.3 in 1940 and 75.9 in 1941.[46] Between September 1939 and June 1941, over half a million Polish Jews died in ghettos and labor camps.

For the Nazis, the aim of the sealed ghetto policy was ultimately to get rid of the Jews. The sealed ghetto was on the same imaginary spectrum of the various plans to remove the Jews territorially. On the level of open policy plans, the Nazis discussed the ghetto as a temporary solution until the final removal of Jews after the war. But on the level of the imagination, the Jews were already dead. This duality was manifested in the debate between "moderates" and "extremists" over the issue of ghettoization among the Nazi policy makers in Warsaw and Lodz between 1939 and 1941.[47] The "moderates" wanted to keep the ghetto as a productive unit to help the German war effort, and thus to allow Jews to survive without starvation and disease so long as they remained useful to the economy. The "extremists" rejected this possibility. Alexander Palfinder, an official in the ghetto administration in Lodz, argued that "especially in the Jewish question the National Socialist idea ... permits no compromises," and hence "a rapid dying out of the Jews is for us a matter of total indifference, if not to say desirable."[48] In late 1940 and early 1941 the "moderates" won the debate, before the policy was changed in late 1941 and early 1942 to extermination. The debate shows the complexity of the ghettoization policy (there were Jews who remained in rural areas where no ghettos were created, and in eastern Upper Silesia, which was annexed to the Reich from Poland, ghettos were not created until 1943), even as it affirms the argument made here about the Nazi imagination reflected in the sealed ghettos.

Whether some Nazis were "moderates" or "extremists," what was crucial was the very discussion itself: the Jews had no right to live as human beings; they were either to die or to remain alive as productive units to support the German war. At the level of imagination, the participants in this debate had already internalized that Jews should not conduct full, creative, healthy, and emotionally satisfactory lives. In this respect, the creation of sealed ghettos in 1940–1941 and the extermination of the following years were on the same spectrum of imaginary possibilities to solve the Jewish Problem. The ghettoization policy was made not only by administrative measures and practical implementation carried out by the German officials in Poland but also by their subterranean fantasies that at times were not totally clear to, or could be explicitly expressed by, the Nazis themselves.

The sealed ghetto was thus not only about a transition policy or an experimentation measure. Rather, it manifested a state of mind that accomplished a German world without Jews not by killing them outright but by setting an undefined expiration date on their existence. "Logically, we must die out," wrote Kaplan in 1940. "According to the laws of nature, we are doomed to destruction and total annihilation. How can a whole community feed itself when it has no anchor in life? There is no occupation, no profession that is not limited and circumscribed for us! . . . Total segregation from all life's professions. Segregated and separated from the world we shall atrophy in our poverty, suffering, hardship, and filth, we shall rot until our end will come."[49]

Oskar Rosenfeld, an author, journalist, and man of letters in his mid-fifties who had earned a doctorate from the University of Vienna, was deported from Vienna to the Lodz ghetto on November 4, 1941. He kept a remarkable diary between February 17, 1942, and July 28, 1944, as an active member of the archive group that documented ghetto life. He was a steady contributor to the daily ghetto chronicle. What he identified as the essence of the sealed ghetto in May 1942 is true to its history from the beginning:

Every community will breathe, flourish, grow, create. It's part of the animal instinct, law of nature. To come into being, to grow, to pass away, every renewing life, parallel to nature. . . . [The] ghetto [is] the exception. People . . . are granted just enough air to vegetate. They don't plant crops . . . you cannot produce. When the suit becomes worn, you have to walk in rags. . . . The bolts get rusty, the colors fade. . . . There is no growth, everything falls apart step by step. And without work, starving here are the engineers, chemists, mathematicians, botanists, zoologists, pharmacologists, physicians, architects, teachers, writers, actors, directors, musicians, linguists, administrative officials, bankers, pharmacists, handicraftsmen like electricians, woodworkers, carpenters, metal experts, upholsterers, house painters, furriers, tailors, shoemakers, textile manufacturers, turners, watchmakers. . . .[50]

In the Reich, meanwhile, Jews lived in isolation and fear. From early September 1939 they were prohibited from owning a radio and were allowed to shop only at designated stores. Hunger and poverty became a way of life. Jews were not issued ration cards for clothing. From July 1940 in Berlin they could shop for food only between four and five o'clock in the afternoon, which meant that women, who did most of the shopping, had to rush after work to the baker, butcher, and other shops, where they found long lines and little on offer. In Breslau, Jews could shop for food between 11:00 a.m. and 1:00 p.m., a period when most women worked. In January 1940, rationing for Jews became more restricted, and they could not receive legumes, most fruit, and meat. A Jew doing heavy labor received seven ounces of meat a week compared to almost two pounds for a German.[51]

The anti-Jewish legislation and decrees continued during the war, attenuated but always present. From September 1 to December 31, 1939, the Nazis promulgated 55 new laws and decrees; in 1940, an additional 101. The years 1941 and 1942 were the apex, with 135 and 169 new laws, respectively. This reflected the shift to the policy of extermination as the fixation with the Jews reached new heights. Even though Germany was at war with half the world, Germans were annihilating Jews across Europe, and there were scarcely any Jews left in Germany following the deportations, it was important to decree in 1942 that Jews were prohibited from buying cakes. Then, with no Jews remaining in Germany, the stream of laws dried up: 37 in 1943, 22 in 1944, and just 3 in 1945.

As the war began, from September 1 to December 31, 1939, Nazis found new restrictions to impose on the Jews, some related to the military effort, others to the fear of the Jewish word.

Jews are prohibited from participating in air-raid drills. Jews should build and finance their own air-raid shelters. Atonement fine: Jews are fined 250 million Reichsmarks needed for the armament industry. Minister of education: Writers of doctoral dissertations should avoid citing Jewish authors; when it is absolutely necessary, writers should put in special quotation marks any citation from these authors. 1940: Jews are placed under night curfew and are prohibited from being out in the streets from 9:00 p.m. to 5:00 a.m. during the summer and between 8:00 p.m. and 6:00 a.m. during the winter. Ration cards for Jews are marked by an additional J. Jews are excluded from private medical insurance plans.[52]

In May 1940, the Klemperers rented out their home in Döltzschen because Jews were forced to move from their private accommodations to Dresden's Jews' House. Eva and Victor could take few belongings with them and had to dispose of many things and pack the remainder into storage. The days of the move coincided with the German attack on the Low Countries and France. On Thursday evening, May 16, Klemperer wrote: "Perhaps the gloomiest wedding anniversary we have ever celebrated. The chaos of the move has begun, nine tenths of our furniture has to go into storage, much written and printed matter, which we had preserved for so long, is being destroyed as ballast. . . . The successes in the West are prodigious, and the nation is intoxicated." A few days later, on Tuesday, May 21, he added, "We are both most deeply depressed by the incomprehensible course of events. It destroys our future. Eva [is] badly worn down by all the moving work." The next day he summed up world and personal affairs: "French defeat is becoming a catastrophe. . . . We try hard not to despair."[53]

Hitler's stunning victory in the West against Holland, Belgium, and France, in addition to the German occupation of Denmark and Norway in April, extended the German empire from Paris to North Cape, Norway, to Warsaw. The collapse of France in a mere six weeks was the most spectacular of Hitler's victories. German troops entered Paris on June 14, and the French signed an armistice at Compiègne on June 22 in the same railway carriage in which German forces had surrendered in 1918. Hitler had vanquished the negative memory of the First World War and had eliminated as a European power Germany's most powerful military opponent. He was venerated by Germans, and his mastery on the Continent seemed unchallenged. Only Britain, now under the resolute leadership of Winston Churchill, remained to fight the Third Reich. Hitler proceeded with plans to invade the British Isles. From August 1940 the Luftwaffe, the German air force, staged massive air attacks on military installations, cities, and ports. The Battle of Britain raged in the fall and winter of 1940–1941. The inhabitants of cities such as Coventry and London were subjected to constant German bombing, which took a heavy toll. But Britain held firm. This did not seem a battle Hitler would win.

For Jews in Germany, the restrictions suffocated their last breath of air, but for Germans they made little difference, for they had already stopped noticing the presence of the Jews. In Kippenheim in southern Germany a lively community debate took place in April 1940 over what should be done with the synagogue, which had stood in ruins since Kristallnacht, and its plot of land. The National Socialist mayor, Friedrich Spielmann, wanted to raze it to the ground. Others hoped to profit from the commercial possibilities of the lucrative land. In addition, there were legal intricacies to resolve. All in all, it took two years for the town to become, in October 1942, the legal owner of the property. The town bought the land not from the Jewish community but from Heydrich's RSHA, which was now the legal owner of all Jewish property in Germany.[54] A small community of Jews still lived in Kippenheim when the affair began in April 1940. Soon afterward, in October 1940, they, together with the entire Jewish community of Baden and the Saar-Palatinate, were deported to Vichy, the nonoccupied zone of France. The Jews of Alsace-Lorraine had already been expelled to Vichy on July 16, 1940. Seven years after coming to power, the Nazis had succeeded in making the first regions in Germany *Judenrein*, or free of Jews.

Just around the time when parts of Germany became free of Jews and as a genocide of Polish Jews was under way, two important films interpreted for Germans the state of German-Jewish relations. *Jew Süss (Jud*

Süss) premiered in Berlin at the Palast-am-Zoo theater on September 24, 1940, while *The Wandering Jew* (*Der ewige Jude*) was released on November 28, 1940. Both films were masterminded by Goebbels and were intended to instruct and indoctrinate Germans about the Jews. But they should not be seen simply as an ideological tool made by the regime for the public. The films interpreted the evolving relations of Germans and Jews since September 1, 1939—for the public, for the Nazis, and for Goebbels himself.

In their message and visual language, the two films were linked, but otherwise they were not at all similar. *Jew Süss* told the story of Joseph Süss Oppenheimer, the court Jew and financial adviser of the duke of Württemberg in Stuttgart between 1733 and 1737. Played by Ferdinand Marian, Süss exhibited any number of basic Nazi anti-Semitic motives from extorting money to seducing German maidens. In a happy ending, justice prevailed and Süss was sentenced to death. The final scene is the banishment of all the Jews of Württemberg. An anti-Semitic eighteenth-century costume drama, the film was hugely popular. Twenty million viewers had seen it by the end of 1942.[55] The film fit the general, widely shared anti-Jewish imagination made between 1933 and 1939: a Germany without Jews and Judaism, but also without excessive visible violence (compared to Poland).

The Wandering Jew was a documentary ostensibly showing the evil influence of the Jews in the world. It went through many revisions because Goebbels did not know how strongly to visualize the Jewish danger. At the end, the film was released in two versions, one for adult men, including revolting scenes such as the ritual slaughter of animals, and a sanitized version for women and children. Before the war, Goebbels wanted to send a crew to Poland to film Jews on location, but he did not get permission from the Polish authorities. After September 1939, he went himself to Lodz with a crew to supervise shooting in the ghetto and then sent Fritz Hippler, the director, as well. Hippler later recalled that Goebbels told him to "capture everything of Jewish ghetto life, before its demise. The Führer will have all of them moved to Madagascar or some other area."[56] Whether Goebbels actually said this or not, the film includes a much more ominous scene than anything shown in *Jew Süss,* a sickening visual of the Jews as a horde of rats. The final scene is a newsreel footage of Hitler delivering his prophecy to the Reichstag on January 30, 1939. *The Wandering Jew* was a commercial flop; it opened in Berlin in at least thirty-six cinemas, but by mid-December only one theater was still screening the film.[57] The public obviously rejected the upfront, candid illustration of the fate of the Jews under National Socialism.

Why did the German public recognize itself in the depiction of the fate of the Jews in *Jew Süss* but had difficulty acknowledging the depiction of *The Wandering Jew*? *The Wandering Jew* is explicit and violent, but burning a synagogue is quite explicit and violent as well. Why did Hitler's prophecy, which created an instinctive emotional bond between the Führer and his public in January 1939, fail to achieve the same effect in the film in November 1940?

The public reception of the two films indicated the evolving anti-Jewish imagination during the war. In *Jew Süss,* Germans recognized their prewar anti-Jewish policies. Most Germans could identify with the banishment of the Jews at the end of the film as an accurate illustration of the situation in Germany. *The Wandering Jew,* on the other hand, with its menacing hints and visual evocations of mass murder, brought to mind not the prewar policies (these did not need hints and evocation because they were known to and seen by all) but the post-September 1939 treatment of the Jews. Hitler's speech now elicited different emotions. In January 1939, the prophecy linked Hitler and his public in the shared project of removing the Jews. But in September 1940, with the Nazi persecution of the Jews in Poland under way, the prophecy was understood as an image of annihilation that went well beyond what had transpired in the Reich between 1933 and 1939. Between the images of rats and Hitler's prophecy there was little left for the viewer to imagine about the fate of the Jews in occupied Europe. *The Wandering Jew* provided a description of the present as well as the future fate of the Jews that implicated the German viewer directly. This is why the public turned from the film.

Most Germans knew from afar the fate of the Jews in Poland, and by extension in Europe, but the films made it clear, direct, and personal. The anti-Jewish policies in Poland were public and official. Press reports and newsreels brought to the attention of the public the situation of the Jews. More important perhaps, a flow of soldiers and civilians visited Poland and the ghettos, producing a torrent of letters and photographs of the conditions of the Jews: emaciated adults, begging children, Jews in side locks and beards being humiliated, and many others. Photographing piles of corpses in the Warsaw Jewish cemetery while complaining about the low Jewish death rate, as described by Ringelblum, was not exceptional. Germans at the front and on the home front knew the fate of the Jews. Knowledge brought a new and different awareness: a hardening of anti-Semitism as a way to justify the genocide but also a sense of surprise and horror at how changed the new treatment of the Jews was from the prewar persecution. It was one thing to make a Germany free of Jews by expelling them—as had been done in the prewar years and was represented in *Jew Süss*—but quite another to murder and starve thousands of Jews—as had been done since September 1939 and was represented in *The Wandering Jew*.

Melita Maschmann, a young activist in the League of German Girls, the female wing of the Hitler Youth, was sent in later 1939 as press officer to the Warthegau, the area in western Poland that was annexed to the Reich and was destined for German resettlement. She passed by a Jewish ghetto in Kutno, north of Lodz, and saw the miserable, starving people who looked more dead than alive: "The wretchedness of the children brought a lump to my throat. But I clenched my teeth. Gradually I learned to switch off my 'private feelings' quickly and utterly in such situations. This is terrible, I said to myself, but the driving out of the Jews is one of the unfortunate things we must bargain for if the 'Warthegau' is to become a German country."[58] For Maschmann, the treatment of the Jews was justified, even as intense emotions of horror and shock reveal a sense of disquiet, even doubt, creeping in. She justified the genocide on national resettlement grounds, even though her inner self was horrified by what she was discovering about herself and her fellow Germans. She now faced the consequences of the prewar imagination that made these deeds and sights possible. There would be no persecution-light: "only" getting rid of the Jews and of Judaism in one's little hometown. Nazism's promotion of the destruction of Judaism as the basis for the new national identity meant a project on a European scale: a new racial empire based on the uprooting of Judaism everywhere.

Maschmann expressed pity about what she saw, but she had no problem speaking about and imagining it, contradicting the long-standing view after 1945 among scholars and the public alike that Germans could not imagine or speak about the murder of the Jews. If the anti-Jewish policies in Poland were talked and written about, as well as photographed, for many Germans who acquired this knowledge a gap opened between the "good" persecution of the prewar years and the "excessive" persecution of the war. The result, as Maschmann wrote, was to switch off their private feelings about the mass murders and to try not to think or talk about them. Maschmann's sense of shock shows that she clearly perceived the fate of the Jews. This commingling of shock and recognition was also behind the public's rejection of *The Wandering Jew:* audiences chose to ignore the film precisely because they knew how to read its message of annihilation. From the outset of the war some Germans began to keep silent and feel perturbed about the mass murders in the East, a behavior that would expand in the years of total extermination from 1941 to 1945. They kept silent, not because they did not know what was happening, but, on the contrary, precisely because they did know something and could imagine what was happening. They did not need to know the exact details of the deaths in the Lodz ghetto or, later, in Auschwitz in order to understand—to *sense* is the accurate word—that the Jews were being made to totally vanish, this way or another.

"I am virtually ravaging my past," wrote Victor Klemperer on May 21, 1941, as he was "burning, burning, burning for hours on end" all his past life in preparation for the move to the new quarter at the Jews' House. In the prewar years, the Nazis persecuted the Jews because they represented a present modernity and past roots, but Jews could still seek, and indeed were encouraged by the Nazis, to emigrate and start a new life. But between September 1939 and June 1941 the Nazis made the Jews into people without time, who were still alive (for a short time) but fundamentally without the right to have a history, a past, present, or future.

The sealed ghettos in Poland epitomized this Nazi state of mind. "We have entered then a new life and one cannot fathom the anxiety and fear in the Jewish quarter," wrote Kaplan on November 17, 1940. "Suddenly we saw ourselves fenced from all sides, segregated and separated from the whole world, exiled from the company of humans, a disgusting people to be banished, like polluted people and lepers that it is a mitzvah to distance and separate from human society so they will not pollute and contaminate the surrounding."[59] In Lvov, shortly after the Nazi invasion of the

Soviet Union in June 1941, the Germans sealed the ghetto from all sides, and the Jews had to establish a kind of municipality to handle their affairs. Lvov Jews called it "the municipality of bizarre death."[60] The Nazis denied the Jews the key element that makes social life possible, a sense of time: the ability to link memories of one's individual and collective past into a story that builds on the present and projects into the future. "I do not feel alive," wrote nineteen-year-old Genka Wimisner in 1940 from Kraków to a relative in New York, expressing a sentiment that Jews were suspended in time with no use of the past, no activity in the present, and no future prospects. "Those who are alive often envy the dead ones now," added Klara, Genka's mother.[61] "Our human emotions have become so dull," noted Kaplan painfully, "that we stopped hav[ing] feelings."[62] Perhaps more than the deportations of Polish Jews into the ghettos and of German Jews into Vichy France, more than the deaths by slave labor, shooting, and starvation, the sealing of the Jews from human time indicated the Nazis' conscious and unconscious intentions.

A sense of time—that is, of history and memory–permeated the perceptions of both Jews and Germans about the disappearance of the Jews: a sense that the Jewish people had become a thing of the past, of memory and commemoration, while the Nazis had replaced them and had appropriated the image of the Jew as associated with morality, historical origins, and being chosen, thus laying the foundation for a new Nazi civilization. In Kippenheim several people in the community joined the debate over the future of the synagogue by arguing that the building should be kept as an architectural monument that belonged to the historic heritage of the town. Erasing the Jewish community in Kippenheim and killing its Jews did not mean for Kippenheimers obliterating the memory of the local Jewish community. On the contrary, keeping the synagogue relegated the Jews to the past as objects that belonged in a museum and as a subject of commemoration, even as in turn it accentuated the mastery of the Germans over the Jews.

Local events were matched by institutional and professional policies. The Institute for the Study of the Jewish Question and the Institute for the Study and Eradication of Jewish Influence on German Church Life were two among several research centers whose activities, including conferences, publications, and the allocation of funds, aimed to forge a Nazi history of the Jews. The new Institute for Research on the Jewish Question was inaugurated in Frankfurt on March 16, 1941, with Wilhelm Grau as director (he was made to leave the Institute for the Study of the Jewish Question, which he originally directed, after a professional and personal fallout). The new institute was part of Alfred Rosenberg's larger plan for a National Socialist university to be founded after the war. In his inaugural address, Rosenberg explained the reason for the institute's creation in terms of historical memory: "If the Jewish question is solved in Germany—and one day in all of Europe—then perhaps a new generation who will come after us might be unable to remember what actually transpired during these decades. Our grandchildren, liberated from Jewish influence, might then fall victim to fanciful ideas and might not be able to evaluate the potency of the Jewish people amidst the Europeans as we must do today. Human memory is very short."[63] Killing the Jews and keeping their memory alive—that is, the Nazi version of their memory—were commingling Nazi tasks.

The Nazis sought to tell Jewish history anew and to insert it within a new German narrative. This had already happened, of course, in the prewar years. In 1935, the Jewish physician Walter Heinemann of Braunschweig emigrated to Palestine and asked the local authorities for permission to take with him the Judaica collection of the local Hornburger synagogue. He planned on giving it to the Hebrew University in Jerusalem, assuming that the Nazis would have no interest in this stuff. He was surprised when Johannes Dürkop, an art historian, party member, and director of the Heimat Regional Museum, denied the request. Dürkop motivated his position in a letter to the local minister of popular education on November 30 that "the synagogue stands in the Heimat history collection of the museum as a foreign body but precisely because of this it is such an illustrative example for the role that Judaism has played in our area as well as everywhere." The minister concurred. Dürkop planned to introduce to the museum a permanent exhibition about the Jews that "will show not only the racial image of the Jews in our area, but also the way they operate, and how the 'objective' researchers of older generations" failed to capture this meaning. As a result, further requests to remove Jewish objects from the area were also denied.[64]

By 1939–1940, the essence of Nazi appropriation of Jewish history changed dramatically. In 1935, Dürkop rewrote Jewish history while letting Heinemann emigrate; after September 1939, the Nazis rewrote Jewish history by killing Jews.

The Nazi story about Germans and Jews included racial and Heimat elements, as by Dürkop, who viewed local Jewish history important enough for the writing of German local history. It also included Christian elements. In 1940, the Jews were erased from one foundational site of memory, whose spirit and essence they had defined since its inception: the New Testament. The Institute for the Study and Eradication of Jewish Influence on German Church Life published a dejudaized New Testament entitled *God's Message*.[65] The Old Testament had of course been eliminated from the Bible several years earlier. All references to Jewish names and places were erased from the new text, as were all quotations from the Old Testament unless they portrayed Judaism in a negative light. Also deleted were the genealogical descent of Jesus from the House of David and his fulfillment of any Old Testament prophecy about the Messiah. The new text told the life of Jesus in militarized, masculine, heroic, Nazified language, focusing on his triumph rather than on his defeat in his fight against his enemies, the Jews, who brought about his death. Some two hundred thousand copies of the new Bible were sold during the war. This blotting of memory did not simply precede the physical annihilation but in some respects imagined it.

In German communities the Nazi fusion of the racial, Heimat, and Christian elements developed their own local character. In Schnaittach, Franconia, in the early years of the war, the Jewish synagogue was incorporated into the local Heimat museum in an act of national and religious memory appropriation. Gottfried Stammler, a local Heimat enthusiast who founded the Museum Association in 1923 and joined the Nazi Party in 1937, wanted already in early 1938 to take advantage of the dwindling Jewish community by integrating the local synagogue into the holdings of the Heimat museum. On Kristallnacht he rushed to the burning synagogue, ordered the firefighters to extinguish the flames, and was able to save some of the interior objects. For this the district leader of the party threatened to throw him into a concentration camp. But Stammler had his way, and the mayor approved handing over the synagogue to the museum.

The Judaica objects were made part of the museum exhibition in 1939 and 1940. Photographs from the period show that they were not accompanied by anti-Semitic text, and there is no evidence that Stammler was motivated by any anti-Semitic sentiments.

Rather, Stammler saw the preservation of local Jewish history as part of his duties as a local Heimat historian; he internalized and regarded as the order of things that Jews and Judaism now belonged to a bygone world. He gave this sentiment a professional edge as a historian and museum activist. With the Jews gone, he collected local Judaica and transformed the Jews from a group that is alive and developing in the real world into a group that belonged in the past, in a museum. It is unclear whether he was perturbed that terror made his Jewish acquisitions possible and that, although he saved the memory of local Jews, he and his community doomed the Jews themselves. In any event, Nazism, the Heimat idea, Christianity, and Judaism blended quite well for Stammler. He took two wide gravestones from the Jewish cemetery and installed them inscription-upward as steps at the Heimat museum entrance. In the synagogue he set in the former place of the Holy Ark a Gothic pietà. He thus acknowledged the place of Judaism in German local and Christian identity even as his actions signaled the death of Jews and the appropriation of Judaism by German and Christian identity. Judaism, submerged within local, national, and Christian identity, was drained of life and, by dying, became an object that illuminated the grand German past and present.

The gravestones were removed from the museum entrance in 1946 after Jewish protests; the pietà was removed in the 1980s.[66]

In the Warsaw ghetto at the same time, a very different person reached similar conclusions to Dürkop and Stammler, to the scholars of research on Jews, and to the theologians who rewrote the New Testament. Chaim Kaplan also saw the key to understanding the Nazi persecution in the inextricable link between Germans and Jews. For him, Nazism was both imitating and replacing the Jews, seeking to take its place:

> We are dealing with a nation of high culture, with the people
> of the book. An article [in the *Deutsche Allgemeine Zeitung*]
> "Books, Books, Books" reported on the mania for reading that

has seized all of Germany. The Germans have simply gone crazy for one thing—books. At every bookstore there are long lines of people waiting for the happy moment when they will be able to buy a book. They are hungry, not for bread, not for water, not for any tangible worldly pleasure, but for the word ... of the German writer.... Germany has become a mad-house—mad for books. Say what you will, I fear such people! Where robbing is based on ideology and on a worldview that is essentially spiritual, then it is unparalleled in its power, dura-bility, and longevity. Such a nation will not perish. The Nazi has robbed us not only of our material possessions but also of our good name as "the people of the book." The Nazi is also [like the Jew a combination of] spiritual and worldly charac-teristics—this is the source of his power and heroism.[67]

In setting up the pietà in the empty former space of the Holy Ark, Stammler created an image whereby Christianity, and by extension Nazism, consumed Judaism. Similar images of Judaism being devoured emerged from Dürkop and from the new New Testament. Kaplan, writing on Christmas Day, 1939, had in mind a related image: "There is a new force in the world, its name is Nazism, and it will found a new world order on the ruins of the old one.... [Its principles] are against the law of nature set since the six days of creation. It aims to create a ... [new] world." And he added, using an image from the chaos of creation: "If we say that the sun has darkened upon us at noon it would not be merely a metaphor."[68]

PART III

1941–1945
The Jew as the Origins of History

Imagining a Genesis

The Jewish question is the key to world history.

The Reich Press Office, February 3, 1944

For us, history had stopped.

Primo Levi, Survival in Auschwitz

P olice Battalion 309 of the German army entered Bialystok without a fight on June 27, 1941. The city, in the Soviet area of northeastern Poland, was home to 100,000 people, half of them Jews. The commander, Lieutenant General Johann Pflugbeil, had orders to "clean up the city of population that is considered a German enemy." An orgy of violence began in the city center, an area inhabited mostly by Jews. In the afternoon, German soldiers led hundreds of Jews into the main synagogue, now surrounded by machine guns. When the building had been filled with more than seven hundred Jews, mostly men, the doors were locked from the outside and the synagogue was set on fire. All were burned alive, except for a few Jews who jumped from the windows and were shot dead on the spot.[1]

Several months later, on Sunday, November 2, 1941, a soldier wrote back home (to his girlfriend, probably) about his experiences somewhere in the occupied Soviet Union in a letter that reads as a sort of commentary on the event in Bialystok: "[There once was here] a massive synagogue built in 1664. Only the walls stand now. It will never be used again for its original purpose. I think that Jews in this country will soon have no use of any synagogue. Why, I have already described to you. For these dreadful creatures this is certainly the only just solution."[2]

On June 22, 1941, Germany invaded the Soviet Union. When it became clear to Hitler that Britain would not be defeated anytime soon, he turned his sights to the East, which, with its vast swaths of land and precious resources such as grain and oil, had always been the main stage for the Nazis' territorial ambitions and racial empire. The scale of the operation was extraordinary: the Germans attacked on a 1,324-mile front with 3,050,000 men and 3,350 armored vehicles.[3] Hitler expected a quick victory, fueled by stereotypes about the dull-witted "Russian character" and a belief in the poor quality of the Red Army opposite the technological superiority of the Wehrmacht. From the beginning this was an ideological, racial war of extermination, against communism, bolshevism, and Jews.

In the short period of the next following months, the Nazis changed their policies toward the Jews several times in a brisk, breathless pace that ultimately ended in the Final Solution. Let us first follow this course of events before turning to the imagination reflected in the extermination. The mass murder of Jews accompanied the invasion from the beginning. A directive from Hitler of March 1941 on basic policies toward Jews, communists, and others, and several orders from Heydrich in June and July, gave German forces a free hand to execute the Jewish civilian population. The directives were important in providing guidelines for action from the highest authorities. But their importance should not be exaggerated. Nazis and other Germans did not kill because Hitler and Heydrich issued directives. For many young soldiers Nazism had been a way of life, and the existence of a universal notion of morality that encompassed all human beings belonged to a pre-1933 old world that for many merely evoked childhood memories. Since 1933, Jewish life had become progressively worthless. Hundreds of thousands of Jews had already died as a result of German policies of ghettoization, starvation, and forced labor since September 1939. On June 22, 1941, other, more violent and immediate means to make the Jews disappear were in the air.

The killers belonged to the Wehrmacht, SS, and police Special Units. Especially important were four Einsatzgruppen (Task Forces). Einsatzgruppe A reported 118,430 executed Jews from the Baltic States and Belorussia by October 15, while Einsatzgruppe B was responsible for 45,467 murdered Jews by October 31. Einsatzgruppe C killed 75,000 Jews by October 20, and the commanders of Einsatzgruppe D reported 55,696 Jews executed by December 12. In addition, independent SS and police Special Units operations combed the rear zones, shooting more than 100,000 Jews. During the initial weeks of the invasion women and children were largely spared from the shooting, but by August 1941, the shooting was extended to include them as well. German units now returned to villages and towns where Jewish men had already been killed in order to execute women and children. From September, the term *Judenfrei,* or free of Jews, began to appear regularly in Einsatzgruppen reports in order to describe whole areas.[4] In the first five months of the Soviet campaign, the Nazis killed around half a million Jews in the newly conquered Eastern territories.[5] The number exceeded 600,000 by year's end. From September 1939 to December 1941, between 1.1 and 1.3 million Jews were killed.

Such vast killings in villages, towns, and cities were public events. Aryeh Klonicki recounted the killings in Tarnopol on June 25, 1941, in his diary: "The Germans, joined by Ukrainians, would go from house to house in order to look for Jews. The Ukrainians would take the Jews out of the houses where the waiting Germans would kill them, either right by the house or they would transport the victims to a particular site where all would be put to death. This is how some five thousand people found their death, mostly men."[6] In a matter of days, weeks, or months, localities were decimated, their Jews rounded up and slaughtered either on the spot or in nearby woods. The massacres, often a concerted effort of locals and Germans, were not secret and were not meant to be. The Jews went to their death in broad daylight, and their property was later meticulously distributed among neighbors and other locals. In Vilna, the "Jerusalem of Lithuania," which had some 60,000 Jews in a city of 200,000 inhabitants, 33,000 Jews were murdered from July to December 1941, mostly in the woods of the nearby village Ponary.

Soldiers shared news of the mass murders with relatives and friends in Germany in conversations and letters. Photographs that left nothing to the imagination often accompanied the letters. Some soldiers described in detail their feelings while murdering, as in this letter of October 5, 1941:

> One more thing I have to write you. I was actually also there the other day in the big mass death. At the first truckload my hand shook somewhat as I shot, but one gets used to it. At the tenth truckload, I already aimed calmly and shot straight at the numerous women, children, and infants. I was mindful that I also have two infants at home who would have been treated by this horde exactly the same, if not ten times worse. . . . Infants flew through the air in high arches, and we did them in already in midair before they [fell] into the pit. . . . Hitler's words are becoming true when he said at the beginning of the war: if Judaism thinks to instigate another war in Europe, then this war will be not its victory but the end of Judaism in Europe. . . . Mogilev lost again [Jews equal to] a number with three zeroes, but this is not a big thing here. I am actually happy, and many here say [the same], that when we will be back in the Heimat it will be the turn of our local Jews.[7]

However extreme the massacres were, they were part of the tradition of anti-Jewish public actions formed in the Third Reich. Of course, the mass murders were on a whole different moral scale from violent actions in prewar Nazi Germany, but chords of emotions and conduct linked the wartime extreme events to prewar practices. The killings were often characterized by sadistic mockery commingled with obsessive anger and horrible violence that nonetheless betrayed a sense of anxiety over the presence of Jews in the world. A sense of transgression hovered over the killings.

Some massacres combined several of the familiar emotions in an almost carnivalesque atmosphere; the murderous scale far exceeded prewar violence, but some of the emotions were not unfamiliar. In Stanisławów, in southern Galicia, murder mixed with drinking and eating in a tableau dominated by mockery. Commanded by the local Security Police chief, Hans Krüger, the town's Jews were led on October 12, 1941, to be shot in the local cemetery. It was Hoshana Raba, the last day of Sukkot, the Feast of Tabernacles that takes place after the Day of Atonement. The first group of a thousand Jews went through the cemetery gates, were ordered to undress, and were then shot into open pits. Krüger took care of refreshments to boost morale. Tables with vodka and food for the killing forces were set next to the mass graves, and Krüger himself went around from time to time offering salami sandwiches and schnapps. The scene was chaotic: panicked Jews, entire families at times, were driven to jump into the pits while alive; others tried to escape by climbing the cemetery walls and were shot dead. When darkness fell, after some ten to twelve thousand Jews had been killed, Krüger announced to the survivors that Hitler had pardoned them.[8]

In the months after June 1941, the Nazis sought to create their world without Jews with much more decisive measures by systematically annihilating Jewish civilians from entire swaths of European lands. That fall, the massacres reached massive proportions as Germans abetted by locals murdered Jews by the thousands—even tens of thousands—in each operation. The killings happened in Kovno, Minsk, Odessa, and eastern Galician towns. In Kiev, 33,771 were executed over a two-day period in the ravine of Babi Yar. In Riga, fifteen thousand Jews were killed from dawn to dusk on November 30 in the Rumbula Forest. There still existed a wide variety of Nazi anti-Jewish policies across Europe: Jews in the eastern occupied territories often found immediate death by execution, those in Poland languished in ghettos, while Jews in western European cities such as Amsterdam, Brussels, and Paris lived precariously but could maintain a vestige of normal life unimagined by Chaim Kaplan and Emanuel Ringelblum. And yet, the massive massacres indicated a mental threshold: Jews would be eliminated, sooner or later, during or after the war, and all violent means were now considered suitable.

But this policy was changed over the fall and winter of 1941 by Hitler and his closest men on the Jewish Question, Himmler and Heydrich, as they formulated a uniform anti-Jewish policy: all eleven million European Jews were to be killed immediately, during the war, and in secrecy. The Nazis obviously had a pressing urgency to get rid of the Jews right away, lest a delay of a few years prove fatal. Starting in September 1941, Jews in Germany had to wear the identifying Star of David. On October 23, all Jewish emigration from the Reich was prohibited, thus putting a legal closure to the fiction of a territorial solution inside or outside of Europe. Also in October began the first deportations of Jews from Germany and elsewhere in central and western Europe to the East for killing that was masked as "resettlement." The first experiments in gassing Jews took place in Mogilev and Minsk from September 3 to 18. In the same month six hundred Soviet POWs in Auschwitz were killed using the cyanide gas Zyklon B; Himmler had decided already that summer to transform the camp into a killing center. In November, mobile gas vans were used to murder Jews in the Kalisch district in the Warthegau in the Polish area annexed to Germany. The killing center at Chelmno (Kulmhof in German), near Lodz, started operation in December 1941.

Meanwhile, in the fall of 1941, Hitler broke his extended rhetorical silence with respect to the Jews. From October 1941 to January 1942, he expressed himself on the Jews often and in detail both in private and in public: all inhibitions were abandoned as he let loose the vilest anti-Jewish tirades of hate that included implicit and explicit threats of extermination, referring to Providence and to his famous prophecy of January 1939. Goebbels soon followed his master. In late October, he visited the Eastern Front and the Jewish ghetto in Vilna. On November 2, he noted in his diary: "Here the Jews crouch among one another, horrible forms to see, not to mention touch. . . . The Jews are the lice of civilized humanity. They have to be exterminated somehow. . . . Only if one proceeds against them with the necessary brutality will we be finished with them."[9] On December 1, the minister of propaganda with a doctorate from the University of Heidelberg gave a speech before the German academy in the new lecture hall of the Friedrich-Wilhelm University in Berlin. He mentioned Hitler's prophecy and revealed to the august audience: "We are now experiencing the implementation of this prophecy. . . . [Jewry] is now suffering a gradual process of extermination."[10] The distinguished guests and professors noted that down.

Supporting this new policy of immediate annihilation, a frenzied spurt of anti-Jewish legislation engulfed the Reich from August to December 1941. The laws included the particular Nazi mix of policy measures and fear of pollution: thus while one decree deported German Jews to their death in the East, another prohibited those still in Germany from using public phones, as if this mattered anymore. It is worthwhile listing chronologically some of these decrees to capture the progression of genocidal imagination of these months.

August 2: Jews are prohibited from using lending libraries. August: Jewish males of working age (eighteen to forty-five) are prohibited from emigrating. August 14: The teaching of Hebrew and Aramaic in higher education institutions is prohibited. September 18: Jews are prohibited from leaving the "area of their residential community" without permission of the local police. In using public transportation, Jews are prohibited from sitting as long as German passengers are still standing. During rush hour, Jews are prohibited from using any public transportation. Jews are prohibited from using sleeping and dining cars, as well as train stations' waiting rooms, restaurants, and shelters for passengers. September 19: Jews are required to wear the Yellow Star. September 24: Jews are prohibited from using checks. October 9: Jews are prohibited from using public transportation during weekends and holidays. October 23: All Jews are prohibited from emigrating. Himmler, October 24: Some fifty thousand Jews from the Reich, Austria, and Bohemia and Moravia are to be sent to ghettos in the east (Riga, Lodz, Kovno, Minsk). November 4: Jews who are not necessary to the workforce will be deported in the next months to the east; their property is confiscated apart from 100 Reichsmarks and 50 kilograms [110 pounds] per person. November 13: Jews are to hand over cameras, optical instruments, record players, bicycles, typewriters, and adding machines. November 14: Jews are prohibited from selling their own books in an open market. November 25, Eleventh Decree to the Reich Citizenship Law: "A Jew shall lose German citizenship if, when this decree becomes law, he maintains his regular place of residence abroad" or if "the circumstances under which [he is staying abroad] indicate that his stay is not temporary"; the decree in effect deprived all German Jews who had been or would be deported of their citizenship. Deported Jews lose claims for social welfare such as pensions. December 12: Jews are prohibited from using public phones.[11]

At the same time, Heydrich and his lieutenant Adolf Eichmann planned a meeting for December 9 at 16 Am Kleinen Wannsee, Berlin, to discuss, as the invitation read, "all necessary organizational and technical preparations for a comprehensive solution of the Jewish Question." Among the participants were representatives from the Ministries of the Interior, Justice, Economics, and Propaganda, the Reich Chancellery, the

Foreign Ministry and the Ministry for the Occupied Eastern Territories. Other guests were from Nazi Party and SS agencies. The meeting was ultimately delayed and took place several weeks later on January 20, 1942, the notorious Wannsee Conference.[12]

The Belzec killing center began operation in March 1942, Sobibor in April, Treblinka in July. By March 1942, Jews were sent to Auschwitz from the surrounding areas to be gassed. At the beginning of 1942, 75 percent of the Jews who would be killed in the Holocaust were still alive. By the beginning of 1943, 75 percent of the victims who would be killed were already dead.[13] The image of Auschwitz epitomizing the Holocaust as a cold, industrial, administrative genocide is not accurate: added to the 1.1–1.3 million Jews killed from September 1939 to December 1941, another 1.5 million were shot in 1942 and 1943. Altogether, almost 50 percent of the victims of the Holocaust were killed in close-range, face-to-face contact. In total, almost 6 million Jews were murdered.

What was the idea that undergirded the total extermination of the Jews and gave it meaning? Historians have given of late two main, related answers to this question: one focuses on anti-Semitic racial ideology, while the other emphasizes the Nazi political paranoia that viewed world Jewry as an international actor that caused the war against Germany. Both are insightful. But how did the extermination fit within the world without Jews constructed by the Nazis since 1933?

This question requires us to seek new ways of perceiving the Holocaust. Popular and scholarly understanding has been based on the idea that the extermination was a radical event whose explanation hinges around the notion of rupture at the expense of the notion of continuity. The story I have told so far, in contrast, has sought to identify cultural continuities that linked the world of Nazis and Germans before and after 1941. The Final Solution was a radical rupture, but not as radical as is commonly portrayed. I would like to ask, what exactly constituted that rupture with respect to previous Nazi anti-Jewish policy? The Nazis established in 1933 that Jews had no place in Germany; in 1938, that Judaism had no place in the Reich and its future empire; in September 1939, that Jews had no place among human beings and were destined to wither away slowly in this or that godforsaken territory; in June 1941, that the mass murder of

Jewish civilians was necessary in order to get rid of the Jews faster rather than letting them perish slowly. Had the Nazis won the war at the gates of Moscow in December 1941, they would have made the Jews disappear from the world either by the Final Solution or by using slower means. The radical element of the Final Solution, therefore, was not the basic decision to create a world without Jews but the decision to create it immediately, in one sweep, during the war. It is from a perspective of continuity, then, that the radicalness of the Final Solution emerged, and it is with this perspective of continuity in mind that we should explore its meaning. The Final Solution was simultaneously a radical rupture and an essential continuity: it was a rupture embedded within the powerful continuity of making since 1933 a Nazi world without Jews.

Let us take this argument a step further. The Holocaust was linked to the vast Nazi imperial, racial project of treating whole groups as people without rights, of labor and concentration camps, and of genocides. The Jews were only one target in the Nazi universe of racial enemies, as the Nazis sought to realize their plans in central and eastern Europe of resettlement, expulsion, and annihilation. But the universe of racial enemies and genocides only begs the question: Why did the Nazis view the extermination of the Jews—but not the extermination of any other group—as the most urgent? What did the Jews symbolize that made it possible for the Nazis to imagine, explain, and justify their extermination? What, in other words, was the image that made the rupture of the extermination both radical and imaginable?

A different way to pose this question is to ask how perpetrators, Germans back on the home front, and Jews made sense of the extermination. We should not recoil from asking about the meaning of the extermination to people at the time: it is jolting for obvious reasons to speak about "making sense" of the extermination, but if we wish to uncover how people in the past made sense of their world, however morally objectionable this world was, then this is the right term and the right exploration to pursue.

Contemporaries did not have a view of the "Holocaust" as we do today assisted by historical work, photographs, and popular culture. The knowledge of the exact process of the extermination was sketchy, and only high Nazi officials knew of the decision taken at the Wannsee Conference.

But contemporaries did know, and at times in great detail, about the deportations, mass murders, and death camps. The question is not about specific "knowledge" of the "Holocaust" but about how Germans and Jews imagined the dramatic events that they experienced or heard about that made their street, neighborhood, town, country, and continent without Jews.

I turned to listen to Nazis, other Germans, Jews, and Europeans. They imagined the extermination of the Jews as an act of creation, in the sense of genesis, in which the Jewish world would be destroyed to make space for the Nazi one. As an act of creation, the extermination was perceived as producing a cosmic result, either salvation or eternal damnation; as being a human experience that lacked historical precedence, as every creation is by definition; and, as such, as a transgression, in the sense that it was a violation of all past known practices. The notion of creation was the organizing metaphor used for Germans, Jews, and Europeans to make sense of what was happening to the Jews after 1941. It allowed contemporaries to represent a radical rupture, for a genesis has no roots in the past, while at the same time it fit within the Nazi evolving imagination since 1933.

However radical the extermination was, then, it shared continuities with the German cultural imagination of the preceding years. There was an inner sense to the Nazi persecution and extermination of the Jews, for the progressive removal of Jews meant the conquering of time—of the present in 1933 through their exclusion from German society; of a moral past in 1938 through the elimination of Judaism and the Bible; and ultimately of history, and therefore of the future, in 1941 through the extermination from the face of the earth of the Jews as the source of all historical evil. The idea of genesis described the symbolic urgency of the Nazis to kill all the Jews immediately. And so, once again, as in 1933 and 1938, the Jews were at the center of the making of Nazi life: it was their extermination that gave meaning to the Nazi empire.

There was a direct link between imagining the extermination of the Jews as a sort of genesis and the transformation of the war into an apocalyptic conflagration that set Nazi Germany against the entire world. After the swift, tantalizing German victories against the Soviet Union in the summer and fall of 1941, the onset of the Russian winter, so dreaded by the German generals, slowed the Wehrmacht's advance toward Moscow. In December the German army stood at the gates of the Russian capital. One more victory, and the war for the Continent would be over. But the Red Army was able to stop the Wehrmacht's advance; the German invasion collapsed outside Moscow.

The failure to achieve a quick victory over the Soviet Union in 1941 profoundly undermined the Nazi war. The Nazi forces were overstretched along a huge and deep front. The Wehrmacht losses were significant and difficult, if not impossible, to replace. More German soldiers were killed in action between June and August 1941 than in the entire war period from September 1939 to May 1941. By December 1941, over a quarter of the entire German army in the East had been either killed (172,722) or wounded (621,308).[14] The Soviets, by contrast, despite suffering massive casualties, could count on an enormous reservoir of men and could call on reinforcements more easily than could the Wehrmacht. They stopped the German advance, stabilized the front, and used the winter months to regroup.

Thousands of miles away, under clear skies, Japan attacked the naval base at Pearl Harbor on December 7, 1941, and thus brought the United States into the war. Since June 1941 Hitler was already facing war against Britain and the Soviet Union, which became allies as Churchill and Stalin set aside their ideological enmity in order to fight Nazi Germany. On December 11, 1941, Hitler declared war on the United States, setting Germany against the universal ideologies of liberalism and communism in a world war of unparalleled fury. He now faced a grand alliance of Great Britain, the United States, and the Soviet Union. However many strains this alliance experienced during the war, Stalin, Churchill, Roosevelt, and later Harry S. Truman kept front and center the aim of defeating Hitler. December 1941 was a turning point in the war from the phase of Nazi victories to a phase of turning of the tide. Until then Hitler had the military upper hand with dazzling victories in Poland, France, Holland, Belgium, Norway, the Balkans, and the Soviet Union. But his attempt to defeat England at the Battle of Britain failed, and his gamble for a quick victory in the East stopped short at the Battle of Moscow. He now faced the prospects of a protracted war against three major industrial powers, including the United States, the number one economy in the world.

This was no ordinary war. Addressing the Reichstag on December 11, when he declared war on the United States, Hitler set out the redemptive character of the struggle from the beginning: "If Providence wanted that the German people not be spared this struggle, then I am grateful to it [Providence] for having entrusted me with the leadership of this historical confrontation, a confrontation that will decisively mold not only the history of our Germany but that of Europe, actually that of the entire world for the next 500 or 1000 years." He then talked about the attack on the Soviet Union as defending Europe from communism and at length about the American responsibility for the war, lying principally with Presidents Woodrow Wilson and Franklin Roosevelt. But, then, toward the end of the speech, Hitler shifted tone and topic, presenting in a tirade of hate the real enemy who caused this world war: "He [Roosevelt] was strengthened in this [decision to enter war] by the circle of Jews surrounding him, who, with Old Testament–like fanaticism, believed that the United States can be the instrument for preparing another Purim for the European nations that are becoming increasingly anti-Semitic. It was the Jew, in his full satanic vileness."[15]

Nazi propaganda viewed the Jews as responsible for originating the war. Goebbels articulated this faith in his article in *Das Reich* of November 16, 1941: "The Jews wanted this war, and now they have it. . . . They started this war and direct it." But Jewish responsibility was not merely political. Wilson and Roosevelt were political enemies, but a war of providential meaning could not be reduced to politics, presidents, and worldly affairs. For the Nazis, the Jews were never a mere political enemy but a redemptive, historical one. The Jews always gave meaning to Nazi political struggles, both in 1933 during the foundation of the Reich and now in a world war of enormous complexity fought from the Atlantic to the Urals to North Africa against very different foes. Neither liberalism nor communism, neither Roosevelt nor Stalin, held the key to this struggle, for they were mortal enemies who would come and go. Rather, the Jews did: "*The Jewish question*," as the Reich Press Office declared in early 1944, "*is the key to world history.*" The Jews incarnated evil historical origins.

Goebbels's article title summed up the ageless responsibility of the Jews that went beyond specific present-day accusations: "The Jews Are Guilty!" Their responsibility for the war was only the most recent manifestation of a bottomless historical guilt, for the Jewish Problem, he wrote, "has occupied mankind for millennia!"[16] The extermination of this enemy was obligatory for the Nazi empire to rise: "In triggering this war, world Jewry completely miscalculated the forces it could muster. It is now gradually being engulfed by the same extermination process that it had intended for us and that it would have allowed to happen without any scruples, had it had the power to do so."[17] By blaming "world Jewry" for triggering the war, Goebbels imagined an abstract entity, unconstrained by time and space, and the exact opposite of a bounded political power that resided in the White House, 10 Downing Street, or the Kremlin. A historical confrontation staged by Providence found its worthy historical enemy of satanic quality.

Such an enemy demanded respect. Liberalism and communism were threats because they commanded state powers in the present, but the Jews were a threat because they commanded powers everywhere spatially and temporally. For Hitler in the speech of December 11, 1941, the Jew associated the Old Testament and satanic vileness. In his speech of January 30, 1942, at the Berlin Sportpalast, Hitler was specific about the Jews as a symbol of an evil past tout court: "And the hour will strike when the most evil world enemy of all times will have ended his role at least for a thousand years."[18] Goebbels, whose anti-Semitic rhetoric was always resourceful, had expressed this idea in numerous ways. One of the last occasions was his final lead editorial in *Das Reich* on January 21, 1945, dedicated solely to the Jews: these were to perish in the war as the historic "source of the world's misfortune."[19]

The Nazis blamed the Jews for everything during the war, for things past and present with no attention to context, facts, or proof. Following Hitler's furious tirade of anti-Jewish hate before the Reichstag on April 26, 1942, Klemperer noted in his diary: "The concentration of hatred has this time turned into madness. Not England or the USA or Russia—*only*, in everything, nothing but *the Jew*."[20] The Nazis created the Jew in the context of the world war as a symbolic manual for historical evil. It was a multifaceted manual of dissimilar political ideas (communism and liberalism) and different registers of historical times (Jewish alleged crimes in the present and the past), but it shared a common belief in the link among Jews, history, and evil. Jews gave the overall meaning to the Nazi fight between good and evil: the messianic struggle to create a Nazi civilization depended on the extermination of the Jews. Creation and extermination were inextricably linked, giving meaning to each other.

The widening German war and extermination of the Jews deepened Klemperer's anguish over who he was and who were the Germans. He recorded in May 1942 with an insistent repetition that assuaged his creeping doubts: "I am fighting the hardest battle for my Germanness now. I must hold on to this: I am German, the others are un-German. I must hold on to this: The spirit is decisive, not blood. I must hold on to this: On my part Zionism would be a comedy—my baptism was *not* a comedy. . . . *I* am German and am waiting for the Germans to come back; they have gone to ground somewhere." But a year earlier, on April 16, 1941, he had to admit: "Once I would have said: I do not judge as a Jew. . . . Now: Yes, I judge as a Jew, because as such I am particularly affected by the Jewish business in Hitlerism, and because it is central to the whole structure, to the whole character of National Socialism and is uncharacteristic of everything else."[21]

The notion of creation included salvation, uniqueness, and transgression. Hitler, Himmler, and Goebbels, who knew exactly what was happening to the Jews, all imagined the extermination after 1941 as an act of creation that would give rise to the new Nazi world. Hitler articulated the extermination as bringing an end to all problems and ushering in a period of world peace in a message read on his behalf in a ceremony for the anniversary of the Nazi Party's founding on February 24, 1942: "My prophecy will be fulfilled that in this war not the Aryans will be exterminated but the Jew will be eradicated. Whatever the battle will bring, or how long it may last, this will be the ultimate legacy of this war. And then finally, after the elimination of these parasites, will there come to a suffering world a long period of brotherhood among nations and true peace."[22] Himmler, in his notorious address to a group of SS officers in Posen in 1943, expressed a sentiment of transgression: "In our history, this [the extermination of the Jews] is an unwritten and never-to-be-written page of glory."[23] The genocide against the Jews was perceived as historically unique.

Goebbels, always expansive when it came to ranting against the Jews, linked metaphors of origins and extermination followed by a sense of transgression. The Reich Press Office, controlled by Goebbels's Ministry of Propaganda, issued weekly directives on how to present the war at home and abroad. On August 8, 1941, it laid the case for the Jews' historical guilt: "What does world Jewry seek? For thousands of years it has aimed at nothing but Jewish world domination. This goal was already present in the Old Testament of the Jews. . . . Repeatedly over the centuries the Jew appeared close to his goal, but then again and again the Aryan people put the Jews in their place. Today Jewry again seeks world domination." On August 19, in his diary, Goebbels noted the consequence of the Jewish guilt: "The Führer believes that his past prophecy in the Reichstag is being confirmed. . . . It is coming to pass in these weeks and months with an almost eerily graceful certainty."[24]

Hitler, Himmler, and Goebbels had no sense of guilt with respect to exterminating the Jews of Europe. But they did obviously have a certain sense of transgression. This is evident in the way they talked and wrote about it: rarely, sparsely, in hints, using code words and insinuation. They avoided describing what really happened not only to others but to themselves. For years they had no inhibition against yelling in public from every rooftop about *the extermination of the Jews,* but when it actually happened, they refrained from putting it into words, sensing the breaking of a taboo.

Goebbels wrote some three million words a year among his speeches, editorials, and fifteen thousand words a night in his diary.[25] A compulsive writer who seemed to come into his own when enraged about the Jews, he never wrote down any details about the Final Solution. His most detailed diary entry on the Final Solution, written on March 27, 1942, is a text that cries for psychoanalysis: "Beginning in Lublin, the Jews are being shipped to the East out of the General Gouvernment. A rather barbaric procedure, which I won't describe in more detail, is used. Not much is left of the Jews themselves."[26] He then proceeded nonetheless to provide quite a lot of information, whose main characteristic is that even in his private moments Goebbels was consciously and subconsciously careful of speaking explicitly about what was happening. The Nazi leaders concealed the extermination from the public not only because they thought, correctly, that Germans would not sign up for this policy, but also because they shared the general cultural sense of breaking a taboo. They, too, belonged to their culture and could not stand outside it. They sensed the transgression in the annihilation of all the members of a group belonging to the origins of Christian European civilization.

Soldiers at the front did not have an overall view of the annihilation policy, and it is therefore significant that they described the part of the extermination they witnessed, participated in, or heard about by using much the same terms of creation. They imagined their killing as unleashing a redemptive period of world peace. "This time we must get rid of or neutralize all the Jews, then it would soon look better in the world," wrote one soldier before the beginning of the mass killings on June 22, 1941. "The city is burning for eight days," wrote another from Kiev in late September. "All is the work of the Jews. So Jews from fourteen to sixty years old are being shot, and also Jewish women will soon be shot. Otherwise, there will be no end to this." This writer had in mind not only Kiev but the alleged troubles Jews created everywhere. Another wrote in 1942: "The great challenge is to exterminate eternal Judaism. . . . The Jews are guilty of everything. This battle is an emergency that has to be fought through and through. Only then will the world find its eternal peace." A common pairing was the opposites of Jews, evil, and destruction as against Germans, Heimat, and peace: "We must and we shall succeed to free the world from this pest . . . the root of all evil. . . . May our wish be fulfilled soon because only then we can unite again in a *happy* meeting [*ein frohes Wiedersehen*], when we shall free ourselves from domestic and foreign Jewish control." "Ein frohes Wiedersehen" was an expression traditionally associated with a union of harmony and peace in the beloved Heimat.[27]

But there were two sides to Germans' imagining the extermination as a new beginning. If it raised expectations of ecstatic salvation, it also conjured sentiments of the end of the world. As such, it first could not be believed only to turn later into an imagination of a moral apocalypse. Captain Wilm Hosenfeld traversed this mental trajectory. A schoolteacher born in 1895, Hosenfeld became a member of the SA in 1933 and of the Nazi Party in 1935, but his Catholic faith slowly led him to question the Nazis. An army officer who could not take part in the fighting because of his health, he was the director of sport activities for Wehrmacht officers in Warsaw. By July 1942 Hosenfeld knew quite a lot about the fate of the Jews deported from the Warsaw ghetto, but the novelty of the systematic extermination led him to refuse to believe it. He wrote on July 25, 1942: "If what they are saying in the city is true, and it does come from reliable sources, then it is no honor in being a German officer, and no one could go along with what is happening. But I can't believe it. The rumors say that thirty thousand Jews are to be taken from the ghetto this week and sent east somewhere. . . . But surely this is madness. It can't be possible." A year later, on June 16, 1943, as the ruins of the Warsaw ghetto smoldered, he wrote of the slaughter of the Jews in the biblical language of a mark of Cain: "With this terrible mass murder of the Jews we have lost the war. We have brought upon ourselves an indelible disgrace, a curse that can never be lifted. We deserve no mercy, we are all guilty."[28]

Three months earlier on March 2, 1943, Goebbels noted in his diary (following a conversation with Göring): "Göring is completely aware of what would threaten us all, if we were to weaken in this war. He has no illusions in this regard. Especially in the Jewish question, we are so fully committed that there is no escape for us anymore. And that is a good thing. Experience shows that a movement and a people who have burned the bridges behind them fight with much greater determination than those who still have a way back."[29] Hosenfeld and Goebbels, two quite different individuals, gave very dissimilar moral meanings to the extermination of the Jews, but they both imagined it—but no other genocides and war crimes committed by the Nazis—as a sort of a new beginning.

Hitler, Himmler, and Goebbels, on the one hand, and German soldiers, on the other, talked and thought about the extermination in similar metaphors of creation. A certain anti-Jewish culture had been created in the Third Reich since 1933 that enabled German leaders and soldiers to understand what was happening to the Jews in shared images. Scholarship of the Holocaust has focused on what Germans knew about the Holocaust and when. Our story has traced anti-Jewish imaginary horizons available to Germans during the Third Reich. It emerges that precise knowledge of the overall policy of extermination, such as information about the Wannsee Conference, was inconsequential for making sense of the killing of the Jews after 1941 in terms of a new beginning. Germans on the fronts sensed what Hitler and his acolytes knew for a fact: that getting rid of the Jews was akin, even in a particularly savage war, to making a clean historical slate.

Jews shared this imagination tangibly. Across Europe, in towns, ghettos, camps, and killing fields, Jews used the notion of a new, destructive creation as the key image to give meaning to what was happening to them. Oskar Rosenfeld, the Viennese man of letters active in literary, theater, and Zionist circles before he was deported to the Lodz ghetto in November 1941, began working on "a cultural history of the ghetto" that was supposed to describe how the Germans gave the Jews "a different morphological form [... achieving among the Jews] a total morphological transformation." In one diary entry, entitled "depiction of the mood," he writes: "This tragedy is devoid of heroes. And why tragedy? Because the pain does not reach out to something human, to a strange heart, but is something incomprehensible, colliding with the cosmos, a natural phenomenon like the creation of the world. Creation would have to start anew, with *berajshit* [Hebrew for "in the beginning," the first word in the Hebrew Bible]. In the beginning," he continued, alluding to another metaphor of creation, this time from the New Testament, "God created the ghetto."[30]

In diaries and letters Jews gave voice to their experiences in expansive, rich language that Germans could not emulate. Germans' descriptions were often sparse, the language laden with Nazi-speak that hid more than revealed, and their understanding blocked by sentiments of guilt and the breaking of a taboo. Still, even under these circumstances the notion of creation emerged among German leaders and soldiers. The victims did not have these constraints, even as they were driven by a compulsive force to explore the tragedy that befell them: the greater was the incomprehensibility toward what was happening, the greater was the urge to recount, record, and give meaning. That Jews wrote as if possessed was linked to notions of historical origins and memory because the obsession to write was driven by the aim to leave a trace, any trace, of a Jewish history that seemed at an end. "We must hurry, we know not our time. At work until the last moment," wrote David Graber, aged nineteen, in August 1942, when tens of thousands were deported to Treblinka from the Warsaw ghetto. His testament was placed in a big milk churn and buried in the ground together with the rest of the Oyneg Shabes archive. It was found after the war.[31]

Jewish history was at an end, and diarists understood what was happening as a new creation that had no reference in the past and belonged with images of universal, natural chaos. Ringelblum wrote in June 1942 that they were "witnessing the death pangs of an old world and the birth pangs of a new," while Rosenfeld noted a month later, on July 24, 1942, a day after the great deportations from the Warsaw Ghetto began, that what was happening was "a *mabul* [the Flood, in Hebrew] . . . destruction of the world . . . apocalypse."[32] Young Noemi Szac Wajnkranc, daughter of an affluent family whose father was a well-known engineer in town, wondered in the Warsaw ghetto: "The foundations of the world [were] crushed with Hitler's wave of the hand. How come these foundations were so weak? Stars in the sky. The Small Dipper and the Big Dipper. . . . Is this a dream or a reality? . . . God, make it that this will be only a dream!"[33]

Diarists understood what was happening by conveying their inability to understand what was happening. They invoked the notions of disbelief, rupture, and exceptionalism, all placed within the metaphor of chaotic creation. Because every creation is both a radical rupture as well as linked to what preceded it, the claim that what was happening surpassed the limits of language was always followed by descriptions of what happened. These descriptions often contained images of acts of cosmic proportions.

Abraham Lewin thus wrote on May 26, 1942: "Only if we were capable of tearing out by the force of our pent-up anguish the greatest of all mountains, a Mount Everest, and with all our hatred and strength hurling it down on the heads of the German murderers of our young and old— this would be the only fitting reaction on our part. Words are beyond us now."[34] Lewin, a forty-seven-year-old educator born to Hasidic parents, taught before the war at the Warsaw private Jewish secondary school for girls, Yehudia, and in the ghetto kept a diary from March 26, 1942, to January 16, 1943. At Yehudia in the mid-1920s Lewin had met Luba, the school's Hebrew teacher. She was a committed Zionist who had emigrated to Palestine in 1921 and worked as a teacher in kibbutz Ein Harod at the Sea of Galilee until compelled to return to Poland in 1923 because of malaria. In 1928, the couple had a child, Ora. In 1934, they all went to Palestine with thoughts of remaining there but returned to Poland because of the poor health of Luba and Ora. In the Warsaw ghetto Lewin was a member of the Oyneg Shabes historical project. He and Ringelblum, former colleagues at Yehudia, helped to establish and maintain the ghetto's underground archives.

The metaphor of creation was so common that it was used by Jews of very different religiosity, culture, class, and background. Young Fela Szeps, a student of philosophy and psychology at the University of Warsaw, was sent in 1942 to a labor camp for Jews inside the Reich near the Silesian town of Grünberg. She challenged God:

> It seems that God created the world for everyone. So why is there no place for us, why was there not enough place for my parents, for all the others, for the children? It is not becoming of you, the highest of all, to play around with your lambs, your own creation. Divide the benefits of your world equally among all lest someone more just than you will come, someone who is better at holding the scepter, and you shall fall from the height of your position and will crumble to dust![35]

The rabbi of Piaseczno, Kalonymos Kalmish Shapira (1889–1943), was one of the leading figures of early twentieth-century Hasidism in Poland. The sermons he gave in the Warsaw ghetto are an invaluable source because religiously devout Jews were less likely to keep a written record of their experiences than secular Jews. The sermons were not personal. They interpreted the specific portion of the Bible read on each week, and only rarely did they discuss directly current events in the ghetto and beyond. When Shapira did use them to explain the present, therefore, they are especially illuminating. At the beginning of the war, Shapira viewed the Nazi persecution of Polish Jews within the familiar framework of God's punishment for the sins of Israel. But he soon realized that this view was wholly inadequate to clarify the magnitude of Nazi persecution and Jewish suffering. He therefore adopted the metaphor of creation to interpret the suffering of the Jews. In his sermon of July 26, 1941, he viewed the current persecution as the "birth pangs of the Messiah" (*havlei mashi'ah*), as a step in a cosmic process of birth and new beginning. This process required a certain death before the rebirth, and because Israel as God's chosen people had been a key figure in this cosmic process, they must suffer the birth pangs in an especially radical way.[36]

But in the summer of 1942, as the deportations to Treblinka began, this view in turn seemed insufficient. Until now Shapira had viewed events as part of the cycle of persecution and redemption that had characterized Jewish history for centuries. He now acknowledged with difficulty that the Nazi persecution was novel for it potentially closed any possibility of redemption. His last sermon was in July 1942. Later that autumn, he wrote a postscript that described a cosmic destruction that created a world without Jews:

> [In 1941] although the suffering was very bitter ... yet it was still possible to lament them and to describe them at least in part.... Not so, however, in the end of [the Jewish year] 5702 [late summer 1942], when our communities are almost completely destroyed.... There are no words with which to lament our suffering; there is no one to admonish, there is no heart to rouse to religious activities. How difficult has prayer become! How difficult is Sabbath observance.... Grieving about the future is out of the question now.... Only He can rebuild what has been destroyed.[37]

The beginning of a new Nazi time depended on the destruction of Jewish time. In the ghettos and camps the Nazis created for the Jews a world without time, where history, as Primo Levi said, "stopped." Hanna Levi-Hass, a Jewish communist from Yugoslavia who was a prisoner in Bergen Belsen, captured this sentiment:

> We have the impression that we're separated from the normal world of the past by a massive, thick wall. Our emotional capacity seems blunt, faded. We no longer even remember our own past. No matter how hard I strive to reconstruct the slightest element of my past life, not a single human memory comes back to me. We have not died, but we are dead. They've managed to kill in us not only our right to life in the present and [... future but also] all sense of a human life in our past.... I turn things over in my mind, I want to ... and I remember absolutely nothing.[38]

In a world without time, social laws no longer applied. Janusz Korczak, the Warsaw educator, pediatrician, and children's author who continued to direct his orphanage in the ghetto, recounted in his diary the following episode in a ghetto store in May or June 1942, a period of high tension just before the beginning of the great deportations: "A small shop-keeper told a complaining customer: 'My good woman—these are not goods, and this is not a store. You are not a customer nor I a merchant. I don't sell to you nor do you pay me because these scraps of paper are not money. You don't lose and I don't profit. Who is cheating today and for what? Only one must do something. Well, am I now right?'" Jewish life became a grand illusion, in which such ordinary social elements as money, trade, and buying were meaningless in a world that had no future and no present and that existed outside normal social order and therefore outside history. Even natural laws no longer applied. "Two of my sensible, know-ing, objective informants and advisers have let me down: the scale and the thermometer," wrote Korczak. "I stopped believing them. They tell lies here too."[39]

The ultimate place with no time, past, and history was the camp. This was true for all inmates, though it applied to Jewish inmates both as individuals and as part of a collectivity destined to disappear soon. The prisoners understood, wrote Primo Levi, "the vanity of every conjecture: why worry oneself trying to read into the future when no action, no word of ours, could have the minimum influence? Our wisdom lay in 'not try-ing to understand,' not imagining the future, not tormenting ourselves as to how and when it would all be over."[40] Jews in the camps and the ghettos often compared their life to that of animals whose single aim was self-preservation. The Nazis aimed to transform the Jews into a people with-out time and without memory. For Jews and Nazis, it was as if time had stopped.

If contemporaries understood the Holocaust as a unique event beyond comprehension and words, so also did laypeople in popular memory and some scholars after 1945. This view is well known and has been expressed by survivors, artists, popular writers, and scholars, namely, that it has been impossible to fully understand the Holocaust and to represent it. But there is a difference that is worthwhile pointing out between this assessment in scholarly and popular culture, on the one hand, and the story told in these pages, on the other.

From the beginning of the extermination in June 1941, the problem of how to describe what was happening became part of the history of what was happening. "If someone will try to describe [the pain]—no one will be successful. If someone will try to experience it—every man will collapse under it," wrote Josef Zelkowicz in his diary in early September 1942 as Jews in the Lodz ghetto received the news of the deportation of twenty thousand children and elderly, a fifth of the ghetto's population. Zelkowicz, born in 1897 near Lodz to a Hasidic family, studied in rabbinical schools and became a rabbi at the age of eighteen before turning to teaching and writing. From the 1920s he published regularly in the Yiddish press in Lodz on Jewish folklore and history. He moved with his family to the Lodz ghetto in the winter of 1940 and continued his literary and cultural activities, especially in the archive of the ghetto that opened in November 1940, being part of the group who wrote the daily account of the ghetto from January 1941 to July 1944.

Contemporaries described the extermination as something indescribable and unprecedented. A German soldier wrote in a letter after the onset of the German invasion in the East: "Emil wrote of the starving children who he recently saw in the Warsaw ghetto.... The truth is worse, more cruel, more bestial than any fantasy."[41] Avraham Lewin wrote in the wake of the great deportations from the Warsaw ghetto: "Our language had no words with which to express the calamity and disaster that has struck us.... This is a slaughter the like of which human history has not seen.... Those who are far away cannot imagine our bitter situation. They will not understand and will not believe [it]."[42] Shortly after the Germans shot 33,700 Kiev Jews in Babi Yar, Iryna Khoroshunova wrote in her diary: "I only know one thing, there is something terrible, horrible going on, something inconceivable, which cannot be understood, grasped or explained."[43]

After the Holocaust some took these sentiments at face value, as attesting that the event was indeed unexplainable and unrepresentable. Others, including some historians, viewed it as one proof that the Holocaust was historically unique, fundamentally different from other historical events. This view has often blocked full-fledged historical research on the Holocaust. Most historians commonly write about the Holocaust by bypassing this sentiment: studies account for what happened, where, and why but do not attempt to understand how the sentiments of disbelief and uniqueness fit in what happened.[44]

In these pages, we have treated the sentiments of disbelief and uniqueness as part of the imagination of the extermination as an act of creation. Precisely these sentiments made it possible for Germans, Jews, and Europeans to internalize the killing of the Jews. We have been interested not in entering the debate over whether the Final Solution was historically unique (it was not, if by "unique" we mean it had characteristics that fundamentally distinguished it from all other historical events) but in understanding how people made sense of it. Imagining what happened to the Jews after 1941 as unprecedented was a vehicle for people to understand what was happening.

When we look from this perspective at the perceptions of disbelief and uniqueness generated during the war—not as a statement of truth but as a reflection of how people understood their experience—we gain new insights: these perceptions change from an obstacle to understanding the Final Solution into being part of its explanation as they reveal the horizons of imagination shared by Germans and Jews (each group giving it different meanings, of course).

One key idea that the Jews shared with the Nazis was that the essence of the Nazi assault was to eradicate Jewish memory and history. In the Majdanek concentration camp, Isaac Schipper told a fellow inmate in the summer of 1943:

> Should our murderers be victorious, should *they* write the history of this war, our destruction will be presented as one of the most beautiful pages of world history, and future generations will pay tribute to them as dauntless crusaders. . . . They may wipe out our memory altogether, as if we had never existed. . . . But if *we* write the history of this period of blood and tears— and I firmly believe we will—who will believe us? Nobody will *want* to believe us because our disaster is the disaster of the entire civilized world. . . . We'll have the thankless job of proving to a reluctant world that we are Abel, the murdered brother.[45]

The role of memory in a post-extermination world preoccupied not only Schipper but also Alfred Rosenberg in his speech of March 1941. Like other Germans and Jews from Goebbels to Hosenfeld to Rosenfeld and Zelkowicz, Schipper understood the extermination as a cosmic event and rendered it comprehensible via a story from the book of Genesis. He personally doubted that the world would believe what had happened, although he was committed to writing its history. But most Jewish diarists wrote "themselves into the future," in Alexandra Garbarini's elegant phrase, precisely to challenge this war on memory.[46] They wrote, recorded, and amassed evidence. Ultimately, they and the Nazis shared a belief in the power of Jewish history and memory.

It was this power the Nazis were set on destroying. For Nazis and other Germans, killing the Jews coexisted with constructing a new memory of the evil Jews; destroying Judaism and rewriting its history reinforced each other. That is why they paid so much attention to Jewish books, libraries, and Judaica in the occupied territories.

In September 1939, special arson squads followed the German army in Poland with the task of burning Jewish synagogues, books, and libraries. What followed was a systematic bibliocide. Wild destruction followed, which at times was reported in the papers. The Great Talmudic Library of the Theological Seminary in Lublin was burned in late 1939. In March 1941, the destruction generated the following comment in the *Frankfurter Zeitung*:

> For us it was a matter of special pride to destroy the Talmudic Academy which was known as the greatest in Poland. . . . We threw the huge Talmudic library out of the building and carried the books to the market-place, where we set them on fire. The fire lasted for twenty hours. The Lublin Jews assembled around and wept bitterly, almost silencing us with their cries. We summoned the military band, and with joyful shouts the soldiers drowned out the sounds of the Jewish cries.[47]

The bibliocide continued during the war elsewhere on the Continent, in the Balkans, France, and Holland, as well as across eastern Europe. In Kovno, the Germans publicly burned the famous Mapu Library, established in 1908 and named after the Hebrew writer Avraham Mapu. A military band played for officials and soldiers as revelers danced around the fire.[48]

But if destruction was one German way to forge a new memory of the Jews, preservation and collecting was another. The library of the Reich Security Main Office, under the title of "investigating the enemies," was established before the war, and focused on collecting reading material on Marxism, churches and pseudoreligious trends, Freemasons, and Jews. From its central home in a Freemason temple in Berlin, it acquired two million books, manuscripts, and journals by the end of the war.

The project chiefly responsible for the confiscation and collection of Jewish material was the operation Einsatzstab Reichsleiter Rosenberg (ERR), or Reichsleiter Rosenberg Taskforce, headed by Alfred Rosenberg, who became in July 1941 the rather powerless Reich minister for the Occupied Eastern Territories but who had full authority on matters of Jewish history and memory. The operation was established on July 17, 1940, when Hitler gave Rosenberg a free hand to pillage and sort Jewish cultural materials from across the Continent for Rosenberg's postwar project of a National Socialist university. The activity range of the ERR was impressive. According to one postwar estimate its staff visited 375 archives, 402 museums, 531 miscellaneous institutions, and 957 libraries across Europe.[49] Another source describes this list as indicating activities only in the conquered areas in eastern Europe in 1943.[50] Rosenberg set up offices in some twenty-five European locations. Books and cultural materials were carefully collected and cataloged by scholars and librarians, and those selected were shipped to the Institute for Research on the Jewish Question in Frankfurt. The Frankfurt city administration had already lured the institute to the city through its donation of a precious local Judaica collection.[51] It is difficult to estimate the number of books collected by the institute during the war. One estimate gives the number of six million volumes, but this could be a postwar figure linked to the power of this number.

The cultural heritage assembled was extraordinary. In Paris the ERR seized the libraries of the Alliance Israélite Universelle (60,000 books), the École Rabbinique (30,000 books), the Biblioteka Polska (130,000 books), and the Rothschild libraries (28,000 books and 780 cases of archival material). In Holland, the Spinoza collections were seized in The Hague and

Rijnsburg, and in the summer and fall of 1941, the Jewish libraries in Amsterdam were impounded. Later in the war, the library of the Rabbinical College in Rome was sent to the institute. Early on the institute collected 280,000 volumes of Soviet and Polish Jewish literature as well as substantial Talmudic literature from Kovno, Vilna, Minsk, Kiev, and Riga. It also opened a branch in Lodz. Other scholarly initiatives were not left behind. The newly founded German university in Posen established in 1941 a professorship for Jewish history with a dream library of 400,000 Judaica volumes—all confiscated from Jewish libraries in Poland.

Collection of Jewish material was methodical. When Jews were deported from Prague and elsewhere in Czechoslovakia, the Nazis set out a special agency to confiscate property left behind in their apartments. Also books were collected; names of former owners and bookplates were removed from them. By March 1943, the agency was able to clear only about half of the empty Jewish residences in Czechoslovakia. It had already collected 778,195 books.[52] In Holland, employees of the ERR received the front-door keys of houses of deportees, entered their apartments, and seized private books and Judaica. In France, the operation's employees searched castles, farms, warehouses, and bank vaults.

One object was no longer of interest to the Nazis. The institute did not bother to collect Torah scrolls, although one official noted that "perhaps the leather can still have some use for bookbinding." Scrolls were used in areas occupied by the Nazis for binding books and making such leather objects as belts and shoes.[53]

A librarian active in the looting of ERR was Johannes Pohl, who became the chief of the Judaica collection in the institute's library. By now his career had spanned Jewish life and death: from being an expert on the Jewish community of Palestine and living in Jerusalem, he now took part in the preservation of Jewish culture in a world destined to be without Jews in order to create a new, "true" history and memory of the Jews. Pohl's zeal for collecting Judaica knew no bounds. Shortly after Greece fell in April 1941, he showed up in Thessaloniki to enrich his collection. In January 1942, he traveled to Vilna with four assistants. He ordered that all the important book collections in the city and nearby localities, altogether from some three hundred synagogues and from private collections, be concentrated and demanded that the Jewish Council provide twenty workers, among them five experts on Judaica, to sort the materials. These workers arranged one hundred thousand volumes by century of publication, from which Pohl selected twenty thousand to be sent to the institute. The rest were sold to a paper mill for nineteen Reichsmarks per ton of paper.[54] At some point during the war, after examining the assembled collection, Pohl summed up with satisfaction: "As far as Jewish literature is concerned, this library holds collections such as have never before been assembled in Europe or elsewhere. The library will be developed (as part of the organization of the New Order in Europe) not only for Europe but for the entire world."[55]

The most concentrated attempt to rewrite Jewish history and memory took place in the Jewish Central Museum in Prague, established in 1942.[56] The project began haphazardly, initially functioning more as a depot center for Jewish items than as a museum. It soon became the central collection site of Judaica from victims of the Final Solution. From a mere thousand items in 1941, it grew to two hundred thousand objects housed in eight buildings and fifty warehouses by 1945. The galloping number of items reflected the progression of the extermination. During the war, the museum was a work in progress and the exhibition was undeveloped. It was oriented more toward arts and crafts than history. Visitors were not allowed into the museum, which planned to open to the public only after the war. This fit the memory meaning of the project. It was not the usual wartime anti-Semitic propaganda; it was not meant for the period of the war, when the extermination of the Jews was taking place. It was meant to teach about Jewish history after the total extermination of the Jews would have become publicly shared knowledge. Members of the ERR already started thinking during the war how to present and exhibit the looted cultural objects after the war. Two exhibitions to that effect were organized in 1942 and 1943.[57]

In this sense, although the overall intention to appropriate and rewrite Jewish history was evident in a range of Nazi actions, these attempts could not develop sufficiently in the short span of the war. The necessities of the military effort were more urgent, and more important, it was not clear to the Nazis themselves what new image of the Jew to forge, given the acceleration of the mass killings, as well as the tension of managing the knowledge of the extermination among silence, insinuation, and public information. The period was too short (1942–1945) and too intense for a full-fledged Nazi presentation of evil Jewish history and memory. The Nazis considered that this articulation would have to wait for the period after the victorious war and would presumably have included such vehicles of memory as school textbooks, history books, films, and perhaps even monuments.

But by collecting Jewish books and Judaica the Nazis did set out to determine the story of Jewish history after the war. They would tell this history, what it meant, and how it finally ended. This is why the Nazis had such deep appreciation of the power of books, for good or evil. Ultimately, they forbade Jews to have any books at all. On February 18, 1942, the ERR operation in Kovno announced a ban on all books in the ghetto starting in ten days' time. Regardless of their content or language, books were to be handed over, announced a man named Benker, a representative of the operation. Anyone found possessing books after that date would be shot. Benker was aware of the ghetto's rich library, and he ordered the Jewish Council in the ghetto to seal the library so that important books in the collection would not get lost because, he explained, "the Germans, you understand, are cultural men."[58] On February 28, Jews handed over tens of thousands of books to the Nazis. Thousands more were saved as Jews hid or buried them. The Nazis sent the most valuable Judaica to the institute in Frankfurt, the rest to a paper factory. Book reading did not stop, of course; Jews read in hiding, and books passed from hand to hand in secret. But the Nazis did make the ghetto for all intents and purposes a society without books. It fit perfectly with their imagination of and policies about the Jews: the people without time, whose life in February 1942 had a very short expiration date, had no use for books, that art of storytelling that makes us human, allows us to dream, and places our experiences in a narrative.

But stories have life of their own, and even the Nazis could not be masters of their own story. They did not foresee an unintended consequence of their massive, European-wide looting of Judaica. The institute in Frankfurt stored the huge quantities of material in several depots in the city and in nearby villages, in effect keeping them from being destroyed in the fury of the war. During the last months of 1943, when Allied bombing of German cities threatened the collection, a large part of it was removed to nearby Hungen, an isolated castle thirty-two miles from Frankfurt. Many Jewish treasures thus survived the war.

In mid-1942 the Second World War raged in all its destructive wrath from East Asia to North Africa to Europe. Germany was still master of the Continent, ruling from Paris to deep in the heart of Russia to the North African desert. But German forces were spread thin. They staged a few counteroffensives in the East but failed to break through Soviet lines. They had to administer an empire throughout occupied Europe, and they were engaged in battles in the Balkans and North Africa. But the Allies had major difficulties as well. The Soviets were only beginning to recover from their disastrous beginning of the war, and the European part of Russia was still in German hands. The British army was extended across the empire from Europe, to North Africa and the Middle East, to Asia with hardly any military achievement anywhere, while the United States was fighting a hard war in the Pacific and had no intention of opening a second front in Europe. Who would win this war?

No one knew the answer to this question in 1942, but the Nazis were determined to win their war against the Jews, which they continued and intensified. The mass shootings in the East during the invasion of the Soviet Union were followed by plans for implementation of the murder of all European Jews discussed at the Wannsee Conference in January 1942. SS troops and auxiliaries moved methodically in 1942 and 1943 to clear the ghettos in eastern Europe by deporting most of the Jews to Auschwitz, Treblinka, Sobibor, Chelmno, Majdanek, and Belzec. The death toll in 1942 was 2.7 million, with the annihilation of Polish Jewry and the widening of the Final Solution across Europe. The death toll in 1943, with Polish Jewry practically eliminated, was 500,000.

Deportations from various European countries started in late 1941 and intensified in mid-1942, from Germany, France, Holland, Belgium, Slovakia, the Czech Protectorate (the regions of Bohemia and Moravia), and Austria. Trains left Paris, Amsterdam, Brussels, Prague, and Warsaw transporting Jews in sealed freight cars to death camps regardless of bad weather, Allied bombing, or the military needs of the Wehrmacht.

German Jews also now faced deportation and extermination. In Regensburg, on April 2, 1942, all Jews under the age of sixty-five, 106 souls, were deported to a camp near Lublin allegedly for resettlement in the East. On that day, the Nazis ordered the Jews to gather in a specific site in town, from which they proceeded by foot to the railway station and from there by train eastward. Each was allowed to carry one suitcase, hardly a good omen for a successful professional, social, and personal resettlement. Someone took a photo of the Nazis and Jews on the site of the gathering place. It was the same spot where the town's synagogue had once stood before it was set on fire in November 1938.[59]

The Nazis originally planned the deportation of German Jews for the period after the war; this was in 1939–1940, when it was thought by many that the fighting would soon end. But with the expansion of the war in 1941 and the decision to kill the Jews faster one way or another, a Germany cleansed of Jews made for a coherent policy. If dozens of localities in eastern Europe were becoming free of Jews, why keep the local Jews in the Heimat? Some regions had already become *Judenfrei* (Alsace-Lorraine in July 1940 and Baden and the Saar-Palatinate in October 1940). There were also practical rewards. The beginning of the Allied air raids on German cities in 1941 led the regional Nazi leaders of Berlin, Hamburg, Vienna, and other places to press for the immediate deportation of Jews to free up living space for bombed citizens.

In September 1941, as we have seen, the identifying Star of David was introduced; on October 15 the first deportation of Jews from localities in Germany and the Czech and Moravian Protectorate to ghettos in former Poland and Russia began. Hitler had made the decision to deport the German Jews in the previous weeks, perhaps as early as September 2. Transports left Vienna to Lodz on October 15, Prague and Luxemburg on the sixteenth, and Berlin on the eighteenth. Twenty transports carrying 19,593 Jews were completed by November 5. By mid-January 1942, 22,000 more Jews were deported in twenty-two transports to ghettos in Riga, Kovno, and Minsk. Five thousand deportees, shot immediately on arrival, never reached the ghetto.[60] Completing the deportations was only a matter of time. In January 1943, Leo Baeck and other leaders of the Jewish community, the last remaining Jews, were deported to Theresienstadt. Exactly ten years after their seizure of power, the Nazis realized their plan of a Germany without Jews.

The deportation of the Jews from German towns belonged to a Third Reich tradition of anti-Jewish public actions. From January 1933 to November 1938 this tradition was characterized by local, popular, public, interpersonal violent actions against Jews that came from the locals as much as from the regime. Kristallnacht was the peak of this tradition, and the last significant such event. Thereafter, the number of Jews in Germany dwindled, and they disappeared from public sight. But the deportations continued this basic tradition (without the personal violence) while bringing it to a close: they were the last local, public, visible anti-Jewish actions in the Reich. They had other revealing characteristics. Even if the local police at times attempted to keep the deportations secret, local news spread quickly, the events took place in public, and, as the Security Service of the SS in Bielefeld reported, were "talked about in all sections of the population."[61] It is doubtful whether the local police actually wished to keep the deportations secret: they occurred in broad daylight, the local Jewish community received notification well in advance, and the local Gestapo knew of it even before that in order to prepare the logistics. These were not the makings of a covert operation.

Everywhere the deportations raised great interest. Scores of curious locals assembled at the gathering site of the Jews, which was often the center of town; in small Lemgo near Detmold, Nazis, Jews, and many locals gathered in the town's marketplace. Many others lined the streets as the Jews made their way through town. Herta Rosenthal, sixteen years old, recounted the deportation from Leipzig to Riga in January 1942 when "everybody saw it. . . . All the Jews were leaving Leipzig and they [the Germans] were happy, a lot of them. They were standing there laughing. . . . They brought us up during the day, not at night."[62] Photographs show how public was the sending off of local Jews in a parade of humiliation. In Hamburg the parade of the Jews from the Jews' House was accompanied by cheering schoolchildren, while the Jews were then paraded on trucks to the applause of the crowd. After the deportation of November 29, 1941, in Nuremberg, local Nazis including their secretaries and cleaning ladies organized a small party with drinks, snacks, and dancing while dividing up the items found in the stolen bags of the evacuated Jews.[63] Goebbels planned on filming the deportation in Berlin, while those in Nuremberg and Stuttgart were filmed by the local authorities in November 1941. The deportation in Bad Neustadt was filmed in a long series of pictures by local Nazis, who took souvenir photos on site before leading the Jews to the train station. Enlarged photographs of the event were later hung in the center of town.[64]

The deportations became an important part of the evolving local and national Heimat history of the end of the Jews in Germany. Local historians made the deportations into the last chapter of the history of the Jews in the Heimat. The deportation in Bielefeld on December 13, 1941, was photographed in twenty-six pictures with permission of the Gestapo for a project of local historians entitled "War Chronicle of Bielefeld." The Jews were transported to the train station during the day on buses hired from the local bus company; a truck followed with their bags and suitcases. Their destination, Riga. In Eisenach, as well, the deportation was photographed for a book recording the history of the town during the war.[65] Chronicles like these had been a familiar feature of local identity since the early nineteenth century and were an integral part of Heimat history, developing since the unification in 1871 as the essence of local identity. They chronicled the important events in the life of the community.

The parade, the participation of children, the public mockery, the photographs—all these were essential elements of prewar anti-Jewish actions. The public humiliation of Jews in German localities followed a script from 1933 through the deportations in 1941–1943. Germans knew this script and followed it as they deported the Jews. It was familiar and recognizable, and it enabled them to place the deportations within the story of the local community and the nation. They thus owned the deportations and made them their own. Each deportation was recognized as an important event in the life of the community and therefore a historic topic worthy of being documented. The script included not only those Germans who actively acted against Jews but also those who kept silent or who opposed what was happening. Not all Germans took part in the public deportations. Indeed, as on Kristallnacht, most did not. But they knew and understood what happened and were thus complicit.

It is precisely because locals knew the script of Jewish humiliation of previous years that they perceived the deportations as something particular that deviated from the usual anti-Jewish measures. It was not violence that made the deportations special, for they were not accompanied by systematic brutality or bloodshed. On the contrary, they were all very organized, all sides played their part, including the helpless Jews, and they often transpired in silence as the Jews marched along the town's streets watched by locals. But locals knew they were witnessing a finality, a dramatic act in local, German, and Jewish history. After years of persecution, no one in the community could mistake the meaning of deporting the Jews to the East. Who could imagine building a new life with one suitcase in tow? The awed silence was fitting. The distribution of Jewish property made these sentiments tangible. Some helped themselves to the property with no moral qualms. For others, the looting raised a sense of guilt as they refused to take anything lest "they will have no peace anymore," as one woman in the Swabian village of Baisingen said. Still others took care to keep a material object owned by the Jews as an elegiac souvenir reminding them of their former neighbors in a world of yesteryear.[66]

The deportations may have had a role in the anti-Jewish decrees of 1942. One would think that in 1942, when the Nazi policy of deportations and extermination was in full swing, local decrees against the Jews would stop. But this did not quite happen. The Jews continued to haunt the imagination, now perhaps more than before precisely because locals knew the meaning of the deportations and many in Germany knew of the murders in the East. In most of Germany there were no Jews anymore, and still:

Dwellings of Jews are to be marked with a star. Jews are forbidden to keep pets. Jews are prohibited from using the services of German barbers and hairdressers. Jews are to hand over their shaving tools, combs, and scissors. Jewish schools are closed. Jews are not issued ration cards for eggs, tobacco, wheat flour, white bread, milk, fish, meat, and fresh fruits and vegetables. Blind Jews are not allowed to wear the usual yellow armband to prevent Germans coming to their assistance. The sale of newspapers, journals, and periodicals to Jews is prohibited. Jews are prohibited from visiting Aryans in their homes. Jews are prohibited from buying articles of clothing of the traditional German regional and national costumes. Jews are prohibited from using ticket machines in stations. Jews are prohibited from praying in the coming High Holidays. Jews are prohibited from buying books. Jews are prohibited from buying cakes.[67]

There was another reason why locals sensed that the deportations were a final act. A stream of information on the mass massacres in the East coming from soldiers and state and party officials on the front had flooded Germany after June 1941. Even though the deportations were not reported in the press and radio or mentioned in speeches by Hitler and Goebbels when they began in October 1941, there was a dramatic increase of public anti-Semitic rhetoric in the fall of 1941 and winter of 1942, not least by Hitler. The Nazis made things quite clear about the future of the Jews and the proper behavior expected by Germans toward them. After reports of acts of sympathy toward Jews following the introduction of the yellow Star of David, Goebbels announced on October 24, 1941, special punishments for "Jewish-friendly behavior" that could amount in extreme cases to three months in a concentration camp. The decree was printed on a black page with a yellow star reading, "Germans, this is your mortal enemy," and was distributed to every household in Germany together with the monthly food ration cards.

Throughout 1942 the Reich was swamped by information, rumors, tales, and anecdotes of what was happening to the Jews. State and party officials were especially well informed. Colonel Ernst Ebeling, stationed in Hamburg, wrote on March 22, 1942, that "[one knows] what was done for example with the deported Jews of Hamburg that were supposed to reach a ghetto in the East. They were gunned down en masse by Latvian soldiers eight kilometers [five miles] from Smolensk."[68] But simple folk with no special access to information were also well informed. Herman Frielings-dort, a craftsman from Hamburg, wrote in his diary on July 19, 1942: "In recent weeks the last Jews in Hamburg have been deported, where to—no one knows. But lurid stories circulate among the people. The Jews are said to be killed in large groups, including women and children, by mass executions in open graves or in open fields. . . . One can hardly bear hearing of such horrors. . . . Our deeds cry to heaven."[69]

Victor Klemperer, in his state of social isolation in Dresden's Jews' House, first heard of Auschwitz in March 1942. "In the last few days," he noted on March 16, "I heard Auschwitz (or something like it) near Königshütte in Upper Silesia, mentioned as the most dreadful concentration camp. Work in a mine, death within a few days. Kornblum, the father of Frau Seligsohn, died there, likewise—not known to me—Stern and Müller." This description was surprisingly accurate, given that in March 1942 Auschwitz was just becoming an extermination center. On Saturday, October 17, 1942, late in the afternoon, he noted that it was a "swift-working slaughter-house."[70]

Such knowledge was not an exception. On Tuesday morning, June 1, 1943, Klemperer noted what he heard about the April Warsaw ghetto uprising:

On Sunday Lewinsky related as an entirely vouched for and widespread rumor (originating with soldiers): there had been a bloodbath in Warsaw, revolt by Poles and Jews, German tanks had been destroyed by mines at the entrance of the Jewish town, whereupon the Germans had shot the whole ghetto to pieces—fires burning for days and many thousands of dead. Yesterday I asked several people at Schlüter about it. Widespread reply: yes, they, too, had heard the same or similar, but had not dared pass it on. Eva, coming from the dentist, reported that Simon stated with certainty, 3000 German deserters had also taken part in the revolt, and that battles lasting weeks (!) had taken place before the Germans had mastered the situation.

Simon's credibility is limited. Nevertheless: *that* such rumors are in circulation is symptomatic. . . . Just at the right moment, Eva told me that there is a new poster in town—two people whispering to each other—with the caption: "Anyone who whispers, is lying."[71]

But the whispers, even if exaggerated and at times inaccurate, were not lies, and they made the regime and the Gestapo, which wanted to control the information, nervous. Germans heard news and scraps of information from family, relatives, friends, and coworkers in widespread social unofficial channels. They did not know about the "Holocaust" in the same way we know about it today. For a long time scholars have searched for the elusive "knowledge" about the "Holocaust"—how much Germans knew and when—but this in itself is a research topic driven by historians' post-1945 knowledge of what the Holocaust was, not by the experience of contemporaries. Germans did not know of the "Holocaust," but they did know of the massive slaughter of the Jews. This could not have been a secret: the combination of the incessant Nazi propaganda calling for Jews' extermination, the local deportations, and the stream of information from the occupied territories made the mass murder of the Jews a constant presence in the public sphere. In truth, the Nazis wanted not to conceal the facts of the Holocaust but to "manage" them.[72] For the Nazis the Holocaust was not and could not be a secret; rather, it was a precious fact that symbolized and touched on essential elements of their identity, history, and humanity. A fact of this magnitude could not simply be hidden, but given its transgression, it could not yet be revealed with total frankness either.

On one occasion the Nazis used the disguise of alleged rumors to spread the truth about the extermination. On April 30, 1942, the *Völkischer Beobachter* ran an article by its war correspondent, a man named Schaal, about operations in the East: "The rumor has spread among the population that it is the task of the Security Police to exterminate the Jews in the occupied territories. The Jews were assembled in the thousands and shot; beforehand they had to dig their own graves. At times the execution of the Jews reached such proportions that even members of the Einsatzgruppen suffered nervous breakdowns."[73]

The extermination remained a deeply disturbing presence. One reason that *knowledge* is the wrong term to capture the mentality of Germans in the Reich with respect to the murder of the Jews is that it is too direct and cerebral; we should look in fact for sensibilities and emotions that are crucial but cannot quite be expressed openly. That the mass murder of the Jews was a transgression different from other murders perpetrated by the Nazis was clear to the public from the dissonance that emerged between the official attempt to manage the knowledge about the Jews, on the one hand, and the flow of information about what was happening, on the other. That which happened could not be named. The police and legal authorities were so concerned by the continuous spread of information after 1942 that speaking the truth about the killing of the Jews became telling "insidious horror-lies," a punishable offense. Something nasty was happening to the Jews, this much people knew, and whatever it was, people sensed, the regime deemed it transgressive enough to shroud it in mystery. Germans' attitude toward the mass killing was laden with emotions: fear, hatred, brutality, transgression, guilt, regrets, shame, and a hopeless attempt to repress. It was under these circumstances that Germany became a Reich of rumors about war, Germans, and the mass murder of the Jews.

Rumors about the Jews during the war came in two basic forms. One was typified by Hosenfeld, who wrote in July 1942:

> Rumors say that thirty thousand Jews are to be taken from the ghetto this week and sent east somewhere. In spite of all the secrecy people say they know what happens then: Somewhere not far from Lublin, buildings have been constructed with rooms that can be electrically heated with strong current similar to the electricity in a crematorium. Unfortunate people are driven into these heated rooms and burned alive. Thousands can be killed like that in a day, thus saving all the trouble of shooting them, digging mass graves, and then filling them in. The guillotine of the French Revolution can't compete, and even in the cellars of the Russian secret police they hadn't devised such virtuoso methods of mass slaughter. But surely this is madness.[74]

Rumors like this, denoting the mystery and unbelievability of the extermination, focused on what was happening to the Jews. They started in 1942
and their impact depended on the course of the war. As long as Germans
still thought they were going to win, they evaluated this information as a
fait accompli. Some thought the Jews got what they deserved. Many registered various levels of moral or tactical discomfort, but the anticipated
victory assuaged misgivings. A Germany without Jews had already been a
reality, and if one were to believe the rumors, a Europe without Jews would
soon be one, too.

The other type surfaced in 1943, when Germany began to lose the
war and the Allied air bombing devastated German cities and brought the
war home. Now the extermination was viewed in a very different light,
and the air bombing was rumored to be a Jewish retaliation and payback.
"Our entire position on the Jewish problem," challenged a homeless
Frankfurt resident and official of the Security Service, "especially the solution to this problem, has been the ground for the results and repercussions
the German people must today pay for. Had one left the Jews in Germany,
no bombs would have fallen on Frankfurt today."[75] Rumors like this
focused on what happened to Germans because of what they had done to
the Jews. On one level the new rumors reflected the internalization of Nazi
anti-Semitic propaganda in the belief that the Jews controlled the war
effort against Germany. But on another level the rumors reflected a guilty
conscience and the fear of revenge emerging from a lucid sensibility that
Germany's policy toward the Jews ended in mass murder.

In previous centuries, rumors about Jews posed the Jew as the murderer, often of children for alleged ritual purposes. As a social occurrence,
anti-Jewish rumors had a formula consisting of origins, dissemination,
and the threat of mob violence. But Germans' rumors during the war
about the murder of the Jews were different: they were not about what the
Jews did to "us" but about what "we" did to them; not about the guilt of
Jews but about the guilt of Germans. They had an origin and a dissemination, but no conclusion in anti-Jewish mob violence. In general, rumors
emerge in a state of curiosity and mystery, and they are a mixture of fable
and reality. The rumors about how the Jews were being exterminated, with
stories that at times were accurate and at other times fantasy tales, had an
important cultural function: they made the unimaginable stories of the

extermination imaginable; they gave the events a narrative framework. They entered the cultural space between the frequent yelling of Nazi propaganda about exterminating the Jews and the deep official ambiguity about speaking of the actual policy of extermination, about what happened in Auschwitz and Treblinka. In this respect, rumors about the extermination emerged because enough was known about the act to engender a sense of breaking a taboo, while at the same time the rumor put this taboo in words to make it understandable. The rumors reflected a profound doubt about the official representation of truth about the Jews. They are thus evidence in the hand of the historian that Germans palpably sensed that something horrendously immoral was happening to the Jews.

Germans told rumors about the mass murder of the Jews that made them into perpetrators and victims all at once. By producing rumors that undermined official announcements, they distanced themselves from the regime. By arguing that the solution to the Jewish Question was the reason for the bombing, they admitted responsibility and guilt. By blaming the Jews for the air raids, they emphasized their own suffering and victimhood. But even in blaming the Jews, they showed the raw awareness of guilt, for they placed their own suffering within a sense of fear of the consequences of what they had done and condoned.

The background to the Germans' new preoccupation with their recent anti-Jewish actions, as well as to the increased rumors, was the turning point in the war at the end of 1942, when Germany lost two crucial military battles. In North Africa, the German forces under the command of Field Marshal Erwin Rommel lost to the British army of Field Marshal Bernard Montgomery at El Alamein in November 1942. The defeat ended Hitler's dream of seizing control of the Middle East and its oil fields from the British Empire as well as of advancing in a pincer move toward the Soviet oil fields in the Caucasus. Soon thereafter came the devastating defeat at Stalingrad in the winter of 1942–1943. The German southern army attacked the Caucasus with an eye to the oil fields. The German Sixth Army under General Friedrich von Paulus struck Stalingrad. The campaign was of unparalleled brutality. It is estimated that it cost Germany 300,000 men and the Soviet Union 470,000 dead soldiers (the American losses in the entire war were 418,000). On January 31, 1943, Paulus capitulated.

The defeat ended any hope of winning against the Russians. Equally criti-
cal was its impact on public morale in Germany. In spite of Goebbels's
relentless propaganda, many Germans now began to doubt the possibility
of a Nazi victory.

The losses at El Alamein and Stalingrad, together with the landing
of Allied forces in Morocco and Algeria in November 1942, left Germany
effectively without a military strategy, although it still occupied most of
the Continent. Strategically, the war was over. Germany's forces could not
successfully conclude the war on their own. They could not deliver victory. All Hitler and the Wehrmacht could promise was war until the bitter
end. That is what happened. For another two and a half years Germany
fought a desperate battle that became ever more radical and destructive.
Unable to start any significant operation, the Wehrmacht could only react
to military events initiated by the Allies.

Following Stalingrad, Soviet troops soon regained Kursk, Rostov,
Charkov (Ukraine's second largest city), and Rzhev, located a hundred
miles west of Moscow. On November 6, 1943, the Red Army reclaimed
Kiev. The slow, step-by-step westward advance of the Red Army, which
would end in Berlin in April 1945, was no longer stoppable. In the southern
Mediterranean, the Allies started their invasion of Axis-controlled Europe
with landings on the island of Sicily on July 10, 1943. Mussolini was over-
thrown several days later. On June 6, 1944, the Allies landed in Normandy
to open a second front in Europe. It took another eleven months to end
the war, largely because the German soldiers fought with incredible tenacity until the end. Germany had no chance of winning, but during this
period, according to estimates, three million German soldiers died, a futile
death in a fanatic war.

The war would be lost, but no hurdle could stop the deportation of
Jews from across the Continent. Klemperer and his acquaintances in the
Jews' House had no doubt about that. On October 23, 1942, he recorded in
his diary: "One can conclude how bad things look for the National Socialist
cause. But all conversations among Jews again and again lead to the same
reflection: 'If they have the time, they'll kill us first.' One said to Frau
Ziegler yesterday: He felt like a calf at the slaughterhouse, looking on, as
the other calves are slaughtered, and waiting his turn. The man is right."
Jews understood the bitter truth, but the heart refused to believe, grasping

at any available scrap of hope. A month earlier, on September 21, Klemperer wrote: "Today is Yom Kippur, and this very day the last 26 'old people' are sitting in the Community House, from where they will be transported early tomorrow. So on Saturday afternoon we made our farewell visit to [them]." The friends scheduled for deportation left things behind, and Klemperer received a jacket and a vest. Frau Arendt, an Aryan friend, brought cakes, and there was "real tea." "'Funeral meal,'" said Klemperer, to which Neumann, among those to be deported, answered, "'Yes and no.' [To which Klemperer answered to himself,] On the one hand, the corpses themselves were there. On the other they were really going into a beyond, from which as yet there had been no reliable news." Then he ended with the following words: "The mood of Jewry here is without exception the same. The terrible end is imminent. *They* will perish, but perhaps, probably, they will have time to annihilate us first."[76]

The Nazis' decrees confirmed that. Only a handful of anti-Jewish laws were passed in 1943 and 1944, but two of them significantly reflect Nazi policies and state of mind. A main decree of 1943 was: *The German press is required to discuss the Jewish problem relentlessly.* A decree of March 1944 simply stated the fact that, eleven years after the seizure of power, Germany was without Jews: *The evacuation and isolation of the Jews and gypsies, now implemented, has made the publication of special orders and decrees, as previously practiced, meaningless, and such publication should cease.*[77]

The Nazis acted to replicate this condition all across Europe. A bowshot's distance from the pope's residence in Saint Peter's Square, on October 16, 1943, shortly after the occupation of Rome, the Germans arrested 1,030 Jews, among them some 200 children under the age of ten, and sent them two days later from the Tiburtina railway station to Auschwitz. Fifteen survived the war. A bowshot from Michelangelo's *David*, 311 Jewish residents from Florence and Siena, as well as Jews from other locations who hid in the countryside, were deported in November 1943 and on June 6, 1944, from Santa Maria Novella railway station. Fifteen returned. Of the twenty-seven children who were deported, none survived; the youngest was Fiorella Calà, born on September 1, 1943, and barely four months old when "arrested" with her family. Today, a plaque commemorates the deportations right at the start of platform 6.[78]

In Hungary in mid-May 1944 the authorities in coordination with the Germans began deporting the Jews; 440,000 were deported in 145 trains, mostly to Auschwitz. Then, three days after the Allies landed in Normandy, on June 9, 1944, the Germans found the presence of mind to deport the Jews from the remote Mediterranean island of Corfu. The Jewish community, existing in good number from the fourteenth century, included Sephardic Jews from Greece, Spain, and southern Italy. Their deportation could not assist the military effort. Indeed, it hurt this effort because it demanded special gasoline for boats that was very expensive. But on June 7, 1944, the Allies entered Rome, the German hold on Corfu seemed short-lived, and they did not want to leave the island with the Jewish community alive. On Friday at 5:00 a.m. the Germans knocked on every Jewish door on the island. The entire community, 2,000 people, was assembled in the main square. Allied planes hovered above, but the Germans continued. The Jews were forced to surrender their valuables and hand over the keys to their homes, which the Germans later looted, selling what they did not want to locals. Several days afterward the Jews were placed on barges pulled by motorboats and transported first to Patras and then to Athens, where they were put in cattle cars bound for Auschwitz. Ninety-one percent of the Jews of Corfu died in the Holocaust.[79]

The collection of Judaica also continued. A report of the Institute for Research on the Jewish Question from November 28, 1944, noted that materials had just been received from Minsk and Rome.[80]

It was appropriate that the extermination, imagined as a sort of genesis in an apocalyptic war, was accompanied by a messianic prophecy. "I have often been a prophet in my life and I was mostly laughed at," thundered the prophet from Berlin in the Reichstag on January 30, 1939. "The Jewish people received with nothing but laughter my prophecy.... I want to be a prophet again today.... The result will be ... the annihilation of the Jewish race in Europe." There was only one prophecy in wartime German society, and it meant one thing: Hitler's promise to annihilate the Jews. In January 1939, the prophecy was still a declaration of purpose, but as the war developed and with it the mass murder of the Jews, it became a common, shared, universal idiom among Germans and Jews to describe the evolving extermination.

Goebbels, the voice of the prophet, made this prophecy into a key metaphor in his writings and speeches about the Jews. He first confided to his diary on August 19, 1941: "The Führer believes that his past prophecy in the Reichstag is being confirmed." He then went public. He gave Germans a clear idea about the mass killings by informing them in an article published in *Das Reich* on November 16, 1941, that the prophecy was now in a stage of implementation: "We are seeing the fulfillment of the prophecy."[81] On December 1, he made a similar announcement to the German academy. Some two years later, on May 8, 1943, he interpreted the prophecy further in his article "The War and the Jews": "None of the Führer's prophetic words has come so inevitably true as his prediction that if Jewry succeeded in provoking a second world war, the result would be. . . . This process is of vast importance, and will have unforeseeable consequences that will take time. But it cannot be halted."[82]

Soldiers used the prophecy to describe and justify the mass murder in letters to relatives at home: "One particular chapter is the fact that the Jewish question is being solved at present with massive thoroughness," wrote one soldier from the Eastern Front in August 1941. "As the Führer indeed said in his speech shortly before the beginning of the war: 'If Jewry. . . . ' "[83] The prophecy appeared in army newsletters and other propaganda writings. One such publication, an army newsletter for the Mosel region, explained in November 1941 the difference between metaphor and reality: "[The prophecy] was a hard, pitiless statement that many did not take seriously[,] interpreting it only in an allegorical manner. But the Jews knew that a death warrant stood behind this prophecy and that it would inevitably come to pass if plutocracy and Bolshevism one day collapsed and were replaced by a new world order."[84]

For Jews, regardless of their religious or secular inclinations, prophecies were part of a cultural heritage, and the one from Berlin was listened to very carefully. "The day before yesterday we read the speech of the 'leader' in connection to the commemoration of January 30, 1933," wrote Chaim Kaplan in the Warsaw ghetto on February 2, 1942, with respect to Hitler's speech at the Berlin Sportpalast referring to the Jews as the world's most evil enemy. "He boasted that his prophecy is beginning to come true: had he not said that if a war would break out in Europe the Jewish people would be annihilated? *This process has already begun and will continue until the end is reached....* There is [in Hitler's words] a sort of justification to the whole world. But in particular there is a hint to us that all the stories about the atrocities are not wild rumors but true and existing facts."[85]

The prophet himself, of course, used the idiom in his dialogue with Germans throughout the war, especially in key speeches and declarations that were closely followed in Germany and the world. Hitler used it on at least seven occasions to inform and interpret for Germans what was happening to the Jews: in speeches commemorating the Nazi seizure of power on January 30 in 1941 and 1942; on Nazi Party Foundation Day on February 24, 1942; in the Berlin Sportpalast speech on October 1, 1942, and shortly thereafter at the Munich commemoration of the 1923 putsch on November 8, 1942; on February 25, 1943, several days after Goebbels's speech announcing total war; and in his New Year's speech of January 1, 1945. (Hitler explicitly mentioned the extermination of the Jews in public speeches and declarations at least a dozen times.)[86]

Hitler's use of the prophecy reveals a great deal about the imagination of the mass murder formed in Germany after 1941. The prophecy created a direct link between the war and the mass murder of the Jews. During the war Hitler moved the date of the prophecy from January 1939 to September 1, his declaration of the war before the Reichstag. The soldier cited above also got the date wrong, linking it to the beginning of the war. Whether Hitler confused the dates or changed them intentionally, the meaning was the same: in this war, the Jews would perish.

The prophecy created an important link with the anti-Jewish imagination of the prewar years. Its emotional context was rooted in the period around Kristallnacht (and whether Germans remembered this chronological fact or thought the prophecy was given in September 1939 was irrelevant to its emotional impact). The prophecy reiterated shared emotions about the Jews, such as anger, mockery, vengeance, sarcasm, and brutality, that in the past had already created an emotional link between Hitler and Germans. The recent deportations revealed similar emotions. Hitler thus shared with his audience in the years 1941–1945 new, radical information by placing it within a shared, familiar narrative. In arguing this I do not wish to place Hitler as an all-powerful agent who shaped culture but stood outside of it. He was as much part of his culture as he had a decisive role in shaping it. He, too, looked to find the right words to tell Germans clearly enough, as well as to tell himself, about a policy that could not be named. It is significant that he chose to articulate to his fellow Germans the mass murder of the Jews during the war with a prophetic speech from the period before the war.

Hitler used the prophecy to inform Germans of new stages in the murder of the Jews. In 1942, the peak year of the Holocaust, he communicated to Germans the extermination of the Jews no fewer than four times. On February, 24, 1942, Hitler for the first time said that the war might be lost but that the Jewish Problem nonetheless would be solved: "My prophecy will be fulfilled that in this war not the Aryans will be exterminated but the Jew will be eradicated. Whatever the battle will bring, or how long it may last, this will be the ultimate legacy of this war." The element of Jewish laughter was important. On October 1, 1942, he announced that some who formerly laughed do not laugh anymore: "The Jews in Germany once also laughed about my prophecy. I don't know whether they still laugh today or whether the laugh already died away. I can also now simply assure [you]: their laugh will die away everywhere. And I shall be proven right also with this prophecy." A week later, Hitler announced in a witty sentence the extermination as a fact: "Of those who once laughed, scores do not laugh today, and those who still laugh, will probably soon enough also not do so anymore." The leader and his audience in the hall were as one: the crowd of party officials burst into wide laughter and applause as everybody got the joke.[87]

As the military situation became increasingly desperate, so Hitler's declaration about the Final Solution became clearer: he informed Germans about the extermination of the Jews not as a propaganda, threat, or future plan but as a fact that had been happening. On January 3, 1944, he declared that although the end of war was not clear, the end of Jewish life in Europe was "beyond any doubt."[88]

The prophecy shaped a sensibility of guessing and suspecting, of presentiments and allusions, that together made the extermination quite clear. Hitler and other Germans made frequent use of the prophecy precisely because it spoke to an element of life that could not be named but was nonetheless massively present. By making it into a common idiom in wartime society, Germans showed that they understood very well the mass murder of the Jews. After the war Germans claimed that they had not known about Auschwitz, thus dividing the world into those who knew and those who did not. But life is more complex. Many indeed did not know the details about the extermination in Auschwitz but still understood clearly that Germans had been bringing Jewish history to an end. By understanding the meaning of the prophecy, Germans became complicit, whatever they knew about Auschwitz and whatever they thought about the extermination.

The war drew to a close. Nazism was defeated on all fronts. In the West, the British and Americans liberated Paris in August 1944 and Brussels in September. On March 7, 1945, American troops crossed the Rhine River at Remagen. The road to central Germany was open. In the East, the great Soviet offensive in January 1945 on the front from East Prussia to southern Poland crushed the Wehrmacht; the road to Berlin was open. Auschwitz was liberated on January 27. But the Wehrmacht fought with renewed, suicidal tenacity. In January 1945, the number of German soldiers killed in a single month reached its apogee—over 450,000; in each of the following three months the number of German military killed exceeded 280,000, which is much more than the 185,000 Wehrmacht soldiers who died in January 1943, the month of the German defeat at Stalingrad.[89]

The war against the Jews also knew no letup. Germans in Schwerin followed closely the occupation of Budapest and the fate of its Jews in May 1944. They were outspokenly brutal in support of anti-Jewish measures: "The SS is already succeeding in taking care of the Jews!"[90]

Victor Klemperer's prediction that the Nazis would perish but would still have time to annihilate the Jews first seemed to have become a reality. In the first months of 1945 the Nazis found time for a handful of anti-Jewish decrees. One of them deported Jews who had been spared before because they could work and were married to Aryans:

January 10: Bad Kreuznach's Gestapo headquarters: Jews who live in mixed marriages and are able to work are to be deported to Theresienstadt.

This decree had direct consequences for Klemperer. Though the end of the war was in sight, on February 12, 1945, the remaining Jews of Dresden were ordered to report for labor duty in three days' time. The destination was probably Theresienstadt. Klemperer was not included in this transport, although he was one of those who delivered the orders. Among those summoned were children under the age of ten. Everyone knew that the summons meant death; Klemperer expected to be included in the following transport. On the night of February 13, however, an Anglo-American air raid reduced Dresden to rubble, including the Gestapo headquarters—with all its offices, files, and lists. Most city Jews survived the attack. They removed their yellow stars and destroyed documents that identified them as Jews. "I sat in restaurants," Klemperer wrote on February 19, "I traveled by train and tram—as a Jew in the Third Reich all of it punishable by death. I constantly told myself, who could recognize me."[91] The link between summoning the Jews and bombing Dresden was not a contingency of major historical importance, but for Victor Klemperer on that day it meant the world.

Germans now faced a commingling of their continuous knowledge of the crime, vain attempts at denial and repression, and nightmares of revenge and punishment. In fact, Germans had been thinking about the fate of the Jews and about their own fate for some time now. From 1942, the combination of the increased rumors about the fate of the Jews in the East and the devastating Allied air raids at home led many Germans to search for meaning. Sentiments of victimhood and guilt coexisted in shifting proportions. As they looked back at the Third Reich's anti-Jewish policies, many viewed one event in particular as the cause of Germany's suffering at the air raids. After Frankfurt was bombed in 1943 evacuees saw the bombing as "retaliation to the nth degree for the Jewish action of 1938."[92] Local sources confirm that Kristallnacht came to represent a moral turning point because, as one person put it, "with this action Germany began the terror against the Jews."[93] Some Germans viewed the destruction of the churches in the bombed cities as retribution for the destruction of the synagogues. When Würzburg was spared following a spate of air raids on German cities, some inhabitants in Ochsenfurt, a town some twelve miles south of the city, believed that it was because "in Würzburg no synagogues were burned."[94]

Since September 1939 Germans had perpetrated atrocities against Jews that were infinitely more horrible than having burned synagogues in November 1938. Why of all events did Kristallnacht come to represent a key meaning of Nazi anti-Semitism? People often perceive abstract, big ideas in a local, experiential way: Kristallnacht was the last local, public, violent anti-Semitic action in the Reich, actively participated in by many, and it was a way to link one's memory to the wider case. Many Germans also thought that Kristallnacht was the first violent deviation from a justifiable policy of anti-Jewish discrimination in 1933–1938 that removed Jews from professions, citizenship, and public life.

But there is more to it. The rumors that linked the air raids, the murder of the Jews, and Kristallnacht contained no explicit racial ideas. What gave meaning to Germans' suffering and guilt in this case were the attacks against the synagogues. By referring to Kristallnacht, Germans showed that they knew they had been the aggressors in the campaign against the Jews and that their crime against the Jews, which had earned them such fury from the skies, was at least in part the attempt to eradicate the Jew as a historical, moral, religious being.

Fear from past deeds was tangible. One soldier wrote to his wife on August 27, 1944:

> Mami, I want to write you something and please don't laugh. . . . The war is going to end soon, but not for us, I think. You surely know that the Jew will carry on a bloody revenge, in particular against Party members. I was unfortunately also one of those who wore Party uniforms. I already regret this. I plead with you to stash the uniforms away. No matter where and when, burn the whole thing. I can no longer sleep at night because of this matter. It worries me so much, you cannot imagine.[95]

In January 1945, the SS organ, *Das Schwarze Korps,* ran an unusual article, in veiled language, on the fate of the Jews and the responsibility of German society. With respect to the Jews, stated the paper, "Basically, no one in Germany is 'not guilty.'" The piece contained an element of self-exculpation, but also one of truth. Everyone in Germany during the war could imagine the fate that awaited the Jews. The statement reflected a moment of heightened self-consciousness that came with defeat and anxiety.[96]

After the landing in Normandy, Aachen was the first German city to fall into Allied hands in October 1944. Cologne surrendered on March 6, 1945. Rumors spread in both cities and as far as Berlin of Jewish revenge against Germans. It was told that in retaliation for the yellow star, Jews assembled local Nazi leaders, had their heads shaved, and marched them through the streets of town in a parade of humiliation.[97]

Epilogue
A World with Jews

The war ended, sorting out lives and fates. The Germans now faced a world without Nazism but with Jews. Hitler committed suicide in Berlin on April 30, 1945; Goebbels and his wife, Magda, after arranging to kill their six children, on May 1; Himmler, while in British custody, on May 23; and Göring, sentenced to death at the Nuremberg Trials, on October 15, 1946, a day before he was to be hanged. Walter Frank, the historian and president of the Reich Institute for History of the New Germany, committed suicide on May 9, believing that the world no longer held meaning.

Good deeds were not necessarily rewarded. Wilm Hosenfeld was captured by the Soviets and sentenced to twenty-five years' hard labor for war crimes committed by his unit. Jews and others pleaded his case, but the Soviets refused to change the sentence. He died in captivity in 1952.

Others fared much better as they reinvented themselves to fit the new circumstances. Otmar von Verschuer, after a distinguished academic career in the Third Reich propagating racial science, presented himself following the war as a genetic researcher, receiving in 1951 the professorship of human genetics at the University of Münster. He was honored by the German scientific community after his death in a car accident in 1969. His best-known assistant, Josef Mengele, disappeared after the war. Eugen

Fischer, Verschuer's teacher, retired in 1942 and continued to hold his views about racial anthropology. After the war he wrote a memoir that made no mention of the link between his theories and Nazi atrocities. In 1952, he was made an honorary member of the German Anthropological Society. He died in 1967. Johannes Pohl also showed resourcefulness, deleting the most anti-Semitic writings from his publications list and using a pseudonym to sign his new writings. A frequent contributor to the journal of the Catholic German Association of the Holy Land, he obtained a position at Duden publishing house in Wiesbaden. He died in 1960.

Siegfried Leffler, who wondered how to exterminate the Jews with minimal emotional tribulation, was held in a Denazification prison between 1945 and 1948. He then entered the service of the Protestant Church in Bavaria, serving as a priest in Hengersberg until his retirement in 1970. A year later he received the town's highest civil award. He died in 1983. His boss at the Institute for the Study and Eradication of Jewish Influence on German Church Life, Walter Grundmann, remained in East Germany and held various important theological and teaching positions, although his professorship was taken away because of his activity in the Third Reich. In the Regional Church of Thuringia Grundmann was responsible for the theological education of priests: his task was to teach the Bible. He retired in 1975. Church authorities conferred an honorary title on him to acknowledge his work and to enable him to claim a larger pension. After the fall of East Germany in 1990, it was discovered that he was an informer for the Stasi, the communist regime's secret police.

Jews had very different life stories. Betty Scholem emigrated to Sydney, Australia, in March 1939. She joined her sons, Reinhold and Erich, who had already emigrated there with their families in the summer of 1938. She wrote Gershom on April 26, 1941: "Gerhard, I'm fascinated by the news of your book and your other scholarly activities. If I could, I'd have come to hear you speak about the secrets of this world and the next! I'm enormously interested in the Messiah—though I think he should hurry up. I regret to say it, but for now the only one in charge down here is his powerful antagonist."[1]

Arnold Zweig left Berlin's Opera Square and Germany to spend the war years in Palestine. Disillusioned with Zionism, he turned to socialism, moving in 1948 to East Germany and dying in 1968 in East Berlin. Joseph

Roth also left Nazi Germany, spending most of the 1930s in Paris, where he died prematurely in 1939. Victor Klemperer, having survived the bombing of Dresden, became a leading cultural figure in East Germany, where he died in 1960. His diary was published in 1995 to great acclaim.

For most of the Jews we have encountered in these pages, the war meant death, but not before they told their story. Emanuel Ringelblum, the leader of the Warsaw ghetto historical archive Oyneg Shabes, escaped with his family shortly before the ghetto uprising. The Gestapo discovered their hiding place on March 7, 1944, and he and his family, together with those who hid them, were executed amid the ruins of the ghetto. When it became clear that the Jews were destined for total extermination, the Warsaw ghetto archive was concealed in milk churns and thrice hidden in 1942 and 1943. The first section of the archive was found on September 18, 1946, the second on December 1, 1950. The third has never been found.

The diary of Abraham Lewin was found in those milk churns, fragmented, part in 1946 and part in 1950; another section of the diary was only recently identified.[2] Lewin's wife, Luba, was deported to Treblinka in 1942; he died in the ghetto or was deported to Treblinka along with his fifteen-year-old daughter, Ora, sometime in January 1943. Josef Zelkowicz was deported to Auschwitz in August 1944 together with the remaining sixty-five thousand Jews in the Lodz ghetto. One of the Jews who was left behind by the Nazis to clean up in the eerie, deserted ghetto, Nachman Sonabend, took advantage of the opportunity and hid most of the ghetto archive, with which Zelkowicz had been active. Twenty-seven notebooks of his diary were found after the war together with a rich collection of documents, diaries, and photographs. Oskar Rosenfeld wrote the last entry in his diary at the Lodz ghetto on July 28, 1944, just before the final deportation; he was transported to Auschwitz in August. His diary, twenty-one Polish school notebooks, was buried in early August by his friend Moishe Lewkowicz, who retrieved it in the summer of 1945. Lewkowicz kept the diary until his death in 1970, bequeathing it to a writer friend in Australia who then donated it to Yad Vashem in Jerusalem in 1973.

Noemi Szac Wajnkranc survived the Warsaw ghetto, where she lost her parents and husband. In the last days of the war she joined a unit of the Red Army that entered liberated Lodz. A stray bullet hit her and she died. Her diary was taken to Moscow by a Jewish Soviet officer and then found its way back to Poland, where it was published in 1947. Fela Szeps survived the death march from her labor camp Grünberg in Silesia. She died of exhaustion and hunger one day after her liberation. The diary she kept with her for four years was collected by her sister, who endured the war years with her. She brought it to Israel, where it was published.

Chaim Kaplan and his wife were murdered in Treblinka. The last line of his diary, written in the evening hours of August 4, 1942, reads: "If my life ends—what will become of my diary?"

An unexpected protagonist has emerged in our story—the book, as a physical and profound object of meaning. I did not expect this when I started writing, but stories take on a life of their own. I recalled a text Franz Kafka, only twenty-one years old, wrote to his friend in January 1904:

> I think one should absolutely read only those books that bite and sting. If the book we are reading does not wake us up with a fist to the skull, then why read this book? So that it would make us happy, as you write? My God, we would also be happy even if we had no books, and those books that make us happy we could ourselves write when needed. Instead, we need books whose impact on us is like a disaster that causes us much pain, like the death of someone we love more than ourselves, like being driven into the woods far away from any living soul, like a suicide; a book must be the ax for the frozen sea within us. That is what I believe.[3]

We read these words with an almost physical sense of pain. Kafka was uncompromising, only partly because of the radicalism that accompanies youth. I have to disagree, in part. Of course books offer us hope, happiness, even a smile and a laugh, that enrich our life. Books can and should offer hope as well as a painful punch; there is no reason to limit the impact of books to one attitude at the expense of the other. But Kafka was of course insightful that books and stories shape our innermost identities. Nazis and Jews shared a belief in the power of the book and in the necessity of stories to give meaning to life. That is why the Nazis wanted to destroy the Jewish Bible, history, and memory, and why Jews clung to them.

Stories give life, and stories kill as well.

Now that we have told our story, an overall meaning of the Holocaust emerges in surprisingly clear fashion. In the Holocaust, the Nazis defined and attempted to solve the problem of the origins of historical evil. All the problems of the world, from the dawn of humanity via the time of ancient Christianity, of Germany in the Middle Ages, and finally to the modern period were caused by one group, the Jews. The Jews were intrinsically evil; moral corruption, decay and degeneration, and, in the modern world, communism, capitalism, and liberalism were all inherently Jewish. The Nazis thus offered a modern salvation worldview that defined evil lucidly and consistently: significantly, it did this by blending science, morality, and identity, that is, by mixing modern race theories, moral religious sentiments associated with a tradition of Christianity, and key elements of Heimat and German national identity.

Nazism, like all great modern ideologies, promised redemption, but unlike Marxism and liberalism, it defined the origins of evil in a sharp, clearly understandable way.[4] Marxism located evil in the vague story of the alienation of labor and mode of production. It promised to eradicate historical evil, but the journey to achieve redemption—via the predestined historical journey that would bring about a classless society—was always obscure about the specific role of the individual in this process.

Liberalism located evil in political tyranny, a concept that applied more successfully to the modern world than to history as a whole and could never be clear-cut because it depended on shifting ideas of what "tyranny" meant. It promised a redemption of sorts via personal self-fulfillment and the pursuit of happiness, but its failure to provide a clear moral and social map of how to behave ultimately burdened the modern individual with the primary responsibility for attaining his or her own happiness, a task that could never be wholly fulfilled and caused a concomitant sense of personal failure and guilt.

We should add Freud and psychoanalysis to this discussion. Freudianism located evil in the individual inner self and offered a procedure to redress it but, like liberalism, offered no hope for social and political perfection. Evil could be negotiated but never eliminated.

Nazism shared with Marxism and Freudianism the commingling of transcendental revelation and the language of science; this was the source of their power. Made in the crucible of the twentieth century, they all offered implausible fantasies about human history, promising salvation in a classless or racially pure society or in the universal, timeless psychological traits of the human soul. Their conceptions of history also shared similarities. They all believed in their scientific credentials, in presenting a universal truth, and in discovering the essential element of history, be it class, biological heredity, or the psychic repetition in human history.

But Nazism went beyond Marxism, Freudianism, and liberalism by providing a secular solution to the problem of the origins of historical evil. It identified the devil in our own world, here and now, in a universe inhabited by human beings: a specific historical group of human beings, the Jews, thus became the first modern human devil (but not the last, alas). The Nazi mixture of past and present, tradition and innovation, gave this fantasy its power. The language of science lent modern legitimacy to the image of this devil, as did the linkage between Jews and all modern phenomena objectionable to the Nazis. But the power of tradition also determined the fantasy: Jews already belonged to a lengthy Christian, moral, and religious tradition that identified them with evil and whose defeat carried transcendental meaning. The Nazis thus gave a secular answer to the problem of original sin by combining the tradition of the sinful Jew with modern ideas about Jewish ideological corruption. This devil had a physical, tangible existence, and overcoming it through persecution and extermination was a doable, measurable task.

There was another significant difference between Nazism and Marxism, Freudianism, and liberalism. The three worldviews offered universal truths with the purpose of ameliorating the conditions of all human beings. Nazism was a German national movement that believed it had found universal truths, in race as the key to human history and in the Jews a worldwide, timeless devil, but its aim was to use these truths to offer a remedy only to Germans and at the expense of all others.

Here Nazism offered a fundamental break with Jewish and Christian traditions of the end of days as a wonderful, universal vision. Nazism rejected this tradition by offering a redemptive, wonderful vision only for Germans. It took elements prevalent in general German, European, and Christian culture—racial ideas about the origins of humankind, the importance of historical memory to national identity, the redemptive fight between good and evil, and a tradition of anti-Semitism—and mixed them anew, creating an idea of the German nation whose redemption was dependent on and justified the domination, enslavement, and extermination of other Europeans.

We can now articulate anew why several interpretations of the Holocaust, discussed in the Introduction, have been insufficient to explain the Nazi genocide of the Jews. The approach that has viewed the Holocaust as a result rather than a goal of Nazism, growing out of the specific circumstances of the war, can account neither for the consistent apocalyptic role of the Jews in the Nazi imagination nor for the Nazi urgency to kill all the Jews but not all the members of other persecuted groups. The same is true for the approach that has seen the Holocaust as a result of the linked genocidal policies of Hitler and Stalin in eastern Europe. These views ignore that—while the Holocaust was obviously a genocide that shared fundamental features with other genocides—the Nazis perceived it alone as offering them a solution to the problem of historical evil.

The interpretation that emphasized the redemptive character of Nazi racial ideology got a great deal right but did not capture the full emotional and identity depth of Nazi redemptive imagination about the Jews, which, as I have said, combined science with Christianity, past and present. Finally, the interpretation that viewed the Holocaust as produced by the accumulation of centuries of anti-Semitism got the relations of past and present wrong: it is not the past that produced the Nazi imagination but rather modern human beings in Germany in the 1930s and 1940s who, seeking an answer to the problem of evil in modern times, endowed their present with a novel meaning by reading anew the Jewish past.

There is one final reflection to raise about Nazism and Freud. There is of course a most fundamental difference between the two. Race (and class as well) was a state ideology in whose name millions were murdered. Attempting to realize its fantasy paved the way to an all-too-real human suffering. Now, at the dawn of a new century, the Nazi racial fantasy about human history is discredited beyond repair as a project for the improvement of the collectivity and of the individual. Freud's creation, in contrast, has killed no one, has offered emotional remedy to countless human beings, and has been and remained a mainstay of our culture. The "self," "memory," "repression," and "self-knowledge" are beliefs that do not enjoy the support of military divisions, of a state, secret police, and ministry of propaganda and official ideology, but they have remained pillars of our civilization. And they were also part and parcel of German and Nazi culture, of course. This was the territory the Nazis sought to explore in their quest for self-understanding and for their inner self, which they ultimately found in their endeavor to make a world without Jews.

Let us now imagine a different end to our story. After a battle of unparalleled fury, Germany won and now ruled the Continent in an empire that extended from Paris to Vladivostok. Most of the Jews had been murdered during the war, the remnants killed shortly thereafter. In a German and European world without Jews, how would the Jews be remembered, if at all?

It is a common view among scholars and laypeople that the Nazis committed a "memorycide" against the Jews, wishing to erase them from history and memory.[5] But the relation of memory and Nazism is layered with deeper meanings. This view is true when we consider the memorycide as the attempt by the Nazis to expunge Jewish history and memory as viewed by the Jews, as well as when we consider it as the Nazi attempt to sever the historical link of Judaism to Christian and European history. But it is wrong insofar as the Nazis wished, not to erase the Jews from history and memory, but rather to appropriate and rewrite their history, inscribing it with new meaning.

Thinking about the Holocaust as a Nazi memory project opens new ways to understand it. The topic of Holocaust memory *after* the Third Reich ended in 1945 has been of course a mainstay in our culture, represented in museums, commemorations, the arts, and scholarship. We know a tremendous amount about this topic, but this only begs the question: What were the Nazi ideas of time, history, and memory reflected in the persecution and extermination of the Jews *during* the Third Reich? In the Holocaust, the Nazis created new pasts to explain and justify their present. The Nazi project about the Jews was based, not on extermination aimed at forgetting the Jews, but on annihilation for the purpose of historical supersession, of replacing the Jews as holders of a certain historical authority. That is why the Nazis could not have just forgotten about the Jews after winning the war. For the Nazis, their historical existence and Jewish annihilation commingled in a way unlike their relations to any other victim group. With the Nazis victorious, the reasons and inhibitions that led to the secrecy about the murder of the Jews would have probably eased. Hitler is said to have thought of a monument to commemorate the extermination of Polish Jews. Even if the exact methods of Auschwitz may not have been publicly displayed (and we should consider that after the fact the Nazis may well have decided to speak openly about it), a museum modeled after the one in Prague would have most likely been established to showcase the Nazi victory over the evil Jews.

Remembering the Jews after the victorious war would have been important precisely because total liquidation of the Jew could not have been achieved by physical annihilation alone; it required as well the overcoming of Jewish memory and history. A win in the war would have extinguished the alleged power of world Jewry in the White House and the Kremlin and eliminated the Jewish racial menace from German society, but the Nazi struggle against the Jews was never principally about political and economic influence. It was over identity and was waged by means of Nazi appropriation of Jewish history, memory, and books.

What would a world without Jews look like? How would millions of believers across the Continent, including the pope, have received a dejudaized Christianity? Would the Hebrew Bible have become illegal everywhere, and how would this have influenced issues of Christian liturgy and dogma beyond Germany? The Jews were after all everywhere in European art, literature, and the physical environment, all of which would have had to be altered. Would objects of art have been purged of Jewish and biblical scenes, thus removing *David* from Piazza della Signoria and painting over the ceiling frescoes of the Sistine Chapel? And what about literature: Would all books that mentioned the Jews have been banned, much as the Nazis prohibited scholars from citing Jewish scholars in academic works, or perhaps they would have been edited in a manner similar to the rewriting of the New Testament?

How would the Nazis have administered these policies across their empire? We cannot know for certain how the Nazis would have commemorated the murder of the Jews, but we do definitely know that no one has a copyright on memory. In a Europe ruled by the Nazis, no one could have decreed a single memory of the crime. The extermination of the Jews happened in too many different places, nations, and traditions across Europe. The Holocaust was not only a Nazi memory but a European one. A Nazi-pronounced memory from above would have had no chance of being universally accepted and received. The memory of the crime would have festered and become inflamed, its consequences unpredictable. Perhaps the Nazis would have chosen to give local governments the autonomy to deal with Jewish cultural issues, now that the Jews were gone. This would have left an open space for the memory of the crime to live on and disturb further.

Germans and Europeans did not think profoundly about these moral and historical issues when they deported the Jews to their death. But the Jews, I would like to suggest, would have continued to live in European culture even after their extermination because they were part and parcel of its identity. Their memory would have lingered. The crime committed against them would have festered. The Nazis would have understood this perfectly because they knew that physical annihilation was no assurance for memory victory.

The Nazis knew the value of history and memory, and this insight enables us to understand what motivated them. One of the disquieting questions after 1945 was how a nation of poets and thinkers such as Germany could perpetrate a genocide. But this seems to me the wrong way to attempt to understand Nazi Germany and the Jews. Germany went after the Jews and their Book not in spite of being a nation of high culture but because it was such a nation. The new morality of the master race depended on the elimination of the old morality witnessed in the Book of Books. The Nazis perpetrated the Holocaust in the name of culture.

Here lies a paradox embedded in the Nazi extermination of the Jews: the Nazis exterminated the Jews because they viewed them as representing key registers of time in German, European, and Christian history, but precisely because of this role of the Jews, it was impossible to simply forget, ignore, or totally repress their genocide. The link among Jews, time, and morality meant that their annihilation was viewed as a transgression that violated previous accepted norms. The Nazi memory project was built on contradiction: by assigning the Jews historical importance that merited total extermination, they also ensured that the crime would not and could not be forgotten, be it in a world with or without Jews.

This way of thinking leads us closer to understanding why the genocide against the Jews has reverberated so profoundly in the past decades. We have pointed out that the Holocaust must be understood within a history of modern genocides, thus rejecting claims for uniqueness, even as we have posed the question why the genocide against the Jews has been perceived by Germans, Jews, and other Europeans as different from other genocides. The answer that has emerged from our story is that the Holocaust included the particular blend of three elements. The genocide was not limited to one nation or region, or to a specific economic, social, territorial, or political motive, or to a vision bounded by its present-day ideological concerns. It was a genocide that extended across an entire continent, unlike, for example, the genocides against Poles and Russians perpetrated in eastern Europe (Germans did not deport to Auschwitz Poles who lived in Paris). It was driven by a desire to extinguish an identity and to rewrite history, not by practical concerns. And, perhaps most important, the motives and consequences of the murder went beyond contemporary historical circumstances of the 1930s and 1940s: the genocide dictated a new history of Christianity and of European civilization, right from its origins.

Of course, identity is key to any case of genocide. Even if there were practical reasons for conflicts in the case, say, of Germans and Poles (Poles resisted the occupation), of Armenians and Ottomans (small numbers of Armenians joined revolutionary movements that defied the state), or more recently of Hutus and Tutsis in Rwanda (issues of land and political power), the jump from conflict to genocide always requires fantasy-thinking to justify the claim that the "enemy" includes women, children, and the elderly, who must also be eradicated.[6] The case of the extermination of the Jews was an extreme version of this thinking, and it stands squarely within the history of global genocides. But the Holocaust has been perceived as particular because of its combination of the three elements, and especially because the consequences of the eradication of the Jews touched not only Germans but European civilization as a whole.

I would like to continue along this line of thinking by way of reflection. Whatever Nazis thought about Christianity, the result of the extermination of the Jews was to radically alter its theology, liturgy, and history.

From its inceptions, Christianity harbored deep ambivalence toward Judaism in relations that combined break and continuity, separation and closeness.[7] The Jews have not recognized Jesus as the Messiah, but their Book embedded a certain truth that had to be recognized as such in order to make the claim that Christianity had superseded it. The Christian Bible provided a physical contiguity, joining the Old and the New Testaments in a single volume, two books that were related, though one truth replaced another. This ambiguity has been manifested in part in a Christian tradition that built on Augustine, who made space for Jewish truth within Christian truth by affirming that the first was true for its time and then led to a higher truth in the second. He asserted that the Jews were under God's special protection because they were witnesses to the truth of Christianity.[8]

Nazism broke this ambivalence, an event of potential unexpected and incalculable consequences. Killing all the Jews meant getting rid of the witnesses, cutting Christianity's roots, and liberating it of its dependence on the Hebrew Bible. This act opened the way for a radically new Christianity, perhaps its most profound reformulation since the first centuries after Christ. It is important to set here clearly the relations of Nazism and Christianity. For the Nazis, Christianity was not an urgent task; the Jews were. But by making the Jews the linchpin of their identity, they necessarily affected Christianity. The Nazis' aim was to refound German Christianity as a national church, and they had no intention of bringing a change to Christianity as a whole. But that is what was about to happen when their policies on the Jews commingled with their European empire building, when the Holocaust engulfed the entire continent. During the Third Reich, churches in Germany and throughout Europe, including the Catholic Church, headed by Pope Pius XII, were preoccupied with the Nazis' attempt to curtail their earthly influence. But for the long run, had the Nazis won the war, not the Nazis' policies to limit this or that power of the churches, but the making of a world without Jews, would have been of enduring significance for Christianity. And that is one reason the Holocaust has been perceived by Europeans after 1945 as a profound rupture and a genocide like no other.

When we consider the Holocaust as a memory project, it enables us to link the Holocaust during the Third Reich to its memory after 1945. For the Nazis, the Holocaust was a positive memory of origin because the creation of a new humanity started with the Jews, not with any other group. In the postwar world the Holocaust also became a memory of origin—a negative one, of course. In our own society, we view it as a historical rupture, a foundational story, and a point of historical beginning because the extermination called into question what it means to be human. Kaplan, Korczak, Hass, Lewin, Ringelblum, Rosenfeld, Szac, Szeps, and Zelkowicz viewed the extermination as an act of destruction and creation, as did, in their own way, Hitler, Himmler, Goebbels, Hosenfeld, and the soldiers who wrote from the front. The extermination as a foundational metaphor of origins, a sort of genesis, has thus stood at the center of how Germans, Jews, and others understood the Holocaust during the event and after 1945. If the Holocaust has been remembered after 1945 as a point of origins it is because Germans' notion in the Third Reich of the Jew as a symbol of historical origins was a key motivating reason for the extermination in the first place.

The Holocaust has haunted the postwar imagination because the European-wide extermination provided for Jews, Germans, and Europeans a story of origins and new beginning that, horribly, happened in the real world of human experience of perpetrators and victims, cruelty and immeasurable suffering: it elicited thoughts about where they came from, how they arrived there, and where they were going. As such it was not unconnected, in a sense, to the European tradition of such great narratives as Genesis and *The Odyssey*—only it superseded them, to the disbelief of people both then and now, by really happening.

Notes

Introduction

1. Quoted in Martin Gilbert, *Kristallnacht: Prelude to Destruction* (New York, 2006), 110–111.

2. Ibid.

3. *Haiti Holocaust Survivors: Kristallnacht Memories of Edgar Rosenberg,* http://haitiholocaustsurvivors.wordpress.com/anti-semitism/kristallnacht/kristallnacht-memories-of-edgar-rosenberg/.

4. I should qualify this by noting that Kristallnacht is often presented as "the beginning of the end," in which case the sudden outburst of violence is forced into a narrative of radicalization of Nazi policies that ends with Auschwitz. But the narrative of radicalization functions more as a rhetorical device to move the story forward than as an explanatory one and always runs the risk of viewing Kristallnacht as the preliminary stage in the inexorable march toward the Final Solution.

5. J. Keller and Hanns Andersen, *Der Jude als Verbrecher* (Berlin, 1937), 11–12.

6. Daniel Jonah Goldhagen, *Hitler's Willing Executioners: Ordinary Germans and the Holocaust* (New York, 1996).

7. Christopher R. Browning, *Ordinary Men: Reserve Police Battalion 101 and the Final Solution in Poland* (New York, 1992).

8. Primo Levi, *Survival in Auschwitz* (New York, 1996), 103.

9. Donald Bloxham, "The Holocaust and European History," and A. Dirk Moses, "The Holocaust and World History: Raphael Lemkin and Comparative Methodology," in *The Holocaust and Historical Methodology,* ed. Dan Stone (New York, 2012), 233–254, 272–289.

10. Mark Mazower, *Hitler's Empire: Nazi Rule in Occupied Europe* (New York, 2008).

11. Timothy Snyder, *Bloodlands: Europe Between Hitler and Stalin* (New York, 2010).

12. Ian Thomson, *Primo Levi: A Life* (New York, 2002), 227–235.

13. Michael Ruck, *Bibliographie zum Nationalsozialismus* (Darmstadt, 2000). The first edition was published in 1995.

14. Saul Friedländer, *Nazi Germany and the Jews: The Years of Persecution* (New York, 1998), 87, 99.

15. Sigmund Freud, *Moses and Monotheism* (New York, 1967). See the discussions of Yosef Hayim Yerushalmi, *Freud's Moses: Judaism Terminable and Interminable* (New Haven, 1991); and Jan Assmann, *Moses the Egyptian: The Memory of Egypt in Western Monotheism* (Cambridge, MA, 1997). And see my essay "Freud, Moses, and National Memory," in *Germany as a Culture of Remembrance: Promises and Limits of Writing History* (Chapel Hill, NC, 2006), 159–169.

16. See the insightful book of David Nirenberg, *Anti-Judaism: The Western Tradition* (New York, 2013).

17. Ernest Renan, "What Is a Nation?" in *Nation and Narration,* ed. Homi Bhabha (London, 1990), 19.

ONE A New Beginning by Burning Books

Epigraph: Jorge Luis Borges, "El libro," in *Borges, Oral* (Buenos Aires, 1979), 13.

1. Gershom Scholem, *A Life in Letters, 1914–1982* (Cambridge, MA, 2002), 229 (emphasis in original).

2. Ibid., 7–10.

3. Stephan Schurr, "Die 'Judenaktion' in Creglingen am 25. März 1933: Eine Quellendokumentation," in *Lebenswege Creglinger Juden: Das Pogrom von 1933; Der schwierige Umgang mit der Vergangenheit,* ed. Gerhard Naser (Bergatreute, 2002), 59–82; Hartwig Behr, "Der 25. März 1933—Judenpogrom in Creglingen," in *Vom Leben und Sterben: Juden in Creglingen,* ed. Hartwig Behr and Horst Rupp (Würzburg, 1999), 135–152.

4. Richard J. Evans, *The Coming of the Third Reich* (New York, 2003), 432; Abraham Ascher, *A Community Under Siege: The Jews of Breslau Under Nazism* (Stanford, CA, 2007), 76–78.

5. *Das Schwarzbuch: Tatsache und Dokumente: Die Lage der Juden in Deutschland, 1933,* ed. Comité des Delegations Juives (Paris, 1934); Michael Wildt, *Volksgemeinschaft als Selbstermächtigung: Gewalt gegen Juden in der deutschen Provinz, 1919 bis 1939* (Hamburg, 2007), 101–137; Götz Aly et al., eds., *Die Verfolgung und Ermordung der europäischen Juden durch das nationalsozialistische Deutschland, 1933–1945,* vol. 1 (Munich, 2008), 81–85.

6. Dirk Walter, *Antisemitische Kriminalität und Gewalt: Judenfeindschaft in der Weimarer Republik* (Bonn, 1999); Michael Wildt, "Gewalt gegen Juden in Deutschland, 1933 bis 1939," *WerkstattGeschichte* 18 (1997): 59–80.

7. Armin Nolzen, "The Nazi Party and Its Violence Against the Jews, 1933–1939: Violence as a Historiographical Concept," *Yad Vashem Studies* 23 (2003): 247.

8. I am grateful to Hermann Beck for sharing with me his unpublished paper "Anti-Semitic Violence During the Nazi Seizure of Power."

9. Saul Friedländer, *Nazi Germany and the Jews: The Years of Persecution* (New York, 1998), 19.

10. Ibid., 28.

11. Adolf Hitler, *Mein Kampf* (New York, 1969), 60.

12. Evans, *Coming of the Third Reich*, 355, 360.

13. William Carr, *A History of Germany: 1815–1990*, 4th ed. (London, 1991), 309.

14. Christopher Isherwood, *Goodbye to Berlin* (London, 1966), 311.

15. Peter Fritzsche, *Germans into Nazis* (Cambridge, MA, 1998), 143.

16. André François-Poncet, *The Fateful Years: Memoirs of a French Ambassador in Berlin, 1931–1938* (New York, 1949), 48.

17. Sebastian Haffner, *Defying Hitler: A Memoir* (London, 2002), 87.

18. Marion Yorck von Wartenburg, *The Power of Solitude: My Life in the German Resistance* (Lincoln, NE, 2000), 20.

19. Bruno Walter, *Theme and Variations: An Autobiography* (New York, 1966), 295–300; Evans, *Coming of the Third Reich*, 393; Friedländer, *Years of Persecution*, 9.

20. Michael Kater, "Forbidden Fruit? Jazz in the Third Reich," *American Historical Review* 94 (1989): 18.

21. Evans, *Coming of the Third Reich*, 385–386.

22. Ibid., 423.

23. It took place on May 17, 1933, a week later than in the rest of the Reich.

24. Michael Kater, "The Myth of Myths: Scholarship and Teaching in Heidelberg," *Central European History* 36 (2003): 570–577.

25. Clemens Zimmerman, "Die Bücherverbrennung am 17. Mai 1933 in Heidelberg: Studenten und Politik am Ende der Weimarer Republik," in *Bücherverbrennung: Zensur, Verbot, Vernichtung unter dem Nationalsozialismus in Heidelberg*, ed. Joachim-Felix Leonhard (Heidelberg, 1983), 61.

26. Ibid., 55–84; Gerhard Sauder, ed., *Die Bücherverbrennung: Zum 10. Mai 1933* (Munich, 1983), 198–201.

27. For a full list of participating communities, see Werner Tress, *"Wider den undeutschen Geist": Bücherverbrennung 1933* (Berlin, 2003), 226–227.

28. Sauder, *Bücherverbrennung*, 93.

29. Ibid., 31.

30. Ibid., 31, 107, 152; Klaus Schöffling, ed., *Dort wo man Bücher verbrennt: Stimmen und Betroffenen* (Frankfurt, 1983), 69.

31. Sauder, *Bücherverbrennung*, 105–144; Tress, *"Wider den undeutschen Geist,"* 93–105. Goebbels attempted to formulate a uniform list. The list of October 1, 1935, included 3,601 titles and 524 authors whose works were completely banned.

32. Sauder, *Bücherverbrennung*, 189.

33. Tress, *"Wider den undeutschen Geist,"* 49–56.

34. Sauder, *Bücherverbrennung*, 192–193; Stephan Füssel, " 'Wider den undeutschen Geist': Bücherverbrennung und Bibliothekslenkung im Nationalsozialismus," in *Göttingen unterm Hakenkreuz. Nationalsozialisticher Alltag in einer deutschen Stadt— Texte und Materialen*, ed. Jens-Uwe Brinkmann and Hans-Georg Schmeling (Göttingen, 1983), 95–104.

35. James M. Ritchie, "The Nazi Book-Burning," *Modern Language Review* 83 (1988): 639.

36. Ibid., 627. Ulrich Walberer, ed., *10. Mai 1933: Bücherverbrennung in Deutschland und die Folgen* (Frankfurt, 1983), 42–43.

37. Sauder, *Bücherverbrennung*, 265–267.

38. Walberer, *10. Mai 1933*, 43.

39. For this argument with respect to the books' burning, see Zimmerman, "Bücherverbrennung am 17. Mai 1933 in Heidelberg," 75–77. For the tradition of national celebrations, see Dieter Düding, Peter Friedemann, and Paul Münch, eds., *Öffentliche Festkultur: Politische Feste in Deutschland von der Aufklärung bis zum ersten Weltkrieg* (Hamburg, 1988); George Mosse, *The Nationalization of the Masses: Political Symbolism and Mass Movements in Germany from the Napoleonic Wars Through the Third Reich* (New York, 1975); and Alon Confino, *The Nation as a Local Metaphor: Württemberg, Imperial Germany, and National Memory, 1871–1918* (Chapel Hill, NC, 1997), part I.

40. Sauder, *Bücherverbrennung*, 177–178.

41. Arnold Zweig, "Rückblick auf Barbarei und Bücherverbrennung," in Schöffling, *Dort wo man Bücher verbrennt*, 82.

42. Sauder, *Bücherverbrennung*, 169–171, 196, 209; Walberer, *10. Mai 1933*, 107; Albrecht Schöne, *Göttinger Bücherverbrennung 1933* (Göttingen, 1983), 26; Joseph Wulf, *Literatur und Dichtung im Dritten Reich: Eine Dokumentation* (Gütersloh, 1963), 45; Tress, *"Wider den undeutschen Geist,"* 151. See also H. Simon-Pelanda and P. Heigi, *Regensburg, 1933–1945: Eine andere Stadtführung* (Regensburg, 1984), 22.

43. Evans, *Coming of the Third Reich*, 429.

44. Zimmerman, "Bücherverbrennung am 17. Mai 1933 in Heidelberg," 60.

45. Zweig, "Rückblick auf Barbarei und Bücherverbrennung," 82.

46. Wulf, *Literatur und Dichtung im Dritten Reich*, 51.

47. Ibid., 52. Walberer, *10. Mai 1933*, 143–144.

48. Walberer, *10. Mai 1933*, 150.

49. Sauder, *Bücherverbrennung*, 193.

50. Henrik Eberle, ed., *Letters to Hitler* (Cambridge, 2012), 79–80.

51. Ibid., 1–2, 72.

52. Ibid., 94.

53. Sauder, *Bücherverbrennung*, 192.

54. Ibid., 183.

55. Ibid., 193.

56. Helmut Heiber, ed., *Goebbels-Reden*, vol. 1, *1932–1939* (Düsseldorf, 1971), 108.

57. George Mosse, "Bookburning and the Betrayal of German Intellectuals," *New German Critique* 31 (Winter 1984): 150.

58. Joseph Walk, *Das Sonderrecht für die Juden im NS-Staat* (Heidelberg, 1996).

59. Ibid., 7, 8, 10, 12, 14, 16, 18, 23, 34, 36, 38, 42–43, 46–48, 51, 54, 62.

60. Heiber, *Goebbels-Reden*, 111–112.

61. Sauder, *Bücherverbrennung*, 251.

62. Amos Elon, *The Pity of It All: A History of Jews in Germany, 1743–1933* (New York, 2002), 338, 340.

63. Zweig, "Rückblick auf Barbarei und Bücherverbrennung," 83–84.

64. Sauder, *Bücherverbrennung*, 34.

65. Schöffling, *Dort wo man Bücher verbrennt*, 56.

66. Ibid., 70.

67. Ibid., 55.

68. Heiber, *Goebbels-Reden*, 111.

69. Joseph Roth, "The Auto-da-Fé of the Mind," in *What I Saw: Reports from Berlin, 1920–1933* (New York, 2003), 208–210.

70. Zweig, "Rückblick auf Barbarei und Bücherverbrennung," 81, 88.

71. Roth, "Auto-da-Fé of the Mind," 214.

72. Schöne, *Göttinger Bücherverbrennung*, 31.

TWO Origins, Eternal and Local

1. Gerhard Sauder, ed., *Die Bücherverbrennung: Zum 10. Mai 1933* (Munich, 1983), 93.

2. Abraham Ascher, *A Community Under Siege: The Jews of Breslau Under Nazism* (Stanford, CA, 2007), 96–97.

3. Cited in Anselm Faust, *Die "Kristallnacht" im Rheinland: Dokumente zur Judenpogrom im November 1938* (Düsseldorf, 1987), 39.

4. Werner May, *Deutscher Nationalkatechismus: Dem Jungen Deutschen in Schule und Beruf* (Breslau, 1934), 22.

5. Peter Fritzsche, *Life and Death in the Third Reich* (Cambridge, MA, 2008), 76–81.

6. Joseph Walk, *Das Sonderrecht für die Juden im NS-Staat* (Heidelberg, 1996), 115, 162, 185, 237, 275.

7. Sebastian Haffner, *Defying Hitler: A Memoir* (London, 2002), 189.

8. Christopher Isherwood, *Goodbye to Berlin* (London, 1966), 316–317.

9. Iona Opie and Moira Tatem, eds., *A Dictionary of Superstitions* (Oxford, 1989), 119.

10. US Holocaust Memorial Museum (hereafter USHMM) Photo Archives #59386, #80821.

11. Richard J. Evans, *The Third Reich in Power* (New York, 2005), 540.

12. Ibid., 545–546.

13. See Alon Confino, *The Nation as a Local Metaphor: Württemberg, Imperial Germany, and National Memory, 1871–1918* (Chapel Hill, NC, 1997).

14. *Unsere Heimat in alter und neuer Zeit: Heimatkunde für Schule und Haus* (Giengen an der Brenz, 1914), 50.

15. Hermann Fischer, *Schwäbisches Wörterbuch,* vol. 1 (Tübingen, 1904), vii.

16. *Oettinger Amts- und Wochenblatt,* June 6, 1908.

17. Ibid.

18. D. Hohnholz, "Das Heimatmuseum im Schloss zu Jever," *Die Tide: Monatsschrift für Nord-, Ost- und Westfriesland, Oldenburg, Friesische Inseln und Helgoland* (Wilhelmshafen, 1921), 115.

19. Karl-Heinz Brackmann and Renate Birkenhauer, NS-Deutsch: "Selbstverständliche" Begriffe and Schlagwörter aus der Zeit des Nationalsozialismus (Darmstadt, 1988), 39.

20. Klaus Geobel, "Der Heimatkundeunterricht in den deutschen Schulen," in *Antimodernismus und Reform: Zur Geschichte der deutschen Heimatbewegung,* ed. Edeltraud Klueting (Darmstadt, 1991), 103–104.

21. May, *Deutscher Nationalkatechismus;* Werner May, *Kleine Nationalkunde für Schule und Beruf (Früherer Titel: Politische Katechismus)* (Breslau, 1938), 26.

22. Yehuda Bauer, *Rethinking the Holocaust* (New Haven, 2001), 34. See Götz Aly and Karl Heinz Roth, *The Nazi Census: Identification and Control in the Third Reich* (Philadelphia, 2004).

23. Adolf Hitler, "Nation and Race," in *The Holocaust: A Reader,* ed. Simone Gigliotti and Berel Lang (Malden, MA, 2005), 7; Dirk Rupnow, "Racializing Historiography: Anti-Jewish Scholarship in the Third Reich," *Patterns of Prejudice* 42, no. 1 (2008): 41.

24. Cited in Rupnow, "Racializing Historiography," 41.

25. Max Domarus, *Hitler: Speeches and Proclamations, 1932–1945,* vol. 1: *The Years 1932 to 1934* (Wauconda, IL, 1990), 432.

26. Patricia Heberer, "Science," in *The Oxford Handbook of Holocaust Studies,* ed. Peter Hayes and John Roth (Oxford, 2010), 41–44.

27. Robert Proctor, *Racial Hygiene: Medicine Under the Nazis* (Cambridge, MA, 1999).

28. Heberer, "Science," 40.

29. Allan Steinweis, *Studying the Jew: Scholarly Antisemitism in Nazi Germany* (Cambridge, MA, 2006), 53–54.

30. Mark Mazower, *Hitler's Empire: Nazi Rule in Occupied Europe* (New York, 2008), 5, 182–183.

31. Walk, *Sonderrecht für die Juden im NS-Staat,* 73, 78, 82, 84–85, 87, 93, 101, 105, 115, 121–123, 125–126, 136, 149.

32. Gershom Scholem, *A Life in Letters, 1914–1982* (Cambridge, MA, 2002), 241.

33. Michael Wildt, *Die Judenpolitik des SD, 1935–38: Eine Dokumentation* (Munich, 1995), 66–69.

34. Henrik Eberle, ed., *Letters to Hitler* (Cambridge, 2012), 150–152.

35. Ibid., 130–132.

36. Amos Elon, *The Pity of It All: A History of Jews in Germany, 1743–1933* (New York, 2002), 399.

37. Götz Aly et al., eds., *Die Verfolgung und Ermordung der europäischen Juden durch das nationalsozialistische Deutschland, 1933–1945*, vol. 1 (Munich, 2008), 78.

38. Michael Wildt, "The Boycott Campaign as an Arena of Collective Violence Against Jews in Germany, 1933–1938," in *Nazi Europe and the Final Solution,* ed. David Bankier and Israel Gutman (Jerusalem, 2003), 62.

39. I am following the insights of history of emotions. See, e.g., "Forum: History of Emotions," ed. Frank Biess, *German History* 28, no. 1 (2010): 67–80; and Joanna Bourke, "Fear and Anxiety: Writing About Emotion in Modern History," *History Workshop Journal* 55 (2003): 111–133.

40. Aly et al., *Verfolgung und Ermordung,* 77.

41. BarbaraRosenwein, "Worrying About Emotions in History," *American Historical Review* 107 (2002): 842.

42. James M. Ritchie, "The Nazi Book-Burning," *Modern Language Review* 83 (1988): 633.

43. Petteri Pietikainen, "The *Volk* and Its Unconscious: Jung, Hauer and the 'German Revolution,'" *Journal of Contemporary History* 35 (2000): 530.

44. Ulrich Popplow, "Die Machtergreifung in Augenzeugenberichten: Göttingen, 1932–1935," *Göttinger Jahrbuch* (1977), 177–178; Peter Wilhelm, *Die Synagogengemeinde Göttingen, Rosdorf und Geismar, 1850–1942* (Göttingen, 1978), 46.

45. USHMM Photo Archives #94674.

46. See also Ignaz Görtz, *Kreis Ahrweiler unter dem Hakenkreuz* (Bad Neuenahr-Ahrweiler, 1989), 227.

47. The specific evidence discussed here is from Catholic communities, and Catholics were more inclined than Protestants to limit the role of race in their world-view, but similar representations appeared in Protestant communities all over Germany on other occasions. For more Carnival representations in Catholic communities in, for example, Dresden, Mainz, Nuremberg, and Cologne, see USHMM Photo Archives #59236, #59237, #31464, #30732, #94675, #59230, #59231, #59232.

48. Ibid., #98545.

49. Popplow, "Die Machtergreifung in Augenzeugenberichten: Göttingen, 1932–1935," 178.

50. Michael Wildt, *Volksgemeinschaft als Selbstermächtigung: Gewalt gegen Juden in der deutschen Provinz, 1919 bis 1939* (Hamburg, 2007), 10.

51. Lyndal Roper, *Witch Craze: Terror and Fantasy in Baroque Germany* (New Haven, 2004), 45–46.

52. Richard Evans, *The Coming of the Third Reich* (New York, 2003), 425.

53. Roper, *Witch Craze,* 104.

54. Ibid., 106.

55. Scholem, *Life in Letters,* 228.

THREE Imagining the Jews as Everywhere and Already Gone

1. Bernt Engelmann, *Wie wir die Nazizeit erlebten* (Göttingen, 1993), 107–108.

2. See also the sign posted on a government building in Hameln. US Holocaust Memorial Museum (hereafter USHMM) Photo Archives #19307.

3. See also the anti-Jewish street signs in Frankenberg, Hessen, and at the entrance to the Berlin suburb of Buckow: USHMM Photo Archives #59264, #23022.

4. Gregory Paul Wegner, *Anti-Semitism and Schooling Under the Third Reich* (New York, 2002), 157–180.

5. See, e.g., USHMM Photo Archives W/S #59284 on a tree-lined local road in Franconia.

6. Richard J. Evans, *The Third Reich in Power* (New York, 2005), 540.

7. The photo archive of the United States Holocaust Memorial Museum in Washington has a substantial collection of them, showing how diffused the practice was: in Franconia, Bavaria, Schleswig-Holstein, Lower Saxony, Baden, Brandenburg, and elsewhere.

8. USHMM Photo Archives #59280.

9. Ibid., #59254. See also Wolfgang Benz, "Exclusion as a Stage in Persecution: The Jewish Situation in Germany, 1933–1941," in *Nazi Europe and the Final Solution,* ed. David Bankier and Israel Gutman (Jerusalem, 2003), 44.

10. Klaus Fischer, *Nazi Germany: A New History* (New York, 1995), 375.

11. Christine Keitz, *Reisen als Leitbild: Die Entstehung des modernen massen Tourismus in Deutschland* (Munich, 1997), 248–249.

12. Joseph Walk, *Das Sonderrecht für die Juden im NS-Staat* (Heidelberg, 1996), 153–154, 159, 162, 170, 185, 190, 198, 204.

13. Haig Bosmajian, *Burning Books* (Jefferson, NC, 2006), 166.

14. Michael Marrus, "Killing Time: Jewish Perceptions During the Holocaust," *The Holocaust: History and Memory: Essays in Honor of Israel Gutman,* ed. Shmuel Almog et al. (Jerusalem, 2001), 12–13.

15. Gretchen Schafft, *From Racism to Genocide: Anthropology in the Third Reich* (Urbana, IL, 2004), 16–17.

16. Herbert Schultheis, *Die Reichskristallnacht in Deutschland nach Augenzeugenberichten* (Bad Neustadt, 1985), 344–345.

17. Ibid., 345–346.

18. Dirk Rupnow, *Vernichten und Erinnern: Spuren nationalsozialistischer Gedächtnispolitik* (Göttingen, 2005), 114–118.

19. Walk, *Sonderrecht für die Juden im NS-Staat,* 219, 221, 228, 235, 237, 244–245.

20. Joseph Goebbels, *Die Tagebücher von Joseph Goebbels,* ed. Elke Fröhlich (Munich, 1994), vol. 1, pt. 4, 429.

21. Michael Wildt, "The Boycott Campaign as an Arena of Collective Violence Against Jews in Germany, 1933–1938," in *Nazi Europe and the Final Solution,* ed. David Bankier and Israel Gutman (Jerusalem, 2003), 69.

22. Ulrich Baumann, *Zerstörte Nachbarschaften: Christen und Juden in badischen Landgemeinden, 1862–1940* (Hamburg, 2000), 238.

23. Elfriede Bachmann, *Zur Geschichte der Juden in Zeven* (Zeven, 1992), 16.

24. Peter Fritzsche, *Life and Death in the Third Reich* (Cambridge, MA, 2008), 131.

25. Walk, *Sonderrecht für die Juden im NS-Staat*, 62, 73, 105, 204, 245.

26. Siegfried Wittmer, *Regensburger Juden: Jüdisches Leben von 1519 bis 1990* (Regensburg, 1996), 301–302.

27. Walk, *Sonderrecht für die Juden im NS-Staat*, 290.

28. Thomas Hofmann, Hanno Loewy, and Harry Stein, eds., *Pogromnacht und Holocaust: Frankfurt, Weimar, Buchenwald . . .* (Weimar, 1994), 50.

29. Martin Gilbert, *Kristallnacht: Prelude to Destruction* (New York, 2006), 133–134. Ben Barkow, Raphael Gross, and Michael Lenarz, eds., *Novemberpogrom, 1938: Die Augenzeugenberichte der Wiener Library, London* (Frankfurt, 2008), 429–430.

30. Evans, *Third Reich in Power*, 577; Wittmer, *Regensburger Juden*, 314; Wildt, "Boycott Campaign," 69; Hans Reichmann, *Deutscher Bürger und verfolgte Jude: Novemberpogrom und KZ Sachsenhausen 1937 bis 1939*, ed. Michael Wildt (Munich, 1998), 19.

31. Barkow et al., *Novemberpogrom 1938*, 735.

32. Wilhelm Grau, "Die Geschichte des Judenfrage und ihr Erforschung," *Blätter für deutsche Landesgeschichte* 83, no. 3 (1937): 167, 171–173. See also Dirk Rupnow, " 'Judenforschung' im 'Dritten Reich': Wissenschaft zwischen Politik, Propaganda und Ideologie (Habilitationsschrift, University of Vienna, 2008); and Dirk Rupnow, "Racializing Historiography: Anti-Jewish Scholarship in the Third Reich," *Patterns of Prejudice* 42, no. 1 (2008): 29–30.

33. Allan Steinweis, *Studying the Jew: Scholarly Anti-Semitism in Nazi Germany* (Cambridge, MA, 2008), 113.

34. Volkmar Eichstät, "Das Schrifttum zur Judenfrage in den deutschen Bibliotheken," *Forschungen zur Judenfrage* 6 (1941): 253–264, quotation on 264. See Rupnow, "Racializing Historiography," 37.

35. Steinweis, *Studying the Jew*, 115–116.

FOUR   Burning the Book of Books

Epigraph: Ben Barkow, Raphael Gross, and Michael Lenarz, eds., *Novemberpogrom 1938: Die Augenzeugenberichte der Wiener Library, London* (Frankfurt, 2008), 525.

1. Ulrich Baumann, *Zerstörte Nachbarschaften: Christen und Juden in badischen Landgemeinden, 1862–1940* (Hamburg, 2000), 240. All figures for number of inhabitants in Baden are for 1925 (207). For Kristallnacht in Baden villages, see also Historischer Verein für Mittelbaden e.V., ed., *Schicksal und Geschichte der Jüdischen Gemeinden Ettenheim, Altdort, Kippenheim, Schmieheim, Rust, Orschweier, 1938–1988* (Ettenheim, 1988).

2. Barkow, Gross, and Lenarz, *Novemberpogrom 1938*, 22.

3. Martin Gilbert, *Kristallnacht: Prelude to Destruction* (New York, 2006), 47. Barkow, Gross, and Lenarz, *Novemberpogrom 1938*, 153.

4. Barkow, Gross, and Lenarz, *Novemberpogrom 1938*, 222.

5. Gilbert, *Kristallnacht*, 59.

6. Dagmar and Clemens Lohmann, *Das Schicksal der jüdischen Gemeinde in Fritzlar, 1933–1945: Die Pogromnacht 1938* (Fritzlar, 1988), 28.

7. Barkow, Gross, and Lenarz, *Novemberpogrom 1938*, 146, 273.

8. Gilbert, *Kristallnacht*, 93; Mitchell G. Bard, *48 Hours of Kristallnacht: Night of Destruction / Dawn of the Holocaust; An Oral History* (Guilford, CT, 2008), 98.

9. Gilbert, *Kristallnacht*, 98; Bard, *48 Hours of Kristallnacht*, 135.

10. Barkow, Gross, and Lenarz, *Novemberpogrom 1938*, 351.

11. Uta Gerhardt and Thomas Karlauf, eds., *The Night of Broken Glass: Eyewitness Accounts of Kristallnacht* (Cambridge, 2012), 36–37.

12. Barkow, Gross, and Lenarz, *Novemberpogrom 1938*, 380, 782.

13. Baumann, *Zerstörte Nachbarschaften*, 241–242.

14. Barkow, Gross, and Lenarz, *Novemberpogrom 1938*, 449.

15. Baumann, *Zerstörte Nachbarschaften*, 241.

16. Quoted in Saul Friedländer, *Nazi Germany and the Jews: The Years of Persecution* (New York, 1998), 278.

17. Heinz Lauber, *Judenpogrom: "Reichskristallnacht" November 1938 in Groß-deutschland: Daten-Fakten-Dokumente-Quellentexte-Thesen u. Bewertungen* (Gerlingen, 1981), 159; Wolfgang Benz, "The Relapse into Barbarism," in *November 1938: From "Reichskristallnacht" to Genocide*, ed. Walter H. Pehle (New York, 1991), 14.

18. Allan Steinweis, *Kristallnacht 1938* (Cambridge, MA, 2009).

19. For the historiography, see Wolf-Arno Kropat, *"Reichskristallnacht": Der Judenpogrom vom 7. bis 10. November 1938—Urheber, Täter, Hintergründe* (Wiesbaden, 1997).

20. Dieter Obst, *"Reichskristallnacht": Ursachen und Verlauf des antisemitischen Pogrom vom November 1938* (Frankfurt, 1991), 349.

21. Richard J. Evans, *The Third Reich in Power* (New York, 2005), 581, 583, 598.

22. Friedländer, *Years of Persecution*, 277–278.

23. Angelika Schindler, *Der verbrannte Traum: Jüdische Bürger und Gäste in Baden-Baden* (Bühl-Moos, 1992), 128–133. See the map and photographs of the march at 135–142; see also http://www1.yadvashem.org/yv/en/exhibitions/kristallnacht/baden.asp.

24. Barkow, Gross, and Lenarz, *Novemberpogrom 1938*, 145, 157, 265, 273, 295, 352, 426, 428.

25. Bard, *48 Hours of Kristallnacht*, 124.

26. *Das ende der Juden in Ostfriesland: Ausstellung der Ostfriesischen Landschaft aus Anlass des 50. Jahrestag der Kristallnacht* (Aurich, 1988), 50–51.

27. Cited in Friedländer, *Years of Persecution*, 277.

28. Dieter Albrecht, *Regensburg im Wandel: Studien zur Geschichte der Stadt im 19. und 20. Jahrhundert* (Regensburg, 1984), 227.

29. Siegfried Wittmer, *Regensburger Juden: Jüdisches Leben von 1519 bis 1990* (Regensburg, 1996), 329.

30. Lauber, *Judenpogrom*, 159.

31. Doris Bergen, "Nazism and Christianity: Partners and Rivals," *Journal of Contemporary History* 42, no. 5 (2007): 29.

32. Catherine Merridale, *Night of Stone: Death and Memory in Twentieth-Century Russia* (New York, 2002), 137, 129.

33. Marvin Perry and Frederick Schweitzer, *Antisemitic Myths: A Historical and Contemporary Anthology* (Bloomington, IN, 2008), 177.

34. Victoria Newall, "The Jew as a Witch Figure," in *The Witch Figure,* ed. Victoria Newall (London, 1973), 116.

35. Joshua Trachtenberg, *The Devil and the Jews: The Medieval Conception of the Jew and Its Relations to Modern Antisemitism* (New Haven, 1943), 240, n. 38.

36. Ruth Mellinkoff, *Outcasts: Sign of Otherness in Northern European Art of the Late Middle Ages,* vol. 1 (Berkeley, CA, 1993), 103–104, 106.

37. Newall, "Jew as a Witch Figure," 109.

38. See the insightful books of: Susannah Heschel, *The Aryan Jesus: Christian Theologians and the Bible in Nazi Germany* (Princeton, NJ, 2008), here 1–2; Richard Steigmann-Gall, *The Holy Reich: Nazi Conceptions of Christianity* (Cambridge, 2003); and Uriel Tal, *Religion, Politics and Ideology in the Third Reich: Selected Essays* (London, 2004).

39. Cited in Edward Kessler, *An Introduction to Jewish-Christian Relations* (Cambridge, 2010), 129.

40. Cited in Steigmann-Gall, *Holy Reich,* 41.

41. We need to know more about the history of the Nazis and the Bible; we do not yet have a comprehensive study of the topic. A history of the Bible in Germany during Nazism (viewed within broader European culture) would enable us to place religious beliefs in the Third Reich as blended with racial ideas and to shed light on theological and popular anti-Semitism going beyond the totem of ideology and the dichotomy of Nazism vs. Christianity. The excellent study on the eighteenth century by Jonathan Sheehan, *The Enlightenment Bible: Translation, Scholarship, Culture* (Princeton, NJ, 2005), is one possible model. On Nazism and religion, see Heschel, *Aryan Jesus;* Steigmann-Gall, *Holy Reich,* and the debate over the book in a special issue of the *Journal of Contemporary History,* 42, no. 1 (2007), especially the essays by Stanley Stowers and Doris Bergen; Kyle Jantzen, *Faith and Fatherland: Parish Politics in Hitler's Germany* (Minneapolis, 2008); Tal, *Religion, Politics and Ideology;* Kevin Spicer, *Hitler's Priests: Catholic Clergy and National Socialism* (DeKalb, IL, 2008); and Derek Hastings, *Catholicism and the Roots of Nazism: Religious Identity and National Socialism* (Oxford, 2010). For Marcion, see Adolf von Harnack, *Marcion: The Gospel of the Alien God,* trans. John Steely and Lyle Bierna (1921; Durham, NC, 1990). On biblical theology and scholarship, see Shawn Kelley, *Racializing Jesus: Race, Ideology, and the Formation of Modern Biblical Scholarship* (London, 2002); and the important study by Anders Gerdmar, *Roots of Theological Anti-Semitism: German Biblical Interpretation and the Jews from Herder and Semler to Kittel and Bultmann* (Leiden, 2009), which, tracing theological anti-Semitism from the eighteenth century to the 1950s, concludes that, far from being a deviation, National Socialist exegetes "were merely taking more radical steps on a path that had existed for a long time" (xv).

42. Cited in Heschel, *Aryan Jesus,* 9–10.

43. Friedländer, *Years of Persecution,* 296–298, 326–327.

44. Barkow, Gross, and Lenarz, *Novemberpogrom 1938,* 483–484.

45. Randall Bytwerk, *Landmark Speeches of National Socialism* (College Station, TX, 2008), 91.

46. Barkow, Gross, and Lenarz, *Novemberpogrom 1938,* 143.

47. Lauber, *Judenpogrom,* 166.

48. Ibid., 166–168.

49. Ibid., 174.

50. To use the notion of the late Italian micro-historian Edoardo Grendi, "Micro-analisi e storia sociale," *Quaderni Storici* 7 (1972): 506–520.

51. On Kristallnacht and ritual, see Frank Maciejewski, "Der Novemberpogrom im ritualgeschichtlischer Perspektive," *Jahrbuch für Antisemitismusforschung* 15 (2006): 65–84; and Peter Loewenberg, "The Kristallnacht as a Public Degradation Ritual," *Leo Baeck Institute Yearbook* 33 (1987): 309–323.

52. Wittmer, *Regensburger Juden,* 327–328. See also Wilhelm Kick, *Sag es unseren Kindern: Widerstand, 1933–1945, Beispiel Regensburg* (Berlin/Vilseck, 1985), 187–189; *"Stadt und Mutter in Israel": Jüdische Geschichte und Kultur in Regensburg,* Ausstellung Regensburg Stadtarchiv und Runtingersäle (Regensburg, 1989), 102–106; and H. Simon-Pelanda and P. Heigl, *Regensburg, 1933–1945: Eine andere Stadtführung* (Regensburg, 1984), 32–34.

53. Barkow, Gross, and Lenarz, *Novemberpogrom 1938,* 658, 660–661; Kurt Tohermes and Jürgen Grafen, *Leben und Untergang der Synagogengemeinde Dinslaken* (Dinslaken, 1988), 30–36, 65–70; Kurt Tohermes, ed., *Untersuchungen zur politischen Kultur der Dinslakener Juden zwischen 1869 und 1942* (Dinslaken, 1988), 232–233; Jan-Pieter Barbian, Michael Brocke, and Ludger Heid, eds., *Juden im Ruhrgebiet: Vom Zeitalter der Aufklärung bis in die Gegenwart* (Essen, 1999), 503–522; Adolf Krassnigg, "Juden in Dinslaken," in Rüdiger Gollnick et al., *Dinslaken in der NS-Zeit: Vergessene Geschichte, 1933–1945* (Kleve, 1983), 89–113; Fred Spiegel, *Once the Acacias Bloomed: Memories of a Childhood Lost* (Margate, NJ, 2004), 25–28; *Fast vergessen? Erinnerungen an die "Kristallnacht" in Dinslaken am 10. November 1938,* comp. Stadt Dinslaken, 3rd ed. (Dinslaken, 2003); "Mahnmal erinnert an die Nazi-Greueltaten," *Niederrhein Anzeiger,* November 3, 1993; Ralf Schreiner, "Mahnmal weist Spuren in schreckliche Vergangenheit," *Rheinische Post,* October 22, 1993.

54. Uwe Schellinger, ed., *Gedächtnis aus Stein: Die Synagoge in Kippenheim, 1852–2002* (Heidelberg, 2002), 91.

55. Herbert Obenaus, ed., *Historisches Handbuch der jüdischen Gemeinden in Niedersachsen und Bremen,* vol. 2 (Göttingen, 2005), 1602; Elfriede Bachmann, *Zur Geschichte der Juden in Zeven* (Zeven, 2002), 21–22.

56. For example, Ulrich Herbert, "Von der 'Reichskristallnacht' zum 'Holocaust': Der 9. November und das Ende des 'Radau-Antisemitismus,'" in *Arbeit, Volkstum, Weltanschauung: Über Fremde und Deutsche im 20. Jahrhundert* (Frankfurt, 1995), 75.

57. I am indebted to Dr. Andrea Zupancic of the Dortmund city archive for this information.

58. Barkow, Gross, and Lenarz, *Novemberpogrom 1938,* 467–468.

59. Gilbert, *Kristallnacht,* 29–30.

60. Lauber, *Judenpogrom,* 164.

61. Annemarie Haase, ed., *Fragen Erinnern Spuren Sichern: Zum Novemberpogrom 1938 in Aachen* (Aachen, 1992), 39.

62. Evans, *Third Reich in Power,* 589.

63. Barkow, Gross, and Lenarz, *Novemberpogrom 1938,* 26.

64. Haase, *Fragen Erinnern Spuren Sichern,* 38.

65. Wittmer, *Regensburger Juden,* 329.

66. Barkow, Gross, and Lenarz, *Novemberpogrom 1938,* 128–129.

FIVE The Coming of the Flood

1. Heinz Lauber, *Judenpogrom: "Reichskristallnacht" November 1938 in Groß-deutschland: Daten-Fakten-Dokumente-Quellentexte-Thesen u. Bewertungen* (Gerlingen, 1981), 138.

2. Ben Barkow, Raphael Gross, and Michael Lenarz, eds., *Novemberpogrom 1938: Die Augenzeugenberichte der Wiener Library, London* (Frankfurt, 2008), 342.

3. Frank Bajohr and Dieter Pohl, *Der Holocaust als offenes Geheimnis: Die Deutschen, die NS-Führung und die Alliierten* (Munich, 2006), 42.

4. Mitchell G. Bard, *48 Hours of Kristallnacht: Night of Destruction / Dawn of the Holocaust; An Oral History* (Guilford, CT, 2008), 185.

5. Martin Gilbert, *Kristallnacht: Prelude to Destruction* (New York, 2006), 146–147.

6. Avraham Barkai, *From Boycott to Annihilation: The Economic Struggle of German Jews, 1933–1943* (Hanover, NH, 1989), 136, 153. See also Gilbert, *Kristallnacht,* 146; Saul Friedländer, *Nazi Germany and the Jews: The Years of Persecution* (New York, 1998), 280–284; and Wolfgang Benz, "Exclusion as a Stage in Persecution: The Jewish Situation in Germany, 1933–1941," in *Nazi Europe and the Final Solution,* ed. David Bankier and Israel Gutman (Jerusalem, 2003), 50.

7. The original German text is in *Stenographische Niederschrift (Teilübertragung) der Besprechung über die Judenfrage bei Göring am 12. November 1938,* in *Der Prozess gegen die Hauptkriegsverbrecher vor dem Internationalen Militärgerichtshof, Nürnberg, 14. November 1945–1. Oktober 1946,* vol. 26 (Nuremberg, 1948). I used it and with some modifications the Yad Vashem text: http://www.yadvashem.org/odot_pdf/Microsoft%20 Word%20-%203284.pdf. Here, 4.

8. Ibid., 4.

9. Ibid., 9-11.

10. Cited in Barkai, *From Boycott to Annihilation,* 130–131.

11. Richard J. Evans, *The Third Reich in Power* (New York, 2005), 599; Barkai, *From Boycott to Annihilation,* 154.

12. Susannah Heschel, *The Aryan Jesus: Christian Theologians and the Bible in Nazi Germany* (Princeton, NJ, 2008), 1–2.

13. Ibid., 68, 99, 104.

14. Ibid., 17, 28.

15. USHMM Photo Archives #26834, #26835. See also the float in Singen am Hohentwiel, which presented a voracious "Jew Devourer" crocodile who fed on Jews (#95777).

16. Ibid., #30733.

17. Paul Habermehl and Hilde Schmidt-Häbel, eds., *Vorbei—Nie ist es Vorbei: Beiträge zur Geschichte der Juden in Neustadt* (Neustadt un der Weinstrasse, 2005), 104–105, 118.

18. Joseph Walk, *Das Sonderrecht für die Juden im NS-Staat* (Heidelberg, 1996), 255, 258, 260, 262, 268, 270, 275; Friedländer, *Years of Persecution,* 280–291.

19. Claudia Koonz, *The Nazi Conscience* (Cambridge, MA, 2003), 31, 38, 40–45.

20. Friedländer, *Years of Persecution,* 310–311; Evans, *Third Reich in Power,* 604–605, whose translation I use.

21. Friedländer, *Years of Persecution,* 310.

22. Koonz, *Nazi Conscience,* 213, 245.

23. Friedländer, *Years of Persecution,* 292.

24. "Juden, Was Nun?" *Das Schwarze Korps,* November 24, 1938.

25. Friedländer, *Years of Persecution,* 319.

26. Walk, *Sonderrecht für die Juden im NS-Staat,* 283, 285, 289, 290, 295, 297; Jonny Moser, "Depriving Jews of Their Legal Rights in the Third Reich," in *November 1938: From "Reichskristallnacht" to Genocide,* ed. Walter H. Pehle (New York, 1991), 131.

27. Victor Klemperer, *I Will Bear Witness: The Diaries of Victor Klemperer* (New York, 1998), 1:263, 267.

28. Ibid., 302.

29. Chaim Kaplan, *Scroll of Agony: Hebrew Diary of Ch. A. Kaplan Written in the Warsaw Ghetto* [in Hebrew] (Tel Aviv, 1966), 3–4. I use throughout the Hebrew edition of the diary, which was originally written in Hebrew. An English edition, first published in 1965 and then expanded with previously missing material in 1972, is unsatisfactory. The editor, Abraham Katsch, shortened quite substantially the original text but failed to indicate the elided text with three dots according to convention. More important, the translation is often inaccurate and shows a tendency to moderate and indeed to censor Kaplan's observations. Kaplan, a remarkably sensitive witness of the calamity that befell Polish Jewry, formed thoughtful ideas of, among others, God, the Jewish self-image and behavior in the Ghetto, and spiritual and historical relations between Jews and Nazis. Katsch tempered these observations and often left them out. The reason seems to be, from the perspective of the 1960s, a wish to avoid delicate subjects that complicated the Holocaust beyond a memory of Jewish suffering and heroism. Chaim Kaplan, *Scroll of Agony: The Warsaw Diary,* trans. and ed. Abraham Katsch (reprint ed., Bloomington, IN, 1999).

In addition, there is the problem of the incompleteness of all publications. Kaplan kept a diary from 1933 until August 1942; only Kaplan's war diary has been published. The Hebrew edition of the diary does not include the period April 1941–May 1942 (notebooks 10 and 11); the 1972 English edition does not include the period April 1941–early

October 1941 (notebook 10). The Moreshet Archive at the Mordechai Anielevich Memorial in Giv'at Haviva in Israel has a copy of notebooks 10 and 11, which I consulted here. I am indebted to Amos Goldberg for his invaluable help.

30. Kaplan, *Scroll of Agony*, 67–68.

31. Ibid., 162–163. See the illuminating study by Amos Goldberg, *Trauma in First Person: Diary Writing During the Holocaust* [in Hebrew] (Or Yehuda, 2012).

32. I use throughout the Hebrew edition of the full diary: Emanuel Ringelblum, *Diary and Notes from the Warsaw Ghetto: September 1939–December 1942* (Jerusalem, 1999), 285.

33. Yitzhak Arad, Yisrael Gutman, and Abraham Margaliot, eds., *Documents of the Holocaust: Selected Sources on the Destruction of the Jews of Germany and Austria, Poland, and the Soviet Union* (Jerusalem, 1981), 185–186.

34. Klaus-Michael Mallmann, Volker Riess, and Wolfram Pyta, eds., *Deutscher Osten 1939–1945: Der Weltanschauungskrieg in Photos und Texten* (Darmstadt, 2003), 14.

35. Ringelblum, *Diary and Notes from the Warsaw Ghetto*, 19. On Kristallnacht, see Bard, *48 Hours of Kristallnacht*, 107.

36. Jochen Böhler, *Auftakt zum Vernichtungskrieg: Die Wehrmacht in Polen, 1939* (Frankfurt, 2006), 189–190.

37. Jacob Apenszlak, ed., *The Black Book of Polish Jewry: An Account of the Martyrdom of Polish Jewry Under the Nazi Occupation,* 2nd ed. (New York, 1982), 5.

38. Doris L. Bergen, *War and Genocide: A Concise History of the Holocaust* (Lanham, MD, 2003), 104–106.

39. William Hagen, *German History in Modern Times: Four Lives of the Nation* (New York, 2012), 312–313.

40. Steve Hochstadt, ed., *Sources of the Holocaust* (Houndmills, UK, 2004), 87.

41. Saul Friedländer, *Nazi Germany and the Jews: The Years of Extermination, 1939–1945* (New York, 2007), 32–33.

42. Ibid., 82.

43. Ibid., 39.

44. Arad, Gutman, and Margaliot, *Documents of the Holocaust,* 178–179.

45. Ringelblum, *Diary and Notes from the Warsaw Ghetto*, 52, 87.

46. Richard J. Evans, *The Third Reich at War* (New York, 2008), 62.

47. Christopher R. Browning, "Nazi Ghettoization Policy in Poland, 1939–1941," in *The Path to Genocide: Essays on Launching the Final Solution* (New York, 1995), 28–56.

48. Cited in ibid., 36.

49. Kaplan, *Scroll of Agony,* 202, 367.

50. Oskar Rosenfeld, *In the Beginning Was the Ghetto: 890 Days in Łódź,* ed. Hanno Loewry, trans. Brigitte M. Goldstein (Evanston, IL, 2002), 50–51.

51. Marion Kaplan, *Between Dignity and Despair: Jewish Life in Nazi Germany* (New York, 1998), 151–152.

52. Moser, "Depriving Jews of Their Legal Rights in the Third Reich," 133–134; Walk, *Sonderrecht für die Juden im NS-Staat,* 306–307, 320, 324.

53. Klemperer, *I Will Bear Witness,* 1:337–339.

54. Uwe Schellinger, *Gedächtnis aus Stein: Die Synagoge in Kippenheim, 1852–2002* (Heidelberg, 2002), 167–172.

55. David Culbert, "The Impact of Anti-Semitic Film Propaganda on German Audiences: *Jew Süss* and *The Wandering Jew* (1940)," in *Art, Culture, and Media Under the Third Reich,* ed. Richard Etlin (Chicago, 2002), 139.

56. Ibid., 148.

57. Ibid., 151.

58. Quoted in Evans, *Third Reich at War,* 65.

59. Kaplan, *Scroll of Agony,* 392.

60. David Kahane, *Lvov Ghetto Diary* (Amherst, MA, 1990), 14.

61. *Every Day Lasts a Year: A Jewish Family's Correspondence from Poland,* ed. Richard S. Hollander, Christopher R. Browning, and Nechama Tec (New York, 2007), 142, 159.

62. Kaplan, *Scroll of Agony,* 350.

63. Dirk Rupnow, " 'Ihr müsst sein, auch wenn ihr nicht mehr seid': The Jewish Central Museum in Prague and Historical Memory in the Third Reich," *Holocaust and Genocide Studies* 16, no. 1 (2002): 42.

64. Dirk Rupnow, *Vernichten und Erinnern: Spuren nationalsozialistischer Gedächtnispolitik* (Göttingen, 2005), 113.

65. Susannah Heschel, "From Jesus to Shylock: Christian Supersessionism and 'The Merchant of Venice,' " *Harvard Theological Review* 99 (2006): 420–421.

66. Rupnow, *Vernichten und Erinnern,* 108–110; Bernhard Purin, *Die Welt der jüdischen Postkarten* (Vienna, 2001), 50, 123; Gerhard Renda, "Judaica im Heimatmuseum—die Geschichte einer Bewahrung," *Anzeiger des Germanischen Nationalmuseums und Berichte aus dem Forschungsinstitut für Ralienkunde* (1989): 49–56.

67. Kaplan, *Scroll of Agony,* 123.

68. Ibid., 124, 394.

six Imagining a Genesis

Epigraphs: Jeffrey Herf, *The Jewish Enemy: Nazi Propaganda During World War II and the Holocaust* (Cambridge, MA, 2006), 240 (emphasis in original); Primo Levi, *Survival in Auschwitz* (New York, 1961), 107.

1. Klaus-Michael Mallmann, Volker Riess, and Wolfram Pyta, eds., *Deutscher Osten, 1939–1945: Der Weltanschauungskrieg in Photos und Texten* (Darmstadt, 2003), 70.

2. Walter Manoschek, ed., *"Es gibt nur eines für das Judentum: Vernichtung": Das Judenbild in deutschen Soldatenbriefen, 1939–1944* (Hamburg, 1995), 49.

3. Richard Bessel, *Nazism and War* (New York, 2004), 112.

4. Peter Longerich, "From Mass Murder to the 'Final Solution': The Shooting of Jewish Civilians During the First Months of the Eastern Campaign Within the Context of the Nazi Jewish Genocide," in *The Holocaust: A Reader,* ed. Simone Gigliotti and Berel Lang (Malden, MA, 2005), 207–212.

5. Ibid., 198–199, 205.

6. Aryeh Klonicki and Malwina Klonicki, *The Diary of Adam's Father: The Diary of Aryeh Klonicki (Klonymus) and His Wife Malwina, with Letters Concerning the Fate of Their Child Adam* (Jerusalem, 1973), 22–23, cited in Saul Friedländer, *The Years of Extermination: Nazi Germany and the Jews, 1939–1945* (New York, 2007), 214.

7. Mallmann, Riess, and Pyta, *Deutscher Osten, 1939–1945*, 28.

8. Dieter Pohl, "Hans Krüger and the Murder of the Jews in the Stanislawów Region (Galicia)," *Yad Vashem Studies* 26 (1998): 239–265; Friedländer, *Years of Extermination*, 282; Jonathan Nestel, *There Is an Apple in My Freezer: A True Story* (n.p., 2004), 15–18. I am grateful to Yossi Ofer for bringing Nestel's book to my attention.

9. Joseph Goebbels, *Die Tagebücher von Joseph Goebbels*, ed. Elke Fröhlich (Munich, 1994), vol. 2, pt. 2, 199–200.

10. Herf, *Jewish Enemy*, 125.

11. Jonny Moser, "Depriving Jews of Their Legal Rights in the Third Reich," in *November 1938: From "Reichskristallnacht" to Genocide*, ed. Walter H. Pehle (New York, 1991), 135–138; Joseph Walk, *Das Sonderrecht für die Juden im NS-Staat* (Heidelberg, 1996), 346, 352, 350, 354–355, 360.

12. Mark Roseman, *The Villa, the Lake, the Meeting: Wannsee and the Final Solution* (London, 2002), 56–57.

13. Doris L. Bergen, *War and Genocide: A Concise History of the Holocaust* (Lanham, MD, 2003), 175.

14. Bessel, *Nazism and War*, 117.

15. M. Domarus, *Hitler—Reden und Proklamationen, 1932–1945: Kommentiert von einem Zeitgenossen*, vol. 2 (Neustadt/Aisch, 1963), pt. 2, 1794–1804, cited in Friedländer, *Years of Extermination*, 278–279.

16. See Goebbels's article in Marvin Perry and Frederick Schweitzer, *Antisemitic Myths: A Historical and Contemporary Anthology* (Bloomington, IN, 2008), 192.

17. *Das Reich,* November 16, 1941.

18. Domarus, *Hitler—Reden und Proklamationen*, pt. 2, 1828.

19. *Das Reich,* January 21, 1945, cited in Herf, *Jewish Enemy*, 256.

20. Victor Klemperer, *I Will Bear Witness: The Diaries of Victor Klemperer*, 2 vols. (New York, 1998), 2:45 (emphasis in original).

21. Ibid., 2:51, 63, 1:382.

22. Domarus, *Hitler—Reden und Proklamationen*, pt. 2, 1844.

23. Yitzhak Arad, Yisrael Gutman, and Abraham Margaliot, eds., *Documents on the Holocaust: Selected Sources on the Destruction of the Jews of Germany and Austria, Poland, and the Soviet Union* (Jerusalem, 1981), doc. 161, 344.

24. Quoted in Herf, *Jewish Enemy*, 115–116.

25. Ibid., 146.

26. Goebbels, *Tagebücher*, vol. 2, pt. 2, 431, cited in ibid., 150.

27. Manoschek, *"Es gibt nur eines für das Judentum: Vernichtung,"* 25, 45, 59, 61 (emphasis in original).

28. Wilm Hosenfeld, *"Ich versuche jeden zu retten": Das Leben eines deutschen Offiziers in Briefen und Tagebüchern* (Munich, 2004), 630–631, 719.

29. Goebbels, *Tagebücher,* vol. 7, pt. 2, 454.

30. Oskar Rosenfeld, *In the Beginning Was the Ghetto: 890 Days in Łódź,* ed. Hanno Loewry, trans. Brigitte M. Goldstein (Evanston, IL, 2002), 105–106, 133–134.

31. Michael Marrus, "Killing Time: Jewish Perceptions During the Holocaust," in *The Holocaust: History and Memory: Essays in Honor of Israel Gutman* [in Hebrew], ed. Shmuel Almog et al. (Jerusalem, 2001), 28.

32. Emanuel Ringelblum, *Diary and Notes from the Warsaw Ghetto* (Jerusalem, 1999), 300; Rosenfeld, *In the Beginning Was the Ghetto,* 112.

33. Noemi Szac Wajnkranc, *Gone with the Fire* [in Hebrew] (Jerusalem, 2003), 70.

34. Abraham Lewin, *A Cup of Tears: A Diary of the Warsaw Ghetto,* ed. Antony Polonsky (New York, 1990), 97.

35. Fela Szeps, *A Blaze from Within: The Diary of Fela Szeps; The Greenberg Forced-Labor Camp* [in Hebrew] (Jerusalem, 2002), 46.

36. Nehemia Polen, *The Holy Fire: The Teachings of Rabbi Kalonymus Kalman Shapira, the Rebbe of the Warsaw Ghetto* (Northvale, NJ, 1999), 112; see also Rabbi Kalonymos Kalmish Shapira, *Sacred Fire: Torah from the Years of Fury, 1939–1942,* ed. Deborah Miller (Northvale, NJ, 2000).

37. Polen, *Holy Fire,* 34–35.

38. Hanna Levi-Hass, *Diary of Bergen-Belsen: 1944–1945* (Chicago, 2009), 85–86.

39. Janusz Korczak, *The Warsaw Ghetto Memoirs of Janusz Korczak,* trans. E. P. Kulawiec (Washington, DC, 1979), 54, 70.

40. Primo Levi, *Survival in Auschwitz* (New York, 1996), 106.

41. Manoschek, *"Es gibt nur eines für das Judentum: Vernichtung,"* 29.

42. Lewin, *Cup of Tears,* 232, 133, 157, 183.

43. Karel Berkhoff, *Harvest of Despair: Life and Death in Ukraine Under Nazi Rule* (Cambridge, MA, 2004), 75.

44. Dan Diner is an exception. See Diner, *Beyond the Conceivable: Studies on Germany, Nazism, and the Holocaust* (Berkeley, CA, 2000).

45. Alexander Donat, *The Holocaust Kingdom: A Memoir* (London, 1965), 211 (emphasis in original); Samuel Kassow, "Introduction," in *The Warsaw Ghetto Oyneg Shabes—Ringelblum Archive: Catalog and Guide,* ed. Robert Moses Shapiro and Tadeusz Epstein (Bloomington, IN, 2009), xx.

46. Alexandra Garbarini, *Numbered Days: Diaries of the Holocaust* (New Haven, 2006), 5.

47. Raphael Lemkin mentioned this event in the context of genocide as early as 1944 in his *Axis Rule in Occupied Europe* (Clark, NJ, 2005), 85.

48. Philip Friedman, "The Fate of the Jewish Book During the Nazi Era," *Jewish Book Annual* 54 (1996–1997): 90.

49. Jacqueline Borin, "Embers of the Soul: The Destruction of Jewish Books and Libraries in Poland During World War II," *Librarians and Culture* 28 (1993): 449.

50. F. J. Hoogewoud, "The Nazi Looting of Books and Its American 'Antithesis': Selected Pictures from the Offenbach Archival Depot's Photographic History and Its Supplement," *Studia Rosenthaliana* 26, no. 1–2 (1992): 162.

51. Donald Collins and Herbert Rothfeder, "The Einsatzstab Reichsleiter Rosenberg and the Looting of Jewish and Masonic Libraries During World War II," *Journal of Library History* 18, no. 1 (1983): 24.

52. David Shavit, *Hunger for the Printed Word: Books and Libraries in the Jewish Ghettos of Nazi-Occupied Europe* (Jefferson, NC, 1997), 49.

53. Collins and Rothfeder, "Einsatzstab Reichsleiter Rosenberg," 29.

54. Hoogewoud, "Nazi Looting of Books," 162; Collins and Rothfeder, "Einsatzstab Reichsleiter Rosenberg," 30.

55. Shavit, *Hunger for the Printed Word*, 51.

56. Dirk Rupnow, " 'Ihr müsst sein, auch wenn ihr nicht mehr seid': The Jewish Central Museum in Prague and Historical Memory in the Third Reich," *Holocaust and Genocide Studies* 16, no. 1 (2002): 23–53.

57. Hoogewoud, "Nazi Looting of Books," 161.

58. Rupnow, " 'Ihr müsst sein, auch wenn ihr nicht mehr seid,' " 89–90.

59. *"Stadt und Mutter in Israel": Jüdische Geschichte und Kultur in Regensburg*, Ausstellung Regensburg Stadtarchiv und Runtingersäle (Regensburg, 1989), 118.

60. Friedländer, *Years of Extermination*, 266.

61. Examples are from Frank Bajohr's excellent essay in Frank Bajohr and Dieter Pohl, *Holocaust als offenes Geheimnis: Die Deutschen, die NS-Führung und die Alliierten* (Munich, 2006), 47–48.

62. Friedländer, *Years of Extermination*, 307.

63. Peter Fritzsche, *Life and Death in the Third Reich* (Cambridge, MA, 2008), 257.

64. Ibid., 253.

65. Klaus Hesse and Philipp Springer, *Vor aller Augen: Fotodokumente des nationalsozialistischen Terrors in der Provinz* (Essen, 2002), 154, 159. See the book for information on other localities where the deportation was photographed.

66. Franziska Becker, *Gewalt und Gedächtnis: Erinnerung an die national-sozialistische Verfolgung einer jüdischen Landgemeinde* (Göttingen, 1994), 83, 91.

67. Moser, "Depriving Jews of Their Legal Rights in the Third Reich," 136–137; Walk, *Sonderrecht für die Juden im NS-Staat*, 334, 363, 371–372, 374, 379, 385, 389.

68. Bajohr and Pohl, *Holocaust als offenes Geheimnis*, 62.

69. Ibid., 62.

70. Klemperer, *I Will Bear Witness*, 2:28.

71. Ibid., 234.

72. Fritzsche, *Life and Death in the Third Reich*, 286.

73. Cited in Friedländer, *Years of Extermination*, 337–338.

74. Hosenfeld, *"Ich versuche jeden zu retten,"* 630.

75. Bajohr and Pohl, *Holocaust als offenes Geheimnis*, 66–67.

76. Klemperer, *I Will Bear Witness*, 2:156, 148.

77. Moser, "Depriving Jews of Their Legal Rights in the Third Reich," 138; Walk, *Sonderrecht für die Juden im NS-Staat*, 403.

78. Marta Baiardi, "The Deportation of the Jews from Florence" [in Italian], *Museo e Centro di Documentazione della Deportazione e Resistenza; Loughi della memoria*

Toscana, Prato, http://www.museodelladeportazione.it/modules/smartsection/item.php? itemid=33.

79. Michael Matsas, *The Illusion of Safety: The Story of the Greek Jews During World War II* (New York, 1997), 83, 115–117; Irith Dublon-Knebel, comp., *German Foreign Office Documents on the Holocaust in Greece (1937–1944)* (Tel Aviv, 2007), esp. 188, 190, 208. See also Götz Aly, "Die Deportation der Juden von Rhodos nach Auschwitz," *Mittelweg 36* (2003): 79–88.

80. Collins and Rothfeder, "Einsatzstab Reichsleiter Rosenberg," 33.

81. *Das Reich,* November 16, 1941.

82. *Das Reich,* May 8, 1943, reproduced in "German Propaganda Archive: Calvin—Minds in the Making," http://www.calvin.edu/academic/cas/gpa/rsi60.htm.

83. Manoschek, *"Es gibt nur eines für das Judentum: Vernichtung,"* 43.

84. Randall Bytwerk, "The Argument for Genocide in Nazi Propaganda," *Quarterly Journal of Speech* 91, no. 1 (2005): 52.

85. Chaim Kaplan, Diary, February 2, 1942, Moreshet Archive, Mordechai Anielevich Memorial, Israel. Emphasis in original.

86. Christopher Sauer, "Rede als Erzeugung von Komplizentum: Hitler und die öffentliche Erwähnung der Juden-vernichtung," in *Hitler der Redner,* ed. Josef Kopperschmidt (Munich, 2003), 413–440.

87. Domarus, *Hitler—Reden und Proklamationen,* pt. 2, 1844, 1920, 1937.

88. Sauer, "Rede als Erzeugung von Komplizentum," 434.

89. Rüdiger Overmans, *Deutsche militärische Verluste im Zweiten Weltkrieg* (Munich, 1999), 265–266.

90. Nicholas Stargardt, "Rumors of Revenge in the Second World War," in *Alltag, Erfahrung, Eigensinn: Historisch-anthropologische Erkundungen,* ed. Belinda Davis, Thomas Lindenberger, and Michael Wildt (Frankfurt, 2008), 383.

91. Klemperer, *I Will Bear Witness,* 2:415.

92. Stargardt, "Rumors of Revenge," 378.

93. Bajohr and Pohl, *Der Holocaust als offenes Geheimnis,* 66.

94. Stargardt, "Rumors of Revenge," 378. This was a misperception as two synagogues were destroyed.

95. Manoschek, *"Es gibt nur eines für das Judentum: Vernichtung,"* 75.

96. Bajohr and Pohl, *Der Holocaust als offenes Geheimnis,* 74.

97. Stargardt, "Rumors of Revenge," 377.

EPILOGUE A World with Jews

1. Gershom Scholem, *A Life in Letters, 1914–1982* (Cambridge, MA, 2002), 310.

2. Havi Dreifuss-Ben-Sasson and Lea Preiss, "Twilight Days: Missing Pages from Avraham Lewin's Warsaw Ghetto Diary, May–July 1942," *Yad Vashem Studies* 33 (2005): 7–60.

3. Franz Kafka, *Briefe, 1902–1924* (New York, 1958), 27–28.

4. See the stimulating book by Yuri Slezkine, *The Jewish Century* (Princeton, NJ, 2004), esp. pp. 102–104.

5. Dirk Rupnow argues against this view, which has been articulated in different ways by, among others, Aleida Assmann, Jean-François Lyotard, and James Young. Dirk Rupnow, " 'Ihr müsst sein, auch wenn ihr nicht mehr seid': The Jewish Central Museum in Prague and Historical Memory in the Third Reich," *Holocaust and Genocide Studies* 16, no. 1 (2002): 23.

6. Dan Stone, "Genocide and Memory," in *The Oxford Handbook of Genocide Studies,* ed. Donald Bloxham and A. Dirk Moses (Oxford, 2010), 102–119.

7. Carlo Ginzburg, "Distance and Perspective: Two Metaphors," in *Wooden Eyes: Nine Reflections on Distance* (New York, 2001), 139–156.

8. Paula Fredriksen, *Augustine and the Jews: A Christian Defense of Jews and Judaism* (New York, 2008).

Illustration Credits

The photographers and the sources of visual material are as follows. Every effort has been made to supply complete and correct credits; if there are errors or omissions, please contact Yale University Press so that corrections can be made in any subsequent edition.

42: The burning of the books at Berlin's Opera Square, May 10, 1933. (Courtesy of the Bundesarchiv, Germany, photo: 102-14599 / photographer: Georg Pahl.)

43: Opera Square at the burning of the books in Berlin, May 10, 1933. (Courtesy of the Bundesarchiv, Germany, photo: 183-R70324.)

62: "What the Jew believes is irrelevant, for in his race lies his rascal character" (Was der Jude glaubt ist einerlei, in der Rasse liegt die Schweinerei), Bamberg, August 18, 1935. (Courtesy of Stadtarchiv Bamberg.)

62: "Knowing the Jew is knowing the Devil" (Wer den Juden kennt, kennt den Teufel), Recklinghausen, August 18, 1935. (Courtesy of USHMM Photo Archives.)

63: "Knowing the Jew is knowing the Devil" (Wer den Juden kennt, kennt den Teufel), unidentified German town, 1933–1939. (Courtesy of Stadtarchiv Nürnberg.)

77: "I, the Jew Siegel, will never again file a complaint against National Socialists" (Ich der Jude Siegel werde mich nie mehr über Nationalsozialisten beschweren). Dr. Michael Siegel, Munich, March 10, 1933. (Courtesy of the Bundesarchiv, Germany, photo: 146-1971-006-02/photographer: Heinrich Sanden.)

82: "I have defiled a Christian woman!" (Ich habe ein Christenmädchen geschandet!), Marburg, August 19, 1933. (Courtesy of USHMM Photo Archives.)

83: Thanksgiving Day parade, Altenahr, Rhineland, 1937. (Courtesy of USHMM Photo Archives.)

84: Thanksgiving Day parade, Altenahr, Rhineland, 1937. (Courtesy of USHMM Photo Archives.)

89: "Jews are not welcome here" (Juden sind hier nicht erwünscht), Franconia, 1935. (Courtesy of Bildarchiv Preussischer Kulturbesitz.)

90: "The Jews are our misfortune!" (Die Juden sind unser Unglück!), Düsseldorf, 1933–1938. (Courtesy of Stadtarchiv Nürnberg.)

90: "Whoever buys from Jews is stealing the nation's assets" (Wer beim Juden kauft stiehlt Volksvermögen.)

91: "Jews are our misfortune" (Juden sind unser Unglück), Mannheim, 1935–1939. (Courtesy of Stadtarchiv Nürnberg.)

91: "Jews are not welcome here" (Juden sind hier nicht erwünscht), Nürnberger Tor entrance to the University of Erlangen, November 10, 1938. (Courtesy of USHMM Photo Archives.)

92: "Jews are not welcome in Tölz!" (Juden in Tölz unerwünscht!), 1935.

92: "This house is and will remain free of Jews" (Dieses Haus ist und bleibt von Juden frei), Grüne Tanne Guesthouse, Halle an der Saale, 1935–1939. (Courtesy of Stadtarchiv Nürnberg.)

93: "This will be the end of any member of the national community who buys from Jews, and of any Jew who trespasses into this town!!" (So muß es jedem Volksgenossen gehen der bei Juden kauft und jedem Jude der diese Stadt betritt!!), 1935–1939. (Courtesy of Stadtarchiv Nürnberg.)

93: "In the following houses in Werl live Jews" (In folgenden häusern in Werl wohnen Juden), Werl, 1933. (Courtesy of Bildarchiv Preussischer Kulturbesitz.)

94: "We have three dozen Jews to give away" (Wir haben 3 dtz Juden abzugeben), Reichenberg bei Würzburg, 1935–1939. (Courtesy of Stadtarchiv Nürnberg.)

94: Town hall doorknocker, Lauf an der Pegnitz, 1937. (Courtesy of Stadtarchiv Lauf a.d. Pegnitz.)

95: "Trust no fox in the green meadow and no Jew on his oath!" (Trau keinem Fuchs auf grüner Heid und keinem Jud bei seinem Eid!), telegraph office mural, Nuremberg, 1933–1939. (Courtesy of Stadtarchiv Nürnberg.)

96: "Jews are not welcome here" (Juden sind hier nicht erwünscht), Munich-Landsberg road, May 13, 1935. (Courtesy of Bildarchiv Preussischer Kulturbesitz / Hanns Hubmann.)

96: "German beach Mainz-Ginsheim. Jewish beach only at the Jordan River—1,933 kilometers" (Deutsches Strandbad Mainz-Ginsheim. Jüdisches Strandbad nur am Jordan—1933 klm), Mainz, 1935–1939. (Courtesy of Stadtarchiv Nürnberg.)

97: "Trek further Jews, get out! We do not want you in Neuhaus!" (Zieh weiter Jud, zieh aus! Wir wünschen dich nicht in Neuhaus!), Rennweg am Neuhaus, 1935–1939. (Courtesy of Stadtarchiv Nürnberg.)

116: The contents of the synagogue are burned in Mosbach's Market Square in Baden, November 10, 1938. (Courtesy of USHMM Photo Archives.)

118: The synagogue in Euskirchen with the Torah scroll hanging from the roof, November 10, 1938. (Courtesy of Stadtarchiv Euskirchen.)

123: "God, do not abandon us!" (Gott, vergiss uns nicht!). The Jewish parade in Baden
Baden, November 10, 1938. (Courtesy of Yad Vashem Photo Archive.)

137: "Exodus of the Jews" (Auszug der Juden). The Jewish parade on Maximilianstrasse,
Regensburg, November 10, 1938. (Courtesy of Yad Vashem Photo Archive.)

138: Stormtroopers pose before the destroyed synagogue in Münster, November 10, 1938.
(Courtesy of Stadtarchiv Münster, Fotosammlung Nr. 5168.)

139: Laughing civilians in front of the destroyed Hörder synagogue in Dortmund.
(Courtesy of Horst Chmielarz, private archive, Dortmund.)

149: Carnival at Neustadt an der Weinstrasse featuring a float of the local synagogue in
flames, February 19, 1939. (Courtesy of USHMM Photo Archive.)

213: The deportation of Regensburg's Jews, April 2, 1942. (Courtesy of Yad Vashem Photo
Archive.)

Index

Page numbers in *italics* indicate illustrations.

Judaism, 10, 57, 101, 140–141, 180; appropriated by Christian identity, 179; elimination of, 192; Jesus and destruction of, 148; Jewish holidays, 186–187; link with Christian and European history, 240; Prussian archives on history of, 59; relation to Christianity, 22, 129, 130; rewriting of history of, 207; targeted by anti-Jewish measures, 109; Torah scroll as image of, 121; universal uprooting of, 174

Judenfrei or Judenrein ("free of Jews"), 171, 185, 213

Jung, Carl, 80

Kafka, Franz, 236
Kahlke, Nikolas, 75
Kaiser Wilhelm Institute for Anthropology, 70
Kaplan, Chaim, 158–160, 175, 179–180, 187, 245, 260n29; death of, 236; on Hitler's prophecy, 226–227
Kästner, Erich, 47
Katsch, Abraham, 260n29
Kautsky, Karl, 46
Keller, Helen, 43
Keller, J., 7, 61
Khoroshunova, Iryna, 205
Kissel, Peter, 49
Klemperer, Victor, 156–158, 170, 195–196; bombing of Dresden and, 229–230; on deportations, 223–224; life after the war, 235; on Warsaw Ghetto uprising, 218–219
Klonicki, Aryeh, 185
Koenekamp, Eduard, 166
Korczak, Janusz, 203–204, 245
Kracauer, Siegfried, 43
Kreisau Circle, 37
Kristallnacht, 3–4, 50, 104, 108, 152, 247n4; acting out of emotions in, 136–141; church attitudes toward, 132; destruction of Hebrew Bible and, 115,

118–120; German guilt and fears of revenge, 230–231; German sympathy for Jews during, 125–126, 134–135, 140; Hitler's prophecy and, 227; Jews spared violence of, 157; local history of, 147–148; racial ideology and, 121; tradition of anti-Jewish actions and, 214

Krüger, Hans, 186–187
Kuh, Officer, 57–58, 59, 61
Kunde (local knowledge), 65, 67

labor camps, 4, 163, 167, 191
law, rule of, 29, 31
Law Against Overcrowding in Schools, 51
Law for the Restoration of a Professional Civil Service, 39, 51
Law on Admission to the Legal Profession, 51
Law on Editors, 51
Law on Midwives, 150
Law on Renting to Jews, 156
lawyers, 28, 33, 51, 74, 107
League of German Girls [Bund Deutscher Mädel], 174
League of Nations, 100
Leffler, Siegfried, 131–132, 148, 166, 234
Lenin, V. I., 43, 46, 72
Levi, Primo, 10, 17, 183, 203, 204
Levi-Hass, Hanna, 203, 245
Lewi, Liebe, 162
Lewin, Abraham, 201, 235, 245
Lewkowicz, Moishe, 235
liberalism, 14, 31, 32, 33, 49; on evil as political tyranny, 237, 238; "Jewish spirit" identified with, 41; Jews identified with, 79, 87, 105; Nazi victory over, 56, 85; Nazi violence against, 32–33; Second World War and, 193
"Libro, El" (Borges), 27
Liebknecht, Karl, 43
Lilienthal, Joel, 136
Lippert, Julius, 146

Made in the USA
Middletown, DE
24 May 2021